Simply Divine

A collection of recipes
from the family & friends of
Second-Ponce de Leon Baptist Church
Atlanta, Georgia

Simply Divine is a publication of Second-Ponce de Leon Baptist Church of Atlanta, Georgia. The book was inspired and directed by David P. Lewis, Minister of Recreation, for the purpose of building relationships, sharing beliefs, and strengthening ties with the community.

Proceeds from the sale of ***Simply Divine*** will benefit the Buckhead Christian Ministry and other community projects.

Additional copies of ***Simply Divine*** may be purchased by addressing:

Simply Divine
Second-Ponce de Leon Baptist Church
2715 Peachtree Road, NE
Atlanta, GA 30305-2907
404-266-8111 • FAX: 404-261-6593

All Scripture quotations in this publication are from the HOLY BIBLE, NEW INTERNATIONAL VERSION® NIV® Copyright© 1973, 1978, 1984 by International Bible Society. All rights reserved.

The "NIV" and "NEW INTERNATIONAL VERSION" are trademarks registered in the United States Patent and Trademark Office by the International Bible Society. Use of either trademark requires the permission of International Bible Society.

Copyright 1997
Second-Ponce de Leon Baptist Church
Atlanta, Georgia
All rights reserved

ISBN 0-9658102-0-8
Second-Ponce de Leon Baptist Church

Library of Congress Catalog Card Number: 97-91775

First Printing, October 1997

The Invitation

Jesus offers us a simple but divine invitation: "If anyone hears my voice and opens the door, I will go in and eat with him and he with me" *(Revelation 3:20)*.

The ritual of sharing food is significant. At the table relationships are strengthened, harmony is promoted, and values are communicated: we nourish our bodies and spirits and enrich our lives. In preparing and sharing food, we create the opportunities to know one another better.

Jesus honored the tradition of breaking bread together by accepting the hospitality of friends. Though the recipes in *Simply Divine* can provide for temporal nourishment, Jesus offers eternal sustenance. May He who is the Bread of Life be present at our tables.

Catherine B. Capps

Chairman, *Simply Divine*

Committee

Chairman:	Catherine B. Capps
Editor:	Judith A. Lunsford
Art Director:	Jay Weber
Treasurer:	Shelby Bryant
Recipe Collector:	Jo Shippen
Testing Coordinator:	Pam Corbin
Publicist:	Peggy Lientz
Advisor:	Karen Toholsky
Advisor:	Dorothy Anne Voegeli
Computer Director:	Liz Mann
Artist:	Nancy S. Shippen

About the Artist

Nancy S. Shippen is a local artist, native Atlantan, and member of Second-Ponce. She graduated from Mercer University with a bachelor's degree in art and continued her studies in Italy with the University of Georgia.

Her paintings and murals are currently displayed at Cafe Tu Tu Tango in Buckhead and in many private homes in Georgia and throughout the nation.

Contributors

It has been "simply divine" how hundreds of people in the Second-Ponce community have banded together to work on this project. Nearly one thousand recipes were submitted. After lengthy testing and tasting, some recipes were renamed, adapted, or combined.

Every effort has been made to identify recipe donors, testers, evaluators, typists, and proofreaders. We apologize if a name has been omitted inadvertently. The Committee applauds the efforts of all participants. Special thanks go to:

Stella Abernathy
Judy Acuff
Anita Adair
Barbara Adair
Vivian Aderhold
Rhea Adkins
Trudy Alexander
Lee Allen
Connie Anderson*
Lou Anderson
Bill Angevine
Florence Angevine
Sally Angevine
Widi Arnold
Clarice Ashmore
Bill Bailey
Esther Bailey
Margaret Bailey
Mary Ann Barger
Nancy Barker
Lynn Bartlett
Mamie Ruth Bartlett*
Arvis Bates

Sofia Bauerle
Cecelia Baynes
Rebecca Bedingfield
Betty Belkofer
Teresa Bell
Evangeline Bercegeay
Mary Arnold Binns
Flossie Black
Rhonda Bloschok
Lisa A. Booth
Luther Bootle
Julia Bowden
Paul Bowen
Kim Boyd
Keith Bradley
Connie Brady
Lanoy Branan
Jane Branch
Jean R. Bridges
Elizabeth Brooks
Ellen Brown
Genna Brown
Kay Brown

Mary Lou Bryant
Shelby Bryant
Tricia Buce
Sharla Bufkin
Terri Bunch
Connie Burchfield
Ann Burdette
Doyle Butler
Linda Byars
Betty Byrd
Billie Byrd
Donna Byrd
Jeff Byrd
Helen Cain
Joy Callaway
Gay Campbell
Drema Canterbury
Catherine B. Capps
Hope Mullen Carter
Josephine Castleberry
Sherwood Cates
Dee Caudell
Alyce Cheatham

Ethel Childress
Diane Choyce
Julia Christiansen
Carol Clark
Linda Clark
Iris Cobble
Mary Cohen
Jane B. Coleman
Karen Coleman
Leonard H. Coleman
John Condra
Margaret Condra
Robin Condra
Helen Cooper
Pam Corbin
Kay Cox
Dorothy Craig
Rhoda Craighead
Jim Crawford
Dorothy L. Crowson
Lois Cunard
Hilda Dalton
Judy Darby*

Contributors

Sunny David
Anna Davis
Cantey Deeter
Janet Denison
Ruth Denison
Rita Dennard
Beth Dick
Charles Dickerson
Janet Dickerson
Dr. Jan Disney
Gloria W. Dobbs
Georgeanne Donnelly
Gary Driggers
Kay Dudley
Elizabeth Due
Kathy Dukes
Norma Duncan
Kitty Dunn
Cameron Capps Duree
Peggy Durrett*
Gloria Early
Joyce Ellington
Charles Ellis
Marion Ellis
Deborah Epps
Kathryn Evans
Mary Fambrough
Pam Feagle
Sheryl Ficke
Mildred Flege
Gaye Flynt
Dennis Foust
Paula Foust
Doris L. Franco
Kay Frankum
Elizabeth Freeman
Marcia Gaddis
Vicky Gailey
Nelly Garcia
Palmer Gard
Shirley Garrett
June Garrison
Doris Gaskins
Patti George
Kathryn Girardeau
Myrtis Godbey

Valerie Goetz
Mary Goldsmith
Louise Goodman
Kathy Goodrich
Shirley Goodwin
Amelia Gordon
Linda Lee Gordon
Charlotte Goulding
Jackie Gow
Sarah Gracey
Claire Graham
Tarre Green
Ruth Greene
Barbara Griffes
Babs Gudger
Connie Gunter
Barbara Guptil
Christine Haggai
Ann Hagman
Barbara Haig
Hope Hailey
Jane Hailey
Charlene Hall
Lynda Hall
Mary Ann Hall
Charles Hancock
Martha Hancock
Lynn Handley
Lois Hanke
Pauline Harben
Mary Beth Harbour
Callye Harden
Pat Harmeyer
Helen Harmon
Carolyn Harris
Cathy Harris
Nancy Harris
Sara Harris
Ruth Hartness
Shelley Hayes
Marcine Head
Melissa H. Hellem
Evelyn Helms
Ellen Hendrix
Vernon Hendrix
Hallie Henrickson

Margie Highsmith
Becca Hill
Lisa Hobbs
Sylvia Hodges
Mary Lou Holbert
Janie Holbrook
Jill Holder
Ray Holley
Susan Holt
Charlie Hooper
Marion Howard
Louise Howell
Lovie Howell
Mary Hubert
Sarah Huddleston
Elizabeth Hudson
Holly D. Huneycutt
Erdis Hunkin*
Catherine Hunter
Mary Hurt
Walter H. Inge
Sue Hodges Innes
Beth Irwin
Weezie Jackson*
Wendy Jackson
Nell Jernigan
Delyse Johns
Dorothy Johnson
Janyce Johnson
Joan Johnson
Rose Johnson
Barbara Johnston
Celeste Johnston
Margaret Joiner
Nancy Jones
Betty Justice
Julie Keishian
Necia Kelleher
Nancy Kelly
Sandi Kelly
Joy Ruth Kemp
Lisa Kent
Elizabeth King*
Mary King
Stephanie D.
  Kirkpatrick

Lynn Klein
Mark Knowles
Barbara Korey
Micky Oberry Land
Melissa Langford
Tish Lanier
Dottie Lee
Renee Lefever
Sharron Leland
Edie Lewis
Kelly Lewis
Mary Lewis
Peggy Lientz
Elizabeth Light
Sue Lightner
Bea Lindblad
Anna C. Lindgren
Susan Lindsey
Mattie Lisenby
Gail Love
Sheila Love
Kay Shirley Lovett
Kay Lowe
Susan Lundy
Gary Lunsford
Judith A. Lunsford
Valerie Lyles
Mary Ann Lyon
Kay MacKenzie
Lois Maffett
Sandra Teem
  Maner
Susie Mangum
Liz Mann
Melony Manus
Ann Margeson
Mattie Martin
Rounelle Martin
Susan Massey
Cathy McClure
Katie McClure
Jason McCranie
Jim McCranie
Rae McCranie
Helen Bagley
  McDuffie

Contributors

Susan Angevine McKessy
Mary McNeal
Paul McNeal
Rosalee Meredith
Paige Merkle
Esther Mikhail
William E. Mills
Libby Mims
Gabby Mitchell
Margaret Mitchell
Mary Jane Mitchell*
Ellen Butler Mitchum
Mary Montgomery
Connie Morris
Debbie Morris
Myra Morrison
Rosemary Mosteller
Melody Mulaik
Margaret Mullis
Mary Ellen Murdoch
Mickie Muroff
Ann Murray
Holly Musemeche
Guerry Myers
Annelle Newsom
Ruby Neyland
Phyllis Page
Mary Paschal
Genie Patterson
Mildred Pendergrass
Joe Perry
Judy Perry
Sally Phillips
Rita Picklesimer
Ann B. Platé
Suzy Poole
Sally Pope
Marnie Porson
Marion Poston
Robbie H. Puckett
Gail Pyle
Clay Ramsey
Marianne Ramsey
Jackie Ratledge
Susan Raven

Diane Ray
Frances Ray
Jeanne Redwine
Anne Reed
Sara Ann Reed
Carol Rees
Joyce Rees
Maxine Reeves
Madge Reynolds
Sterling Richardson
Frances Ringl
Janet Roach
Saretta Roberts
Julie Robertson
John R. Roma
Mary Chapman Roma
Susan Rushton
Betty Foy Sanders
Grace Sanders
Betty Jo Sapp
Ouida Sara
Rosalind Sasser
Anna Schaeffer
Carmen Schott
Carol Scott
Diane Scott
Virginia Selph
Dianne Shalibo
Elizabeth Shaw
Jo Shippen
Nancy Shippen
Bonnie Shoemaker
Kathy Simms
Rose Waldron Sims
Jeanne Delany Singer
Jacqueline Slaton
Bobby Small
Robin Small
Betsy Smalley
Betty Jo Smith
Daisy Andrews Smith
Dorothy L. Smith
Helen Smith
Sunny Smith
Arden Starnes
Betty Jo Stephens

Joan Stephenson
Mary M. Stribling
Jeannette Stringer*
Lynn Stuart
Sue Stumm
Nancy Suggs
Gary Suters
Julia Suters
Melissa Suters
Bette Swilley
Magy Tadros
Betty Talmadge
Paul Taylor
Betty Teem
Brenda Terry
Connie Thomas
Dottie Thomas
Christine Thompson
Edward Thorn
Eleanor Thornton
Dottie Tidwell
Lisa Timmons
Karen Toholsky
Margaret Trawick
Janet Trimble
Charlotte W. Troutman
Laura Troy
Debra Tyson
Marianne S. Varley
Katherine W. Veal
Nancy Venezia
Dorothy Anne Voegeli
Carol Warren
Darlene Warren
Marion Wasdin
June Watkins
Allyson Watson
Angie Watterson
Helen Webb*
Jay Weber
Edie Whitaker
Cynthia White
Katherine F. White
Marcia White
Sara B. White

Vicki Whitman
Faye Whitworth
Dolly C. Wiley
Lena Wiley
Ann Williams
Kit Williams
Ruth Renfroe Williams
Claire M. Willingham
Frances Worthy
Beth Wright
Louise Wright
Peggy Wright
Pat Wroten
Jane Wyant
Janet Yerta
LeeAnn Young
Linda Young
Valjean Young
Judy Zellars
Sarah Zimmerman

Writers:
Judith A. Lunsford
Margaret Mitchell
Claire M. Willingham
Sarah Zimmerman

Testing Committee:
Ellen Brown
Pam Feagle
Mary Hubert
Barbara Johnston
Susan A. McKessy
Connie Morris
Debbie Morris
Jo Shippen
Gary Suters
Dorothy Anne Voegeli
Lena Wylie
LeeAnn Young

*deceased

Welcome

Simply Divine is more than a cookbook – it is a ministry. Hundreds of our members have contributed from their kitchens and their hearts to make this book a gift to our community and city.

From its beginnings in 1854, Second-Ponce de Leon Baptist Church has had a heart for people. Our members have helped start some fifty churches and have given millions of dollars to global missions. Our vision has been consistent: to share Christ's love with our community and world.

This book reflects our desire to serve people and their changing needs. Time pressures make sharing meals a formidable challenge. We hope that God will use **Simply Divine** to enrich those times of eating together.

You are welcome to participate in our worship services, the Family Life Center, and our various ministries. The God who gave us our lives and families cares about our every need. His Son died on the cross to pay the penalty for all our sins and mistakes and rose again to give us eternal life. You can call on Him today and He will answer you. He loves us all.

It is a privilege to serve you through **Simply Divine**. May God's richest blessings be yours.

Dr. James C. Denison, Pastor

Contents

"Go and enjoy choice food and sweet drinks, and send some to those who have nothing prepared."
                                        Nehemiah 8:10

Appetizers & Beverages	11
Breads & Brunch	33
Soups & Stews	59
Salads	79
Meat & Game	107
Poultry & Seafood	143
Vegetables & Side Dishes	177
Cakes & Cookies	213
Pies & Sweet Temptations	251
Index	273
Order Forms	287

This book is dedicated to Martha Swilley, whose good humor, gracious service, and love of family, home, and God have endeared her to the community and Second-Ponce de Leon Baptist Church.

As you browse through this book, notice the quotes, tips, and variations accompanying the recipes. In addition, look for two special symbols that are unique to **Simply Divine**:

Heritage Recipe. The Heritage Recipes are our link with the past. The last all-church cookbook was published in 1905 by one of Second-Ponce's parent churches, Ponce de Leon Avenue Baptist Church. The cookbook, called Gate City Cook Book, was underwritten by several Atlanta businesses, including CAPITOLA, a local milling company. More than three dozen recipes from this turn-of-the-century cookbook have been included for your enjoyment.

Kidspeak. Kidspeak is our link with the future. The ritual and enjoyment of sharing food is caught early in life. Woven throughout our recipes are comments and observations about food from the youngsters at Second-Ponce, and no attempt has been made to edit their spelling or phrasing.

Appetizers & Beverages

"So whether you eat or drink or whatever you do, do it all for the glory of God."

I Corinthians 10:31

Appetizers & Beverages

HOT APPETIZERS

Petite Quiche Lorraines	13
Bacon-Wrapped Scallops	13
Cream Cheese Pastry	13
Artichoke Quiche Squares	14
Honey-Mustard Chicken	14
Hot Bacon Roll-Ups	15
Zucchini Triangles	15
Hot Salami	16
Ham Rolls	17

SPREADS AND DIPS

Vidalia Onion Spread	16
Seven Layer Taco Dip	16
Hot and Spicy Bean Dip	17
Mexican Salsa	18
Blue Chip White Salsa	18
Pesto Dip	19
Dilly of a Dip	19
Chèvre Persillade	20
Boursin	20
Liptauer Cheese Spread	21
Smoked Salmon Party Spread	21
Homemade Pimiento Cheese	22
Curried Cheese Log	22
Caviar Mousse	23
Sun-Dried Tomato Log	23
White Cheddar Raspberry Ring	24

COLD APPETIZERS

Marinated Broccoli and Cauliflower	24
Stuffed New Potatoes	25
Open-Faced Veggie Squares	25
Mexican Pinwheels	26
Old-Fashioned Cheese Straws	26

BEVERAGES

Miss Rubye's Summer Punch	27
Patio Punch	27
Mocha Punch	28
SPdL Mint Tea	28
Mint Water	28
Strawberry Punch	29
Peach Punch	29
Almond Tea	30
Cranberry Percolator Punch	30
Cranberry Tea	31
German Coffee	31
Hot Cider	32
Mocha Mix	32

HERITAGE RECIPES

Canapé de Sardines	21
Cheese and Peanut Butter Sandwiches	22
Caviar	23
Cheese Straws	26
Fruit Punch	27

Petite Quiche Lorraines

Make pastry a day ahead.

- ½ cup bacon bits
- ½ cup grated Swiss cheese
- 1 tablespoon parsley
- 2 eggs, well beaten
- ½ cup half-and-half
- ½ teaspoon salt
- ¼ teaspoon dry mustard
- ½ teaspoon Worcestershire sauce
- 1 tablespoon Parmesan cheese
  paprika
- ½ recipe cream cheese pastry

Shape pastry into two dozen balls and press into miniature muffin tins. Layer bacon, cheese, and parsley into unbaked dough. Beat eggs with cream, salt, mustard, and Worcestershire, and add. Sprinkle Parmesan and paprika on top. Bake at 350° for 30 minutes or until brown. These may be frozen. To serve, warm in a 200° oven. Makes 2 dozen.

Appetizers & Beverages

Cream Cheese Pastry

- 1 cup butter, softened
- 1 (8-ounce) package cream cheese, softened
- ½ teaspoon salt
- 2 cups flour
- 1 egg yolk, beaten with 2 teaspoons half-and-half

Beat butter, cream cheese, and salt until blended. Work in flour until smooth. Flatten dough into a rectangle; wrap in foil. Chill overnight. Divide dough and roll between sheets of wax paper. Shape as directed. Chill. Brush tops with egg yolk mixture. Bake as directed. Makes 4 dozen.

Bacon-Wrapped Scallops

- 1 pound bay scallops
- 12 slices bacon cut in half crosswise and lengthwise
- 1¼ teaspoons all-purpose Greek seasoning
- 1 teaspoon freshly ground black pepper
- 2 tablespoons lemon juice

Wrap each scallop with a piece of bacon. Secure with a toothpick. Sprinkle with seasonings and lemon juice. Place on a rack in a shallow roasting pan. Broil 5 inches from heat for 8 minutes or until bacon is crisp, turning once. Serve immediately.

Appetizers & Beverages

Variation:

Add other complementary seasonings, such as chopped parsley, oregano, or lemon juice.

Artichoke Quiche Squares

3   (6-ounce) jars marinated artichokes, drained and chopped
½   pound sharp cheddar cheese, grated
1   medium onion, finely chopped
4   eggs, lightly beaten
6   single saltines, finely crushed
    dash of Tabasco
    salt and pepper to taste

Mix artichokes, cheese, onion, eggs, crackers, Tabasco, and salt and pepper until well blended. Pour mixture into a buttered 8-inch square baking pan. Bake at 325° for 1 hour. Cut into 1-inch squares and serve hot. May also be served at room temperature. Makes 64.

Honey-Mustard Chicken

⅓   cup spicy brown mustard
3   tablespoons honey
2   tablespoons ketchup
1   clove garlic, minced
½   teaspoon Tabasco
1   pound boneless, skinless chicken breast cut into 1-inch pieces

Mix together mustard, honey, ketchup, garlic, and Tabasco. Set aside ¼ of the mixture. Add chicken to the remainder and stir to coat. Cover and refrigerate for at least 1 hour, stirring occasionally. Preheat broiler. Arrange chicken pieces on broiler rack and broil. Turn at least once, brushing with marinade until chicken is tender, about 10 minutes. Serve with the reserved sauce as a dip. Serves 6 as a meal or 15 as an appetizer.

Hot Bacon Roll-Ups

These are easy to make and disappear quickly.

Appetizers & Beverages

1   (8-ounce) package cream cheese, softened
2   teaspoons dried or 2 tablespoons fresh chives
25 slices whole-wheat bread
25 slices bacon, cut in half

Mix cream cheese with chives until well blended. Trim crust from bread and cut each slice in half. Spread 1 teaspoon cream cheese mixture on each half and roll up. Wrap a half slice of bacon around each and secure with a toothpick. Place on broiler pan and bake at 350° for 30 minutes. Turn as necessary to prevent over-browning. Makes 50.

Zucchini Triangles

1   cup buttermilk biscuit mix
½   cup onion, finely chopped
½   cup Parmesan cheese
2   tablespoons chopped parsley
¼   teaspoon salt
½   teaspoon seasoned salt
1   teaspoon dried oregano
     dash of black pepper
½   cup vegetable oil
4   eggs, slightly beaten
3   cups zucchini, grated

Tip:

When marketing, look for firm, heavy zucchini about 5-7 inches in length. Avoid the supersized, overgrown squash which are tasteless and watery.

Mix biscuit mix, onion, cheese, seasonings, oil, and eggs until well blended. Lightly fold in zucchini. Spread evenly in a well-greased 13x9-inch pan. Bake at 375° about 40 minutes or until golden brown. Cut into squares, then into triangles. Serve warm. Makes 4-5 dozen.

Simply Divine

Appetizers & Beverages

Variation:

Rub mushroom caps (stems removed) lightly with olive oil. Stuff caps with mixture. Bake at 375° for 10-15 minutes until nicely browned. Serve hot.

Vidalia Onion Spread

1	cup mayonnaise
1	cup shredded Swiss cheese
1	cup Parmesan cheese
2	cups chopped onion

Mix mayonnaise, cheeses, and onions until well blended. Place in a shallow baking dish. Bake at 325° for 30 minutes. Serve on crackers.

Seven Layer Taco Dip

2	cans bean dip
3	avocados mashed with lemon juice
2	cups sour cream mixed with 1 package taco seasoning
	green onion tops, chopped
	sliced, pitted ripe olives
3	medium tomatoes, chopped

Layer ingredients in order listed in a wide, shallow serving dish. Serve with tortilla chips.

Hot Salami

Variation:

Substitute bologna for salami.

3	cups dark brown sugar
5	tablespoons Dijon mustard
2	pounds salami

Mix sugar and mustard together to make a thick paste. Cut X's halfway through salami and top with sauce. Bake at 375° for 30 minutes. Baste with sauce. Bake another 30 minutes until glazed and the slits open. Serve with cocktail rye.

Ham Rolls

A *"must" for New Year's day football!*

4	packages small party rolls
1	cup margarine, softened
3	tablespoons poppy seeds
1	teaspoon Worcestershire sauce
3	tablespoons mustard
3	pounds sliced ham
1	pound Swiss cheese

Leave rolls whole in foil pan and slice horizontally. Carefully lift top and flip over. Mix margarine, poppy seeds, Worcestershire, and mustard. Spread mixture on both layers of rolls. Place ham and cheese on rolls in pan and replace top section of rolls. Wrap in foil. Bake at 400° for 15 to 20 minutes. Slice and serve while hot.

Hot and Spicy Bean Dip

1	(9-ounce) can bean dip
1	cup sour cream
1	(8-ounce) package cream cheese, softened
1½	ounces dry taco seasoning
20	drops Tabasco
1	cup chopped green onions
¼	cup chopped ripe olives
¾	cup grated Monterey Jack cheese
¾	cup grated sharp cheddar cheese

Mix together bean dip, sour cream, cream cheese, taco seasoning, Tabasco, onions, and olives until well blended. Place mixture in an ungreased baking dish. Top with coarsely grated cheeses. Bake at 350° until cheeses melt and mixture is heated throughout. Serve with tortilla or corn chips.

Appetizers & Beverages

Variation:

For a lighter filling, use 1½ pounds shaved ham and ½ pound shredded cheese. Rolls may be prepared, frozen, and cooked as needed.

Recipe for a Hippopotamus Sandwich

A hippo sandwich is easy to make.
All you do is simply take
One slice of bread,
One slice of cake,
Some mayonnaise,
One onion ring,
One hippopotamus,
One piece of string,
A dash of pepper--
That ought to do it.
And now comes the problem. . .
Biting into it!

                Shel Silverstein,
           Where the Sidewalk Ends

Appetizers & Beverages

Tip:

Serve leftover salsa with grilled chicken, fish, or vegetables.

Mexican Salsa

1½ cups chopped ripe olives
1 cup chopped green olives with pimiento
3 tomatoes, chopped
6 green onions, sliced
¾ green bell pepper, chopped
1 jalapeño pepper, chopped
1 tablespoon olive oil
2 tablespoons vinegar
   dash of Tabasco

Mix all ingredients together until well blended. Chill for several hours and serve with favorite chips.

Blue Chip White Salsa

If you like cilantro, you will love this.

Tip:

This recipe makes a good dressing for taco salad.

1 cup mayonnaise
1 cup sour cream
   juice of 3 limes
4 cloves garlic, crushed
1½ cups finely chopped fresh cilantro
1 (6-ounce) can ripe olives, chopped
1½ cups chopped green onions
½ teaspoon hot pepper sauce
   salt to taste
   white pepper to taste

Mix mayonnaise and sour cream. Add lime juice, garlic, cilantro, olives, onions, pepper sauce, salt, and pepper. Adjust seasonings to taste. Chill about 6 hours and serve with blue corn chips.

18   *Simply* Divine

Pesto Dip

Appetizers & Beverages

2	cups packed fresh parsley sprigs
⅔	cup pecan pieces
⅓	cup Parmesan cheese
2	cloves garlic
1	tablespoon dried basil
1	(8-ounce) package cream cheese, softened
¼	cup milk

In a blender or food processor, blend parsley, pecans, cheese, garlic, and basil until finely chopped. Add cream cheese and milk until well blended. Cover and chill until serving time. Serve with bagel chips or pretzels.

Dilly of a Dip

Also good for topping baked potatoes or grilled fish

1	cup mayonnaise
1	cup sour cream
2	teaspoons lemon juice
2	teaspoons grated onion
1	teaspoon salt
1	teaspoon dry mustard
1½	teaspoons fresh dill or ½ teaspoon dried dill

Tip:

Keep fresh dill in the freezer. As needed, snip off the feathery dill weed and return the unused portion to the freezer.

Mix mayonnaise, sour cream, and all seasonings until well blended. Chill overnight. Serve with celery sticks, carrots, cauliflower, cucumbers, or other raw vegetables.

Appetizers & Beverages

"We may live without friends; we may live without books; but civilized men cannot live without cooks."
-Edward Bulwer-Lytton

Chèvre Persillade

Provençal goat cheese spread

	handful of finely chopped parsley
1	clove garlic, crushed
4½	tablespoons olive oil
1½	tablespoons lemon juice
	dash of freshly ground black pepper
12	ounces soft, fresh goat cheese

Mix parsley, garlic, oil, lemon juice, and pepper. Add cheese to the mixture and mix well. Chill and serve on sliced French baguette or thin crisp toasts.

Boursin

Tip:

Use in place of mayonnaise on turkey or roast beef sandwiches.

1	cup butter, softened
2	(8-ounce) packages cream cheese, softened
2	cloves garlic, crushed
½-1	teaspoon dried oregano
¼-½	teaspoon dried basil
¼-½	teaspoon dried dill
¼-½	teaspoon dried marjoram
¼-½	teaspoon black pepper
¼-½	teaspoon dried thyme

Using food processor or blender, process butter and cheese until smooth. Add remaining ingredients and continue processing until well blended. Refrigerate overnight. Serve with crackers.

Liptauer Cheese Spread

Liptauer cheese is a Hungarian snack.

2   (8-ounce) packages cream cheese, softened
1   small onion, grated
2-3 ounces Roquefort cheese, grated
    drops of hot sauce

In a food processor or with a hand mixer, blend all ingredients until smooth and light. Refrigerate to allow flavors to blend. Serve with rye bread or crackers.

Appetizers & Beverages

Variation:

Add 1 crushed clove of garlic and 1-2 tablespoons of Hungarian paprika.

Smoked Salmon Party Spread

½   cup smoked salmon, or more to taste
12 ounces whipped cream cheese
1   tablespoon lemon juice
2   teaspoons onion, grated
¼   teaspoon salt
½   teaspoon liquid hickory smoke seasoning
3   teaspoons parsley, chopped
¼   teaspoon lemon pepper salt or seasoned salt
    capers

Mix together all ingredients until well blended. Garnish with capers. Chill. Serve with crackers or bagel chips.

Canapé de Sardines.

Cut oblong lengths of toast, spread them with grated parmesan or switzer cheese; lay a boneless sardine, with a square of lemon on it, over each; garnish with alternate rows of chopped olives, bird's-eye peppers and whites of hard boiled eggs. Grate yolks of hard-boiled eggs over all. Dress with mayonnaise if liked.

    Gate City Cook Book

Simply Divine   21

Appetizers & Beverages

Cheese and Peanut Butter Sandwiches.

One pound of grated cheese, one glass of peanut butter, juice of two lemons, one-fourth of a teaspoonful red pepper, two teaspoonfuls salt and enough hot water to make it thin enough to spread on well-buttered bread.

    Gate City Cook Book

Homemade Pimiento Cheese

The real thing

8	ounces extra sharp cheddar cheese, softened
8	ounces Monterey Jack cheese, softened
8	ounces sharp or medium cheddar cheese, softened
1	(7-ounce) jar of pimiento
1-2	tablespoons chopped onion
1	pinch sugar (optional)
1	(4-ounce) can sliced ripe olives (optional)
2-3	cups mayonnaise

In a food processor mix cheeses, pimiento, onion, sugar, and olives until well blended. Place in a large bowl and add mayonnaise as desired for consistency. Serve on crackers or sandwich bread.

Curried Cheese Log

1	(8-ounce) package cream cheese, softened
1	cup coarsely shredded sharp cheddar cheese
½	cup coarsely shredded blue cheese
1	tablespoon butter
½	teaspoon curry powder
½	cup sliced unblanched almonds, finely chopped
	chopped parsley

Combine cheeses and beat until well blended and fluffy. Chill until firm. Melt butter in small saucepan; add curry powder and heat, stirring one minute. Stir in nuts and cool. Shape cheese mixture into 8-inch log. Roll in curried-nut mixture to coat well, and sprinkle lightly with parsley. Wrap tightly and chill. Serve with assorted fresh fruits and crackers. Serves 6-8.

Caviar Mousse

Appetizers & Beverages

2	(4-ounce) jars caviar (black lumpfish)
1	envelope unflavored gelatin
¼	cup cold water
2	tablespoons onion, grated
1	tablespoon lemon juice
½	teaspoon salt
1	cup sour cream
1	cup heavy cream, whipped
	parsley sprigs

Spread caviar gently onto paper towels to drain. Soften gelatin in cold water for 5 minutes in a small saucepan. Place over low heat until dissolved. Cool slightly. Combine onion, lemon juice, salt, and sour cream, blending well. Add gelatin. Gently fold in caviar and whipped cream. Turn mixture into an oiled 4-cup mold. Chill until firm. Turn onto chilled platter. Garnish with parsley. Serve with thin, bland crackers. Serves 50.

Caviar.

Spread Russian caviar (which can be bought tinned) on slices of round or diamond-shaped toast or bread; garnish with chopped beets and chopped parsley making a circle of red surrounded by a circle of green. Chopped hard-boiled eggs may be used.

Gate City Cook Book

Sun-Dried Tomato Log

1	(8-ounce) package cream cheese, softened
¼	cup drained and chopped oil-packed, sun-dried tomatoes
4	green onions, chopped
¼	cup chopped pecans
	dash hot pepper sauce, to taste
	dash Worcestershire sauce, to taste
	chopped parsley

Beat cream cheese until smooth. Add tomatoes, onions, pecans, and seasonings. Mix well. Shape as desired and roll in chopped parsley. Serve with sliced French baguette, crackers, or bagel chips.

Tip:

If you have dry-packed, sun-dried tomatoes, soak them in oil 20-30 minutes before draining and using.

Simply Divine   23

Appetizers & Beverages

Marinated Broccoli and Cauliflower

    florets from 1 bunch of broccoli
    florets from 1 head of cauliflower
1   cup cider vinegar
1   tablespoon sugar
1   tablespoon dried dill weed
1   teaspoon salt
1   teaspoon black pepper
1   teaspoon garlic powder
1½ cups vegetable oil

Blanch the florets, being careful not to overcook. Combine cider vinegar, sugar, and seasonings. Add vegetable oil and stir well. Pour over the vegetables, stirring to coat well. Chill and marinate overnight.

White Cheddar Raspberry Ring

1   (10-ounce) package Vermont white cheddar cheese, grated
2   tablespoons mayonnaise
2   tablespoons minced onion
½   cup chopped pecans
½   cup or more raspberry jam or preserves

Combine cheese, mayonnaise, onion, and pecans. Shape into ring and chill. Fill center with jam and serve with buttery crackers.

Simply Divine

Open-Faced Veggie Squares

Easy and colorful for al fresco entertaining

Appetizers & Beverages

2	cans of crescent rolls
2	(8-ounce) packages cream cheese, softened
1	cup mayonnaise
1	package ranch dressing mix
1	cup grated carrots
1	cup chopped broccoli
1	cup chopped cauliflower
1	cup chopped green onions
1½	cups grated cheese

Spread out crescent rolls into a rectangle on a cookie sheet. Pinch seams together. Bake according to directions. Cool. Mix cream cheese, mayonnaise, and dressing mix. Spread on baked dough. Combine vegetables and press gently into cream cheese mixture. Top with grated cheese. Refrigerate to harden cream cheese. Cut into bite-sized squares and serve.

Stuffed New Potatoes

50	small new potatoes, washed and trimmed
3	(8-ounce) packages cream cheese, softened
3	cups plain yogurt
6	tablespoons fresh dill, divided
1	teaspoon black pepper

Variation:

In place of dill, use parsley, mint, or tarragon.

Simmer potatoes in water to cover until done, about 8-10 minutes. Drain and cool. In separate bowl combine cream cheese, yogurt, 2 tablespoons dill, and pepper. Chill about 30 minutes. Scoop out top third of potatoes and reserve for another use such as potato salad. With a small spoon, place a dollop of filling into center of each potato. Garnish with 4 tablespoons fresh dill. Chill and serve. Makes 50.

Appetizers & Beverages

Mexican Pinwheels

1 (8-ounce) package cream cheese, softened
1 (4-ounce) can chopped ripe olives, well drained
1 (4-ounce) can chopped green chilies, drained
1 teaspoon picante sauce
   garlic powder to taste
   flour tortillas
   picante sauces

Combine cream cheese, olives, chilies, picante sauce, and garlic powder. Spread on flour tortillas and roll up tightly. Refrigerate at least one hour. Slice in ¾-inch lengths. Insert toothpicks and serve with a variety of picante sauces for dipping.

Old-Fashioned Cheese Straws

A new procedure for an old favorite

8   ounces extra sharp cheddar cheese, softened and cut into chunks
¾   cup butter, softened and cut into chunks
1⅓ cups self-rising flour
¼   heaping teaspoon cayenne pepper
½   teaspoon salt

In food processor process cheese until shredded. Add butter and process until mixed, stopping to scrape down sides as needed. Combine flour and seasonings and add to cheese mixture and pulse. Scrape down sides and process until just mixed and mixture begins to gather together. Put room-temperature dough into cookie press. Using saw-tooth tip, press out onto cookie sheets in long strips. Bake at 425° for 8-10 minutes, watching carefully until edges begin to brown. Break into strips of desired lengths and store in air-tight container. Makes about 4 dozen 4-inch strips.

Cheese Straws.

Six heaping cooking spoonfuls of CAPITOLA flour, six heaping cooking spoonfuls of grated cheese, two tablespoonfuls of butter melted, after measuring, a little grated nutmeg, a very little cayenne pepper, sweet milk enough for a thick dough. Mix well, roll thin, cut in straws; bake in biscuit pans.

               Gate City Cook Book

26   Simply Divine

Miss Rubye's Summer Punch

6   lemons, cut into halves
8   cups water, divided
2   cups sugar
1   quart orange juice
1   quart pineapple juice
1   teaspoon almond extract
1   teaspoon vanilla

Squeeze juice from lemons. Set juice aside. Boil lemon halves in 3 cups water for 20 minutes. Remove lemon halves and any seeds. Add sugar to lemon water; stir to dissolve. Then add juices, extracts, and remaining 5 cups water. Cool and store in a large jar. Refrigerate. Makes one gallon.

Patio Punch

2   cups orange juice
2½   cups canned crushed pineapple with juice
2   tablespoons lemon juice
2   cups banana, mashed
10   maraschino cherries
¾   cup sugar
4   quarts ginger ale

Combine juices, fruits, and sugar in a blender. Blend on high until sugar is dissolved. Pour mixture into ice cube trays and freeze overnight. Cubes can be made weeks in advance. To serve, pour unchilled ginger ale over frozen punch cubes. Serves 20.

Appetizers & Beverages

Variation:

In place of fresh lemons, use 1 (12-ounce) can of frozen lemonade concentrate. To prepare, boil 3 cups water, add sugar, and dissolve. Then, add the remaining ingredients, including the lemonade. Because frozen lemonade is sweetened, reduce the amount of sugar.

One local manufacturer of carbonated water was the Harris Lithia Springs Company, headquartered on Peachtree Street. The company advertised lithia water as "Nature's Sovereign Remedy for Stomach, Kidney, Liver and Bladder Troubles."

Fruit Punch.

The strained juice of four dozen lemons, two dozen oranges and one large pineapple grated and strained, one gallon of weak tea; mix these and add sugar to taste—not too sweet. When about ready to serve place large piece of ice in punch bowl, pour in this fluid and let stand till thoroughly cold. Just before serving add a quart bottle of maraschino cherries and a quart of apollinaris or any carbonated lithia water.

                Gate City Cook Book

Appetizers & Beverages

Tip:

"Mocha" originally meant a strong bitter coffee grown in Arabia. Today the word is frequently used to describe a beverage made from a blend of coffee and cocoa. To vary the flavor of Mocha Punch, brew different types of coffee.

Mocha Punch

Makes a hit at summer coffees or receptions

2	quarts cream soda
2	quarts vanilla ice cream
3	quarts chocolate milk
1	quart strong coffee, cooled

Combine soda, ice cream, milk, and coffee; serve. Makes 2 gallons.

Mint Water.

A summer staple
Wash and rinse 1 cup of mint. Twist or bruise leaves and place in a half-gallon container. Fill with fresh water. Refrigerate 4-6 hours. Strain and serve over ice.

SPdL Mint Tea

In the New Testament, the Pharisees paid their taxes with mint, the ancient symbol of hospitality.

11	cups water, divided
4	family size tea bags
15	sprigs of fresh mint
1½	cups sugar
¾	cup lemon juice
1	quart orange juice

Bring 8 cups water to a rolling boil. Remove from heat and add tea bags and mint. Steep 10 minutes. Remove tea bags and mint. Dissolve sugar in hot tea. Add juices and 3 cups water. Refrigerate. Stir before serving as juices tend to settle. Serve over ice. Makes about one gallon of tea.

Strawberry Punch

Until the early 1800s, wild strawberries were so plentiful in America that gardeners did not cultivate them.

Appetizers & Beverages

2	cups fresh strawberries or 2 (10-ounce) packages frozen strawberries
1	(6-ounce) can frozen lemonade concentrate
4	lemonade cans of water
1	cup cranberry juice
1	(2-liter) bottle ginger ale

Puree strawberries in blender. Put puree in a container and add concentrate, water, and cranberry juice. Refrigerate overnight. Before serving put cold juice into a punch bowl and add ginger ale. Makes about ¾ gallon.

Peach Punch

48	(12-ounce) cans peach concentrate
3½	gallons water
4½	quarts ginger ale
6	cups orange juice
1½	cups pineapple juice
1½	cups lemon juice
3	quarts fresh peach halves and slices

Combine liquids. Place peaches into punch just before serving; the floating peaches provide a colorful garnish. Serves 200.

"It's a pleasure to share recipes with people who enjoy Southern hospitality, twentieth-century style."

Betty Foy Sanders

When Betty was First Lady of Georgia from 1963-1967, she often served this punch with Peach Refrigerator Cookies on page 241.

Simply Divine 29

Appetizers & Beverages

Tip:

Flavored extracts, such as almond and vanilla, will keep indefinitely if stored in a dark, cool place.

Almond Tea

A hit with the Rainbow Sunday School Class

10	cups water, divided
2	tablespoons unsweetened instant tea granules
¾	cup sugar
1	(12-ounce) can frozen lemonade concentrate, thawed
1	tablespoon almond extract
2	teaspoons vanilla

Bring 2 cups water to boil; dissolve instant tea. Set aside. Heat 2 cups water and stir in sugar. Boil 5 minutes to make a syrup. Combine tea with syrup, concentrate, extracts, and remaining 6 cups water. Simmer until time to serve. Makes about ¾ gallon.

Cranberry Percolator Punch

Smells spicy and tastes wonderful!

2	cups cranberry juice
2	cups pineapple juice
1¾	cups water
⅓-½	cup brown sugar
1¼	teaspoon whole cloves
2	sticks cinnamon
	pinch of salt

Put juices and water in percolator. Place sugar, spices, and salt in basket. Perk 10 minutes and serve hot. Makes 6 cups.

Cranberry Tea

1   (12-ounce) package fresh or frozen cranberries
1   stick cinnamon
3   quarts water
1   cup sugar
⅔   cup frozen orange juice concentrate
⅓   cup fresh lemon juice

Boil cranberries with cinnamon stick in water until the berries pop. Discard cinnamon stick. Remove berries, reserving liquid. Mash berries through a strainer, discarding skins. Return strained berries to water and add sugar and juices. Serve hot or cold. Keeps in the refrigerator for up to a week. Makes 3½ quarts.

Appetizers & Beverages

Tip:

Cranberry season is October through December. Fresh cranberries can be stored in plastic bags in the refrigerator for 2 months or frozen for up to a year. Before using, discard any shriveled or discolored berries.

German Coffee

½   pound freshly ground coffee
2   tablespoons cocoa powder
¼   teaspoon cinnamon
⅛   teaspoon salt

Combine coffee, powder, cinnamon, and salt. Until ready to use, store tightly sealed, preferably in the freezer. Use 4 tablespoons for 6 cups of coffee.

"My grandmother, Maria Sauerwein, always made her 'kaffee' this way."
                -Barbara Johnston.

Tip:

Salt is used to reduce the natural bitterness of coffee.

Simply Divine

Appetizers & Beverages

Variation:

Add thin strips of orange zest during the last 5 minutes of the simmering process.

Hot Cider

Because of unreliable drinking water, apple cider was a common beverage in colonial America.

2	tablespoons whole cloves
1	whole nutmeg
3	sticks cinnamon
½	gallon apple cider
1¼	cups sugar
2	cups freshly squeezed orange juice
½-1	cup freshly squeezed lemon juice

Put spices in cheesecloth and tie to form a bag. Place spice bag, apple cider, and sugar in a large pot. Simmer 1 hour. Remove spices. Add juices and heat. Makes about ¾ gallon.

Mocha Mix

"*My favorite [food] is chocolate cocoa. It's made from milk, butter, and hershey's chocolate. I like this recipie because my grandmother started this and she is dead now, so my mom makes it.*"

   Rachael Foust, age 12.

2½	cups instant hot chocolate
2	cups non-dairy creamer
1	cup sugar
1	cup instant coffee granules
½-1	teaspoon cinnamon
½-1	teaspoon nutmeg
½-1	teaspoon cloves
	pinch of salt (optional)

Mix all ingredients together; store in airtight container. To serve, place 3-4 teaspoons of mix in mug and fill with boiling water. Makes 6½ cups of mix.

Breads & Brunch

"I am the bread of life. He who comes to me will never go hungry..."

John 6:35

Breads & Brunch

QUICK BREADS
Banana Bread 35
Fruit Bread 35
Apricot Butter 35
Banana Nut Bread 36
Zucchini Bread 36
Poppy Seed Bread 37
Pumpkin Bread 37
Easy Cheese Bread 38

BISCUITS
Aunt Ruth's Cheese Biscuits 38
Cheese Buttermilk Biscuits 39
Mrs. Charles' Scones 39
Egg Wash 39
Butter-Me-Nots 53

CORNBREAD
Country Spoon Bread 40
Grandma Stone's Company Cornbread ... 40
Broccoli Cornbread 41
Corn Muffins 42

YEAST BREADS
Basic Refrigerator Rolls 41
Dinner Rolls 42
Sally Lunn 43
Dill Bread 44
No Need to Knead Wheat Bread 45
Seven-Grain Bread 46

COFFEE CAKES
Ida's Oatmeal Coffee Cake 47
Sour Cream Coffee Cake 48
Texas Coffee Cake 49

MUFFINS
Petite Mayonnaise Muffins 44
Apple Bran Muffins 50
Fig Muffins 50
Orange Spread 50
Morning Glory Muffins 51
Oat and Wheat Bran Muffins 52
Winter Squash Muffins 53

BRUNCH
Granola 49
Baked Blintz 54
Sausage Egg Strata 54
Peggy Durrett's Charleston Cheese Grits 55
Mexican Breakfast Bake 55
Crab Quiche 56
Tomato Gravy and Grits 56
Saturday Morning Omelet 57
Poached to Perfection 58
Ham Hash 58
Ungspankaka 58

HERITAGE RECIPES
Beaten Biscuit 38
Virginia Corn Bread 40
Crumpets 43
Broiled Finnon Haddie 56
Cheese Fondue, or English Monkey 57

Banana Bread

3⅓ cups sifted flour
2 teaspoons baking soda
1 teaspoon salt
1 cup butter, softened
2 cups sugar
4 eggs
2 teaspoons vanilla or 1 teaspoon lemon extract
2 cups mashed bananas
1 cup sour cream
1 cup chopped nuts (optional)

Sift together flour, soda, and salt. Reserve. In a separate bowl, cream butter, sugar, eggs, and extract on high speed for 1½ minutes. Scrape bowl. Add bananas, sour cream, nuts, and reserved flour mixture. Beat on low speed until well blended. Divide batter between three well-greased one-pound coffee cans or two 9x5-inch loaf pans. Bake at 350° about 1 hour or until toothpick inserted in center comes out clean. Cool for a few minutes before removing from containers. Bread freezes well.

Breads & Brunch

Tip:

Use fully ripened bananas when baking cakes and breads. If the fruit ripens before you are ready to bake, store the bananas in the refrigerator. They will keep for several days. While the peel will turn black, the fruit will not be affected.

Fruit Bread

A *delicious combination of cranberries and apricots*

1 package Pillsbury Cranberry Quick Bread
½ cup chopped dried apricots
1 cup water
1 egg

Grease loaf pans (bottom only). Combine all ingredients by hand with a wooden spoon, beating about 50-75 strokes, just until moistened. Put dough in large or small loaf pans. Bake at 350°. Large loaves require 60 minutes to bake; small loaves 45-50 minutes. A doubled recipe makes 5 small loaves of bread. Serve with cream cheese or Apricot Butter.

Apricot Butter

½ cup butter
¼ cup apricot preserves

Beat ingredients together until fluffy.

Simply Divine

Breads & Brunch

Variation:

Add ½ cup currants or dried cranberries.

Banana Nut Bread

⅔ cup shortening
2½ cups flour
1½ cups sugar
2 eggs
1½ teaspoons baking powder
1 teaspoon baking soda
1 teaspoon salt
3 large bananas, mashed
⅔ cup buttermilk
⅔-1 cup chopped nuts

Lightly grease and flour two loaf pans. In a large bowl, mix all ingredients together. Beat at medium speed for 2-3 minutes. Bake at 350° for 35-45 minutes or until golden brown. Makes 2 loaves or 12-18 muffins.

Zucchini Bread

3 eggs
2 cups sugar
1 cup vegetable oil
1 teaspoon vanilla
1 teaspoon cinnamon
1 teaspoon salt
1 teaspoon baking soda
1 teaspoon baking powder
3 cups sifted flour
2 cups raw, grated zucchini
1 cup chopped pecans

Beat eggs until foamy. Add sugar, oil, and vanilla. Mix well. Add cinnamon, salt, soda, and baking powder, stirring until blended. Add flour and mix well. Stir in zucchini and nuts. Pour into two well-greased and floured 9x5-inch loaf pans. Bake at 350° for 1 hour. Makes 2 loaves.

Poppy Seed Bread

1   box butter pecan cake mix
1   small package Royal Instant Toasted Coconut Pudding
4   eggs
½   cup vegetable oil
2   tablespoons poppy seeds
1   cup warm water

Grease and flour loaf pans. Combine cake mix, pudding, eggs, oil, and poppy seeds. Stir well and add water. Bake at 350° for 45-60 minutes. Do not preheat oven. Makes 2 large loaves or 1 large loaf and 3 small loaves.

Breads & Brunch

Tip:

Toasting poppy seeds before cooking with them brings out their nutty flavor. To toast, place seeds in a shallow baking pan. Bake at 350° for 10-15 minutes, shaking the pan occasionally to prevent burning.

Pumpkin Bread

1   teaspoon nutmeg
1   teaspoon cinnamon
3   cups sugar
1   cup vegetable oil
4   eggs
1½   teaspoons salt
1   (16-ounce) can pumpkin
⅔   cup water
2   teaspoons baking soda
1   cup chopped nuts
3   cups flour

Beat together spices, sugar, oil, eggs, and salt. In order, add pumpkin, water, soda, nuts, and flour, and mix well. Divide batter equally between three well-greased, one-pound coffee cans or two 9x5-inch loaf pans. Bake at 350° for 1¼ hours. Cool for 10 minutes in pans. Turn loaves out on racks and cool completely. Makes 2 or 3 loaves.

Simply Divine

Breads & Brunch

Tip:

Because poppy seeds have a high oil content, they tend to go rancid. Store unused seeds in an airtight container in the refrigerator. They will keep for up to 6 months.

Easy Cheese Bread

2½   cups packaged biscuit mix
½   cup shredded sharp cheddar cheese
½   cup finely diced sharp cheddar cheese
2   teaspoons poppy seeds
1   beaten egg
1   cup milk

Combine biscuit mix, cheese, and poppy seeds. Add egg and milk, mixing just until blended. Beat by hand vigorously 1 minute. Turn into a well-greased 8½x4½-inch loaf pan. Sprinkle with additional poppy seeds. Bake at 350° about 50 minutes or until done. Remove from pan. Cool on rack. Serve warm. Makes 1 loaf.

Aunt Ruth's Cheese Biscuits

Aunt Ruth is Mrs. Willie Robbs Cox, who taught Sunday School for thirty-five years. Among her students were teenagers, young adults, and married women. A Sunday School class was named in her honor.

This biscuit dough was beaten with a mallet until it blistered.

Beaten Biscuit.

Sift a teaspoonful of salt into a quart of CAPITOLA flour, mix into a stiff dough with equal parts of sweet milk and water, work in a little at a time, two tablespoonfuls of butter, beat for an hour, wash over with milk, prick and bake.

   Gate City Cook Book

1   cup flour
1½   teaspoons baking powder
½   teaspoon salt
1½   tablespoons shortening
½   cup milk
2   cups grated cheddar cheese

In a mixing bowl, combine flour, baking powder, and salt. Cut in shortening. Add milk and cheese. Roll out to a ¼-inch thickness. Cut out biscuits and place on a greased cookie sheet. Bake at 450° for 10-12 minutes.

Simply Divine

Cheese Buttermilk Biscuits

Breads & Brunch

¼   cup butter or margarine, softened
2   cups self-rising flour
1   cup buttermilk
1½ cups shredded sharp cheddar cheese

Cut butter into flour until mixture resembles coarse crumbs. Add remaining ingredients and stir well. Drop from tablespoon onto a large ungreased baking sheet. Bake at 425° for 12-15 minutes or until golden.

Mrs. Charles' Scones

When Rosalee Meredith's husband was a military attaché to Moscow in 1967, an excellent cook from British Guiana named Mrs. Charles gave her this recipe.

2   cups flour
1   tablespoon baking powder
¼   teaspoon salt
⅓-½   cup sugar
½   cup shortening
1   egg, well beaten
¾   cup milk
½   teaspoon vanilla
½   cup raisins, currants, or dried cranberries

Sift together flour, baking powder, salt, and sugar. Cut in shortening until mixture is crumbly. Set aside. Combine egg, milk, and vanilla. Add to flour mixture, mixing only enough to moisten flour. Stir in raisins. Turn onto a floured board, and pat into a circle about ½-¾ inch thick. Cut into 10 or 12 wedges, or cut with a 2-inch biscuit cutter. (Note: or dough can be dropped from a spoon.) Place scones on a lightly greased cookie sheet at least one inch apart. Brush tops of scones with an egg wash (see recipe). Bake at 400° for 13-15 minutes or until slightly golden. Serve warm with butter and jam. Makes 12 scones.

Variation:

Use 2½ cups flour, ½ cup butter, and no egg.

Egg Wash

1   egg yolk
1-2   tablespoons water or milk

Mix egg yolk and liquid. Brush on pastry or yeast dough before baking to add color and gloss.

Breads & Brunch

Tip:

Because of the danger of salmonella contamination, check eggs carefully. Never use an egg that has an odor or discoloration, especially if the shell has a hairline crack.

Country Spoon Bread

A custard-like bread eaten with a fork or spoon

1	cup yellow or white cornmeal
3	cups milk, divided
1	teaspoon salt
1	teaspoon baking powder
2	tablespoons melted butter or margarine
3	egg yolks, well beaten
3	egg whites, stiffly beaten

In a large sauce pan, cook cornmeal and 2 cups milk until consistency of mush, approximately 10 minutes, stirring constantly. Remove from heat. Add salt, baking powder, butter, 1 cup milk, and egg yolks. Blend well. Fold in egg whites. Bake in greased, 2-quart casserole at 325° for 1 hour. When finished, spoon into small bowls and top with butter or margarine. Serves 4-6.

Virginia Corn Bread.

One pint of cornmeal, ten eggs, one teaspoonful of baking powder, one cooking spoon of lard, whip the eggs lightly, add the meal, lard, salt and baking powder, then a pint of boiling hot water, stirring constantly. Bake immediately in a hot oven.

     Gate City Cook Book

Grandma Stone's Company Cornbread

1½	cups self-rising cornmeal mix
1	small onion, grated
1	cup sour cream
2	eggs
1	small can cream style corn
½	cup vegetable oil

Mix all ingredients together. Spray muffin pan with nonstick cooking spray. Fill ¾ full. Bake at 375° for 12-15 minutes until lightly browned. Serve with butter. Makes 12 muffins.

Simply Divine

Basic Refrigerator Rolls

This recipe belongs to Mrs. Evelyn Blalock, the mother of Sara White. It has been in the family for sixty years.

Breads & Brunch

1 cup fresh mashed potatoes
⅔ cup shortening
½ cup sugar
1 teaspoon salt
2 eggs, beaten
1 package dry yeast
½ cup lukewarm water
1 cup scalded milk
6-8 cups sifted all-purpose flour

Tip:

Refrigerator dough made from a milk base should be used within 3 days. Refrigerator dough made from a water base may be kept up to 5 days.

To the potatoes, add shortening, sugar, salt, and eggs. Dissolve yeast in water and add to milk. Blend liquid into potato mixture. Add flour, mixing thoroughly, to make a stiff dough. Place dough in a large bowl, cover, and let rise until doubled. Refrigerate. When ready to use, roll dough on floured board and cut out rolls. Place rolls on baking sheet; let rise, which takes 1-1½ hours. Bake at 425° for 10-12 minutes. Makes 45-50 rolls.

Broccoli Cornbread

1 (10-ounce) package frozen chopped broccoli, thawed and drained
4 eggs, beaten
½ cup margarine, melted
1 large onion, finely chopped
¾ cup cottage cheese
¾ teaspoon salt
1 (8½-ounce) box cornbread mix

Combine broccoli with eggs, margarine, onion, cottage cheese, and salt. Blend in cornbread mix and pour in greased muffin tins or 13x9-inch pan. Bake at 400° for 25 minutes.

"When it comes to the wonders of cornmeal, I'm strictly an ecumenical believer, an all-souls communicant. I've never met a cornbread I didn't like. Some of that crumbly, yellow, cake-like stuff you get in Northern cafeterias has tested my faith a time or two, but I didn't leave it on my plate."

John Egerton,
Southern Food

Breads & Brunch

"To make plain bread put it in the oven. Cook it for 10 hours. Put some butter on it. Sometimes I put spaghetti on it. Then I put another piece of bread on it. Then I eat it."
Olivia Shoemaker, age 5½.

Dinner Rolls

2	packages dry yeast
1	cup warm water (110°)
1	cup scalded milk
½	cup butter-flavored shortening, melted
3	tablespoons sugar
1	tablespoon salt
2	eggs, beaten
6	cups sifted flour
	butter or margarine, melted

Dissolve yeast in warm water. In a separate bowl, combine milk, shortening, sugar, and salt. Cool to lukewarm. Add yeast and mix well. Stir in eggs. Add flour and mix by hand until dough is well blended. Place in greased bowl, turning once to grease surface, and cover. Store dough in refrigerator at least 2 hours or until needed. When ready to use, roll dough out on well-floured surface and make rolls. Place rolls on cookie sheet. Let stand in warm place (80°-85°) until light, about 1½ hours. Before baking, brush rolls with melted butter. Bake at 400° for 15-20 minutes. After baking, brush rolls lightly again with melted butter. Makes 24 rolls.

"My mother taught me how to make corn muffins. The key to success is to bake them in old, blackened muffin tins."
Beth F. Wright.

Corn Muffins

1½	cups vegetable oil, divided
1	cup self-rising cornmeal mix
1	egg
¾	cup milk

Put 2 tablespoons oil in each cup of muffin tin. Heat tin in oven. Mix cornmeal, egg, and milk. When oil in muffin tins is hot, pour batter into the cups, filling each about three-fourths full. Bake at 400° for 10-15 minutes. Makes 12 muffins.

Sally Lunn

A Southern treat, a cake-like yeast bread that originated in England

1	cup milk, scalded
4	tablespoons sugar
5	tablespoons butter, divided
1½	teaspoons salt
1	package dry yeast
½	cup lukewarm water
4	eggs, beaten
5	cups sifted flour
	shortening

Combine hot milk, sugar, 4 tablespoons butter, and salt. Cool to lukewarm. Add yeast dissolved in lukewarm water. Stir until blended. Add eggs and flour to make a soft dough. Put into a deep bowl greased with shortening. Set bowl in a warm place. When dough doubles in size, about 1 hour, punch down and divide between two greased 9x5-inch loaf pans. Let rise until dough doubles in bulk again. Bake at 350° for 25 minutes, brushing top with 1 tablespoon butter once or twice during baking. Serve hot.

Breads & Brunch

Cooks at the turn of the century not only made Sally Lunn, they whipped up crumpets. A crumpet was a small, unsweetened yeast bread. The crumpet was made by pouring batter into a special mold or "crumpet ring" and cooking it on a stovetop griddle.

Crumpets.

Take one quart of dough from the bread, break three eggs, separate the yolks and whites, both to be well beaten, mix them well in the dough, adding milk-warm water very gradually until a batter about the consistency of buckwheat cakes, beat it well and let rise. Have a hot griddle well greased, pour on the batter in small cakes, bake a light brown.

Gate City Cook Book

Simply Divine

Breads & Brunch

Tip:

Active dry yeast can be refrigerated or frozen. Allow chilled yeast to come to room temperature before using it.

Dill Bread

Delicious toasted!

1	cup cottage cheese
1	package dry yeast, dissolved in ¼ cup warm water
2	tablespoons sugar
1	egg, lightly beaten
1	tablespoon dill weed
1	tablespoon dried onions
1	tablespoon vegetable oil
1	teaspoon salt
¼	teaspoon baking soda
2	cups flour, divided

Heat cottage cheese over low heat, stirring constantly until lukewarm. Do not overheat. Stir in yeast, sugar, egg, dill weed, onion, oil, salt, and soda. Mix thoroughly. Add 2 cups flour and blend well. Turn out on floured board and knead a few minutes, adding more flour if necessary. Put dough in oiled bowl, turning to coat on all sides. Cover and let rise in a warm place (70-80°) about 1 hour. Place in a greased 2-quart casserole. Bake at 350° for 40-50 minutes.

Petite Mayonnaise Muffins

Looks and tastes like a biscuit!

1	cup self-rising flour
¾	cup milk
2	tablespoons mayonnaise

Spray miniature muffin tins with nonstick cooking spray. In medium-sized mixing bowl, combine flour, milk, and mayonnaise, blending thoroughly. Divide dough into equally-sized round balls and place in muffin tins. Bake at 400° for 6-8 minutes. Makes 12 petite muffins.

No Need to Knead Wheat Bread

1½ cups whole-wheat flour
2 packages dry yeast
1 tablespoon salt
1 cup water
½ cup honey
1 cup milk
¼ cup cooking oil
1 egg
2½-3 cups white flour

In large mixing bowl combine wheat flour, yeast, and salt. Set aside. Heat water, honey, milk, and oil over low heat until it reaches 120-130° (use candy thermometer to check temperature). Add egg. Then, add liquid mixture to dry ingredients. Using a mixer, blend on low speed until mixed. Beat three more minutes on medium speed. By hand, stir in white flour until dough is stiff. Cover with plastic wrap, put in a warm place, and allow to rise, about 1 hour. Punch dough and divide in half. Shape loaves and place in two ungreased 9x5-inch loaf pans. Cover pans with plastic wrap. Let dough rise until doubled in size, about 1 hour. Bake at 350° for 40-45 minutes. Makes 2 loaves.

Breads & Brunch

"I like french toast, it taste good. You dip it in cinamon and butter, eggs. You put butter on the pan and on each side of the bread. You flip it every 5 minutes."

Andrew Dick, age 11.

Tip:

Depending on the variety, honey gives baked goods a distinct flavor. Dark buckwheat honey is strong. Orange blossom honey is light and delicate. Generally, the darker the honey, the stronger the flavor, and the less desirable it is for baking.

Simply Divine

Breads & Brunch

Tip:

Old-fashioned oats and quick-cooking oats can be used interchangeably in recipes.

"Man does not live by bread alone, but he also does not live long without it. To eat is to acknowledge our dependence--both on food and on each other. It also reminds us of other kinds of emptiness that not even the Blue Plate Special can touch."

Frederick Buechner,
Wishful Thinking

Seven-Grain Bread

2	cups seven-grain cereal (available in health food stores)
1	cup old-fashioned oatmeal, uncooked
1	cup rye flour
3	packages yeast
4	teaspoons salt
3	cups scalded milk (105-115°)
1	cup water
6	tablespoons brown sugar
½	cup molasses
4	teaspoons melted shortening
5-7	cups white bread flour

Combine cereal, oatmeal, rye flour, yeast, and salt. Add warm milk, water, brown sugar, molasses, and shortening. Mix well and beat thoroughly. Then add 5-7 cups white bread flour, mixing by hand. Place dough on floured board and knead well. Put into greased bowl, cover with damp towel, and let rise 1½-2 hours. Punch down and let rise again 1½-2 hours. Punch down and knead on floured board. Form into 3 large loaves and 1 small loaf. Place in greased loaf pans. Cover with cloth and let rise 1 hour. Bake at 350° for 40-60 minutes. Remove from pans and cool completely.

Ida's Oatmeal Coffee Cake

This coffee cake originated with Ida Barker, the mother of Chris Haggai.

1   cup old-fashioned oatmeal, uncooked
1½ cups hot water
3   eggs, divided
1   cup light or dark brown sugar
½   cup vegetable oil
1½ cups sifted, self-rising flour
1   teaspoon cinnamon
1   teaspoon nutmeg
6-8 tablespoons butter, softened
1   cup chopped nuts
1   cup coconut

Mix oatmeal and water. Set aside to soften oatmeal. Beat 2 eggs; combine with sugar and oil. Set aside. To oatmeal mixture, add flour and spices. Stir in egg mixture. Bake in a greased 13x9-inch pan at 350° for 30 minutes. While cake is baking, mix together butter, nuts, coconut, and remaining egg. Spread on cake and bake an additional 20-30 minutes. Serves 12.

Breads & Brunch

"Let's go and see everybody," said Pooh. "Because when you have been walking in the wind for miles, and you suddenly go into somebody's house, and he says, 'Hallo, Pooh, you're just in time for a little smackerel of something,' and you are, then it's what I call a Friendly Day."

A.A. **Milne**,
The House at Pooh Corner

Simply Divine

Breads & Brunch

Sour Cream Coffee Cake

1	cup margarine, softened
1¼	cups plus 2 tablespoons sugar
2	eggs
1	cup sour cream
1	teaspoon vanilla
2	cups flour
½	teaspoon baking soda
1	tablespoon baking powder
2	tablespoons brown sugar
½	cup chopped pecans
2	teaspoons cinnamon

Beat margarine, 1¼ cups sugar, eggs, sour cream, and vanilla until smooth. In a separate bowl, mix flour, soda, and baking powder. Beat flour mixture into batter. Pour half the batter into a greased tube or large loaf pan. Mix together brown sugar, pecans, cinnamon, and remaining 2 tablespoons sugar. Sprinkle half the nut mixture over batter. Pour remaining batter in pan and top with rest of nut mixture. Bake at 350° for 30-45 minutes. When cool, invert and serve.

Texas Coffee Cake

Great with scrambled eggs, fruit, and hot chocolate

Breads & Brunch

2½ cups sifted flour
2   cups brown sugar
½   teaspoon salt
⅔   cup shortening
2   teaspoons baking powder
½   teaspoon baking soda
½   teaspoon ground cinnamon
½   teaspoon ground nutmeg
1   cup sour milk
2   beaten eggs
     pecan halves (optional)

Mix flour, sugar, salt, and shortening until crumbly. Reserve ½ cup crumbs. Add baking powder, soda, and spices, mixing well. Stir in milk and eggs. Mix well. Pour into a greased and floured 13x9-inch pan. Top with crumbs and pecan halves. Bake at 375° for 25-30 minutes.

"Texas Coffee Cake traditionally has been part of our Christmas breakfast."
        -Perry and Katherine White.

T*ip*:

For a flavor treat, use freshly ground or grated nutmeg. One whole nutmeg yields 2-3 teaspoons of ground spice.

Granola

3   cups quick-cooking oatmeal, uncooked
6   ounces wheat germ
2   cups chopped nuts or seeds
½   pound brown sugar
⅔   cup water
⅔   cup vegetable oil
1   tablespoon vanilla
1¼   cups dried fruits

Mix all ingredients. Spread on large cookie sheet (sides at least 1 inch deep) covered with aluminum foil. Bake at 350° for 30 minutes. Store at room temperature.

Simply Divine   49

Breads & Brunch

Variation:

In place of nuts, substitute raisins, currants, or dried cranberries.

Apple Bran Muffins

3 cups self-rising flour
1 teaspoon cinnamon
⅔ cup whole-wheat bran
1 cup vegetable oil
2 cups sugar
2 eggs
1 teaspoon vanilla
2 cups finely chopped apples
1 cup chopped pecans (optional)

Sift together flour and cinnamon. Stir in bran. In a separate bowl, mix together oil, sugar, and eggs until smooth. Add vanilla and stir. Then, stir egg mixture into dry ingredients until well blended. Fold in apples and pecans. Mix well. Fill muffin tins two-thirds full and bake at 350° for 20-25 minutes. Makes 24 muffins.

Fig Muffins

Orange Spread

1 (3-ounce) package cream cheese, softened
¼ cup sifted powdered sugar
2 tablespoons frozen orange juice concentrate, thawed

Cream cheese until light and fluffy. Beat in sugar and orange juice concentrate. Spread on muffins, toast, or bagels.

¼ cup butter, softened
½ cup sugar
3 eggs
2 cups mashed fig preserves with syrup
1 cup old-fashioned oatmeal, uncooked
1½ cups flour
2 teaspoons baking powder
½ teaspoon baking soda
½ teaspoon salt

Cream butter and sugar. Add eggs, one at a time, beating well after each addition. Add figs. Stir in oatmeal. Sift flour, baking powder, soda, and salt. Add to fig-oatmeal mixture, stirring only enough to moisten dry ingredients. Put into buttered muffin tins. Bake at 375° for 15-20 minutes. Serve warm with Orange Spread. (See recipe.) Refrigerate leftover muffins.

Morning Glory Muffins

¾ cup wheat bran
¾ cup white flour
½ cup whole-wheat flour
1½ teaspoons baking powder
½ teaspoon baking soda
¼ teaspoon salt
½ cup golden raisins
½ cup chopped dates
½ cup chopped dried apricots
1 cup skim-milk buttermilk
⅓ cup molasses
⅓ cup apple butter
1 white from a large egg
3 tablespoons canola oil
1 tablespoon fresh lemon juice
1½ teaspoons grated lemon zest
1 teaspoon vanilla

In a large bowl, stir together bran, flours, baking powder, soda, and salt. Stir in dried fruit. In a medium-sized bowl, whisk together buttermilk, molasses, apple butter, egg white, oil, lemon juice, zest, and vanilla. Stir into the flour mixture just until the dry ingredients are moistened; do not over mix. Divide the batter among greased muffin cups, filling cups nearly full. Bake at 425° in upper third of oven for 15-20 minutes or until a cake tester inserted in the center comes out clean. Turn muffins out onto a rack to cool for 5 minutes before serving. Makes 12 muffins.

Breads & Brunch

Tip:

When buying lemons, choose evenly-colored, yellow ones. Lemons tinged with green are not ripe.

Simply Divine

Breads & Brunch

Tip:

Create a substitute for the buttermilk by putting 5⅓ tablespoons vinegar into a 4-cup measure and adding enough skim milk to make one quart.

Oat and Wheat Bran Muffins

Good for the health-conscious

3	cups All-Bran cereal, divided
3	cups oat bran, divided
2	cups boiling water
1	cup vegetable oil
5	cups unsifted flour
5	teaspoons baking soda
2	teaspoons salt
5	teaspoons cinnamon
2½	cups sugar
2	whole eggs
2	egg whites, unbeaten
1	quart buttermilk
1	(15-ounce) box golden raisins
	fresh apple, chopped
	pineapple tidbits (optional)

In a large bowl, combine 1 cup All-Bran, 1 cup oat bran, boiling water, and oil. Set aside. Sift together flour, soda, salt, and cinnamon. To bran mixture, add remainder of All-Bran, oat bran, sugar, eggs, egg whites, and buttermilk. Then, stir in flour mixture. Refrigerate overnight or until needed. (Basic dough without fruit will last 2 to 3 weeks in refrigerator.) Before baking, add raisins and apples and pineapple to taste. Fill greased muffin tins. Bake at 400° for 20-25 minutes in regular or miniature muffin tins.

Winter Squash Muffins

Use any winter squash in these spicy muffins.

1½   cups unsifted flour
¼   cup firmly packed light brown sugar
1   tablespoon baking powder
½   teaspoon salt
½   teaspoon cinnamon
¼   teaspoon nutmeg
1   egg
1   cup cooked winter squash, pureed
½   cup milk
¼   cup melted butter

Combine flour, sugar, baking powder, salt, and spices. In a separate bowl, combine egg, squash, milk, and butter. Add mixture to flour, stirring until dry ingredients are moistened. Spoon into greased muffin cups. Bake at 400° for 15-20 minutes. Makes 12 muffins.

Breads & Brunch

Tip:

Some popular varieties of winter squash are acorn, butternut, delicata, hubbard, pumpkin, spaghetti, and turban.

Butter-Me-Nots

2   cups self-rising flour
1   cup sour cream
1   cup butter, melted

Mix flour, sour cream, and butter. Put dough in miniature muffin tins. Bake at 400° for 10-12 minutes. Serve hot. Makes 48 miniature muffins.

"I like my mom's homemade biscuts because there real fluffy and good."
Handley Wright, age 10.

Simply Divine   53

Breads & Brunch

Variation:

Sprinkle ½ teaspoon cinnamon over batter before topping with filling.

Tip:

Bake recipe ahead of time and freeze. Thaw and warm before serving.

Baked Blintz

1	cup butter, melted
1	cup sugar, divided
4	eggs, divided
1	cup flour
1	tablespoon baking powder
¼	cup milk
1	teaspoon vanilla
2	(8-ounce) packages cream cheese
2	cups cottage cheese
	juice of 1 lemon
	sliced fresh fruit, sour cream, strawberry jam (optional)

Make a batter by whisking together butter, ½ cup sugar, 2 eggs, flour, baking powder, milk, and vanilla. Spread half the batter evenly into a greased 13x9-inch pan. Prepare filling by combining cheeses, ½ cup sugar, 2 eggs, and lemon juice. Spread filling over batter. Cover with remaining batter. Bake at 350° for 1 hour. Top with fruit, sour cream, or jam. Serves 6-8.

"My brother Taylor (age 9) makes really good scrabled eggs."
  Amy Lewis, age 12.

Sausage Egg Strata

1	pound sausage
6	eggs
2	cups milk
3	slices cubed white bread, crusts removed
1¼	cups shredded sharp cheddar cheese
1	teaspoon dry mustard
1	teaspoon salt

Cook sausage and drain. In a bowl beat eggs and milk. Then add sausage, bread, cheese, and seasonings. Pour into an ungreased 13x9-inch pan. Cover; refrigerate overnight. Bake at 350° for 45 minutes. Serves 10.

Peggy Durrett's Charleston Cheese Grits

Peggy was Emory's first liver transplant recipient. She worked for many years with the children's music ministry at Second-Ponce and always traveled with the Youth Choir Mission Tours.

4½ cups water
1   cup quick-cooking grits
1   teaspoon salt
½   cup butter
2   (6-ounce) rolls processed garlic cheese
    dash Tabasco
    dash Worcestershire sauce
2   eggs, beaten in a measuring cup
    milk
1   cup corn flakes, crushed

Bring water to boil and cook grits, salt, and butter until done. Add cheese, Tabasco, and Worcestershire. Stir until cheese melts. Remove from heat. Add milk to the eggs to make 1 cup liquid and stir into mixture. Pour into a greased 13x9-inch baking dish. Top with corn flakes. Bake at 400° for 1 hour or until set. Serves 10-12.

Mexican Breakfast Bake

6   eggs, beaten
1   (4-ounce) can green chilies, drained
1   (8-ounce) package shredded cheese
1   cup cottage cheese
¼   cup melted butter
¼   cup flour
⅛-¼   teaspoon salt

Mix all ingredients and pour into a buttered 11x7-inch pan. Bake at 375° for 30 minutes. Serves 4-6.

Breads & Brunch

Tip:

A dash is a measuring term which refers to a small amount of seasoning, usually between 1/16 and 1/8 of a teaspoon. When using Tabasco and Worcestershire, remember that each imparts a different flavor. Tabasco is fermented hot peppers, vinegar, and salt. Worcestershire is a blend of anchovies, garlic, lime, molasses, onions, soy sauce, tamarind, vinegar, and other seasonings.

Tip:

To pique the flavor of this dish, use the packaged blends of cheese labeled "Mexican Blend." The blends are combinations of cheddar, Monterey Jack, Pepper Jack, and asadero (also called Chihuahua and Oaxaca). You may experiment with the proportions and create your own blend. An 8-ounce package of shredded cheese equals 2 cups.

Simply Divine

Breads & Brunch

Broiled Finnon Haddie.

Take a large fat haddie of about three or four pounds, soak over night, next morning remove from water, rinse and dry and peel off skin, place on broiler, cut butter over it and season lightly with pepper, no salt necessary, place under light of gas stove and broil about twenty minutes. This is a delicious breakfast dish.

Gate City Cook Book

Crab Quiche

- ½ cup mayonnaise
- 2 tablespoons flour
- 2 eggs, lightly beaten
- ½ cup milk
- 1 (7-ounce) can white lump meat (not flake) crab meat, drained
- 8 ounces grated Swiss cheese
- ⅓ cup chopped green onion
- 9-inch deep-dish pie crust

Combine mayonnaise, flour, eggs, and milk. Add crab, cheese, and onion. Pour into unbaked pie crust. Bake at 350° for 40-45 minutes until set. Makes 6 servings.

Tomato Gravy and Grits

A Southern tradition, grits are finely ground hominy or hulled corn kernels.

- 4 slices bacon
- 3 tablespoons flour
- 1 (14.5-ounce) can tomatoes, undrained
- salt
- pepper
- 2 cups water, lightly salted
- ⅔ cup quick-cooking grits
- ¼ cup milk (optional)

In a pan, fry bacon until crisp. Drain bacon on paper towels. Pour grease from pan except for 3 tablespoons. Add flour and brown, blending and stirring to create a roux. Pour in tomatoes and stir well. Add seasonings to taste. Reduce heat and simmer about 10 minutes until gravy becomes smooth and thick. Bring water to a boil and add grits. Reduce heat and simmer to desired consistency, adding milk for a smoother texture. Ladle gravy over generous servings of grits and serve with bacon. Serves 2.

Saturday Morning Omelet

Delicious with sliced tomatoes and grits or hash browns

8	eggs, lightly beaten
½	cup grated cheddar or Monterey Jack cheese
¼	cup cooked, diced ham
¼	cup crisp fried bacon, crumbled
¼	cup ground beef, cooked and crumbled
2	tablespoons Worcestershire sauce
1	teaspoon salt
½	teaspoon black pepper
4	tablespoons butter or margarine, divided
¼	cup chopped green onions, tops included
¼	cup chopped sliced mushrooms, fresh or canned
⅛	cup chopped green bell pepper or jalapeño

In a large bowl, combine eggs, cheese, ham, bacon, beef, Worcestershire, salt, and pepper. Set aside. In a large non-stick skillet, melt 2 tablespoons butter. Sauté onions, mushrooms, and peppers. Put vegetables into the egg mixture and stir. Wipe skillet clean and melt remaining butter. Pour egg mixture into skillet; cook over medium heat. When eggs start to set, divide into spatula-sized sections and turn each section over to finish cooking. Serves 4-6.

Breads & Brunch

Tip:
Cheese is easier to grate if it is cold.

English Monkey was a dish similar to Welsh rarebit. The term dates in print to 1896. Traditional English Monkey included tomatoes in the cheese sauce.

Cheese Fondue, or English Monkey.

One cup of milk, one tablespoonful of butter, one cup of fine bread crumbs, two cups of finely grated cheese. First put in butter, then cheese, then milk, then bread crumbs. When hot add two well-beaten eggs. Stir the eggs in slowly, and do not let it boil up after adding. Cook slowly for about two minutes. Season with salt and pepper and serve on saltines.

Gate City Cook Book

Simply Divine

Breads & Brunch

Poached to Perfection

6   cups water
1   tablespoon vinegar
1   fresh egg, cracked in a dish
     seasonings

In a saucepan heat water and vinegar to a gentle simmer. Slip egg into water; cook until white is firm, about 3 minutes. Remove with a slotted spoon, season, and serve immediately.

"Ungspankaka is a Minnesota recipe that we use frequently at our cabin up North."

—Julie Robertson

Tip:

For a large crowd, double the recipe, use a 13x9-inch pan, and increase baking time.

Ham Hash

1   (32-ounce) bag frozen hash brown potatoes
1   cup chopped onions
2   cups cubed ham
½   cup sour cream
1   (10¾-ounce) can cream of chicken soup
1   cup shredded cheddar cheese, divided
¾   cup melted butter, divided
1   teaspoon salt
1   teaspoon black pepper
2   cups crushed corn flakes

Mix together potatoes, onions, ham, sour cream, soup, ½ cup cheese, ½ cup butter, and seasonings. Put into 13x9-inch pan coated with nonstick cooking spray. Mix remaining butter, corn flakes, and cheese; spread evenly over mixture. Bake at 375° for 1 hour. Serve with fried or poached eggs. Serves 12.

Ungspankaka

A baked Swedish pancake, pronounced UNGS-pan ka-ka

6   strips bacon
3   eggs
2   cups milk
1   teaspoon salt
⅔   cup flour
2   tablespoons sugar
1-2 tablespoons butter
     maple syrup, warmed

Fry bacon until crisp, and crumble into pieces. Combine eggs, milk, salt, flour, and sugar, and beat with a hand beater. Melt butter in an 11x7-inch pan in 350° oven. When butter is melted, pour batter into pan; add bacon, distributing pieces evenly. Bake at 350° about 40 minutes until pancake is puffed up, firm, and golden brown. Remove from oven and cut into squares. Serve with maple syrup. Serves 4.

Soups & Stews

"Listen, listen to me, and eat what is good,
and your soul will delight in the richest of fare."

Isaiah 55:2

Soups & Stews

SOUPS

Wild Rice Soup	61
Oriental Shrimp Soup	61
Steak and Mushroom Soup	62
Steak Marinade	62
Vegetable Beef Soup	63
Vichyssoise	63
Herb Tomato Broth	63
Barley Soup	64
Nine Bean Soup	65
Nine Bean Soup Mix	65
Cheese Soup	66
Polish Potato Soup	67
Pumpkin Soup	68
Basque Bean Cassoulet	69

CHILIES

Chunky Chicken Chili	70
Cincinnati 5-Way Chili	71
Three Bean Chili	72

CHOWDERS

Corn Chowder	65
Seafood Chowder	73

STEWS

Seafood Gumbo	74
Brunswick Stew	75
Crockpot Brunswick Stew	76
Hunter's Stew	77
Jim Denison's Mexican Stew	77
Oyster Stew	78

HERITAGE RECIPES

Terrapin Soup	61
Pilau	75

Wild Rice Soup

Enjoy the nutty flavor and chewy texture of wild rice.

2	large potatoes, peeled and diced
3	cups chicken stock
9	slices bacon, cut in small pieces
1	medium onion, chopped
1½	cups cooked wild rice
1	quart half-and-half
2	cups American cheese, shredded
	salt
	pepper
	chopped green onions (optional)

Cook potatoes in chicken stock until tender. Puree potatoes and liquid in food processor. In a small skillet, fry bacon. Add onion and cook until tender. In a saucepan, combine bacon mixture with wild rice. Add puree, half-and-half, and cheese. Heat gently, stirring until cheese melts. Add seasonings. Garnish with green onions. Serves 12.

Oriental Shrimp Soup

4	green onions, cut into 1-inch pieces
½	cup carrots, thinly sliced
½	cup fresh mushrooms, thinly sliced
1	tablespoon margarine
4	cups chicken broth
½	pound medium shrimp, peeled and deveined
4	drops sesame oil
½	cup chopped cilantro

In a large pan over medium-high heat, sauté vegetables in margarine until tender. Add broth; bring to a boil. Add shrimp, oil, and cilantro. Cook 3 minutes or until shrimp is done. Garnish with additional cilantro. Serves 4.

Soups & Stews

The choicest of all turtle meat is the East Coast terrapin. The ideal candidate for soup is a three-pound, seven-inch female terrapin.

Terrapin Soup.

Take three terrapins, cut open and clean them, then scald the shells, scrape them, and put into a pot with four quarts of water; boil until tender, then take out and pick to pieces. Place the meat again in the water. Add pepper and salt to taste. Fry a small piece of fat pork, chop it fine, and add to the soup. Thicken with browned flour, CAPITOLA; then add a teaspoonful of mace and one of allspice. When done add the juice of two lemons, one cup of claret. If the soup is not a rich brown from the flour, brown a little sugar for coloring.

        Gate City Cook Book

"Health is the thing that makes you feel like now is the best time of the year."

       -Franklin Pierce Adams.

Simply Divine

Soups & Stews

Steak Marinade

⅔ cup safflower oil
2 tablespoons lemon juice
1 tablespoon dark brown sugar
2 tablespoons dark soy sauce
1 teaspoon Dijon mustard
1 large garlic clove, finely minced

Whisk all ingredients together.

Steak and Mushroom Soup

Marinating the meat enhances the flavor.

1¼ pounds cubed steak, cut in 1-inch cubes
3 tablespoons olive oil, divided
3 tablespoons butter, divided
3 medium onions, half coarsely chopped, half thinly sliced
2 small carrots, minced
2 small celery stalks, minced
1 pound fresh button mushrooms, thickly sliced
 flour for dusting
5-6 cups beef stock
1½ teaspoons salt
¼ teaspoon (or more) freshly ground pepper
1 large bay leaf
1¼ pounds escarole, torn in bite-sized pieces

Marinate steak in marinade (see recipe) for 1 hour, making sure meat is submerged. In a large stock pot, heat 1½ tablespoons olive oil and 1½ tablespoons butter. Add chopped onions, carrots, and celery. Cook over medium to high heat until golden. Add mushrooms and continue cooking until slightly wilted. Remove and set aside. Wipe out pan and add remaining oil and butter; heat. Pat steak dry. Flour the meat, shaking off excess. Brown over medium heat, being careful not to allow the flour to burn. Remove meat; set aside. Return cooked vegetables to pot along with the sliced onions. Add 5 cups stock. Bring to a simmer and add steak, salt, pepper, and bay leaf. Simmer 15 minutes. Add escarole and simmer about 10 minutes, just long enough for escarole to become tender. Do not overcook. Adjust seasonings, adding more stock if the soup is too thick. Serves 6-8.

Vegetable Beef Soup

2   tablespoons oil
1   small onion, chopped
1-2 pounds stew beef
6   cups water
1   beef bouillon cube
3   (14.5-ounce) cans whole tomatoes, chopped
1   cup fresh or frozen green beans
4   carrots, peeled and sliced in coins
2   cups fresh or frozen corn
1   cup fresh or frozen black-eyed peas
1   cup fresh or frozen butter beans
2   bay leaves
1   tablespoon basil
    salt
    pepper
1   teaspoon Worcestershire sauce
2   drops Tabasco

Heat oil. Brown onion until clear. Add beef and brown. Add water and bouillon. Simmer 15-20 minutes until broth has formed. Add remaining vegetables and all seasonings. Simmer for 2 hours, adding water as needed. Serves 8.

Vichyssoise

A quick variation on a classic soup

2   (10¾-ounce) cans potato soup
2   (14½-ounce) cans chicken broth
2¼-3 cups sour cream, to taste
1   teaspoon chopped chives

In a blender, process soup and broth. Add sour cream and chill. Serve very cold. Garnish with chives. Serves 4-6.

Soups & Stews

Herb Tomato Broth

A quick lunch or tasty appetizer

1   (10¾-ounce) can condensed beef broth
1   (10¾-ounce) can tomato soup
1   soup can water
¼   teaspoon ground marjoram
¼   teaspoon thyme
    butter

Combine soups, water, and herbs. Heat to boiling. Simmer 2 minutes. Dot each serving with butter. Serves 5.

Variation:

Substitute other herbs that blend well with tomato, such as basil, dill, mint, oregano, parsley, savory, and tarragon.

Tip:

This soup travels well. Double the recipe and share a batch with a friend or neighbor.

Simply Divine

Soups & Stews

T*ip*:

A ham bone will keep in the freezer for up to six months.

"Do you have a kinder, more adaptable friend in the food world than soup? Who soothes you when you are ill? Who refuses to leave you when you are impoverished and stretches its resources to give you hearty sustenance and cheer? Who warms you in winter and cools you in summer? Yet who is also capable of doing honor to your richest table and impressing your most demanding guests?

"Why, then, do people so mistreat this inestimable friend? They dump it unceremoniously into all the wrong containers, pay no attention to its modest preferences in spoons, tilt it from side to side until it is afraid of perishing in an oceanic storm, make frightful noises at it, and leave spoons pitched into it, like daggers in trusting hearts."

-Judith Martin,
Miss Manners

Barley Soup

The perfect solution for "what to do" with the holiday ham bone.

4	large celery stalks, chopped
4	carrots, chopped
2	onions, chopped
2	tablespoons oil
¾	pound fresh mushrooms, chopped or sliced
1	small turnip, peeled and chopped
1	meaty ham bone
1	teaspoon salt
	pepper
2	beef bouillon cubes
12	cups water
1	cup barley
1	(16-ounce) can tomatoes, chopped
1	(9-ounce) can Italian beans, drained

In a skillet, sauté celery, carrots, and onions in oil. Remove vegetables. Add mushrooms and chopped turnip; sauté. In a large stock pot, place ham bone, salt, pepper, vegetables, bouillon cubes, and water. Heat to boiling. Reduce heat and simmer 1 hour. Add barley and continue simmering 40 minutes. Remove bone and chop ham. Return meat to soup. Add tomatoes and beans. Simmer 20 minutes. Serves 10.

Simply Divine

Nine Bean Soup

2   cups dried bean soup mix
2½ quarts water
1   meaty ham bone
1   large onion, chopped
1   cup celery, chopped
1   (16-ounce) can tomatoes, chopped with juice
1   teaspoon dried basil
2   cloves minced garlic
½   cup picante sauce
½   teaspoon salt

Sort and wash beans; place them in a large soup pot. Cover with water. Soak overnight. Drain beans and return to pot. Add 2½ quarts water and ham bone. Bring to boil. Simmer 3-3½ hours. Remove bone; chop meat and return to pot. Add vegetables, basil, garlic, picante sauce, and salt. Simmer 30 minutes, stirring occasionally. For a thicker consistency, puree a portion of the beans and vegetables and return to pot. Serves 8-10.

Corn Chowder

2   cups diced potatoes
1   cup minced onions
1   cup salted water
1   (16-ounce) can whole kernel corn, undrained
1   (10¾-ounce) can mushroom soup
2   cups milk
1   teaspoon salt
    dash pepper
5   slices crisp cooked bacon, crumbled

Boil potatoes and onions in water until tender. Stir in corn, soup, milk, and seasonings. Cook and stir until thick. Serve topped with bacon. Serves 6.

Soups & Stews

Nine Bean Soup Mix

1   pound dried baby limas
1   pound dried black beans
1   pound dried black-eyed peas
1   pound dried great Northern beans
1   pound dried lentils
1   pound dried navy beans
1   pound dried pinto beans
1   pound dried red beans
1   pound dried split peas (green or yellow)

Combine beans. If you choose, substitute other dried products, such as barley, garbanzos, or kidney beans. One recipe makes about 10 pots of soup, each using 2 cups of mix. Gift idea: layer beans in a glass jar and attach the soup recipe.

Soups & Stews

Variation:

To change the color or flavor of the soup, experiment with the cheese. Cheddars range in color from white to orange and in flavor from mild to sharp.

"Only the pure of heart can make a good soup."
   -Ludwig van Beethoven.

Cheese Soup

2   chicken bouillon cubes
2   cups boiling water
½   cup minced carrot
¾   cup minced celery
2   tablespoons minced onion
4   tablespoons vegetable oil
4½ tablespoons flour
⅛   teaspoon black pepper
2   cups milk
½   pound American or sharp cheddar cheese, grated
    chopped parsley

Dissolve bouillon in water. Add carrot and celery and simmer 10 minutes. In a separate pan, sauté onion in oil until tender. Stir in flour and pepper. Add milk and bouillon mixture. Cook, stirring constantly until thickened. Add cheese; stir until melted. Ladle into bowls and top with parsley. Serves 4.

Polish Potato Soup

Serve with crusty French bread and a green salad.

1	pound green beans, cut in 1-inch pieces
2	pounds boiling potatoes, peeled and cut in ½-inch dice
2	large onions, chopped
2	bay leaves
11½	cups water, divided
10	level tablespoons flour
3	cups sour cream
	salt
	pepper
1	tablespoon fresh minced dill or 1-1½ teaspoons dried

In a soup pot, bring beans, potatoes, onions, bay leaves, and 10 cups water to a boil. Reduce heat, simmer 20-25 minutes until vegetables are tender. Remove pot from heat. Discard bay leaves. In a separate bowl, blend flour with 1½ cups water. Whisk until smooth. Fold into sour cream. Remove 1 cup of hot potato liquid and slowly add to sour cream. Blend sour cream mixture back into the soup, stirring gently. Return pot to heat. Stir until soup thickens. Do not boil. If soup seems thick, thin with more water. If soup seems thin, dissolve more flour in water and add, stirring gently until soup thickens. Remove from heat and season to taste. Serve hot or cold. Flavor improves if soup is made a day ahead and refrigerated overnight. Serves 10-12.

Soups & Stews

Tip:

Always add sour cream at the end of the cooking process, using low heat. Never boil or overstir it.

Simply Divine

Soups & Stews

Pumpkin Soup

For a special presentation, serve in small, hollowed-out pumpkins and top with a dollop of sour cream and a sprinkling of chopped chives.

1	cup chopped onions
1	clove garlic, crushed
¼	cup butter
1	teaspoon curry
½	teaspoon salt
¼	teaspoon coriander
⅛	teaspoon red pepper
3	cups chicken broth
1¾	cups cooked pumpkin
1	cup half-and-half
	sour cream
	chopped chives

Sauté onion and garlic in butter until soft. Add spices and cook 1 minute. Add broth and simmer gently 15 minutes with pan uncovered. Whisk in pumpkin and half-and-half. Simmer 5 minutes, blending until smooth. Serves 6.

"Food should be chosen to give pleasure, and to cheer up people after a hard day's work, to comfort them when they feel down for some reason, to amuse them when things seem a bit dull, or to open up conversation when they feel silent and uncommunicative. It seems to me totally unnecessary for any home, or even institution, to fall into the rut of serving the same thing the same day each week. One should not be able to say, 'Oh, yes, Monday, bread pudding' – anywhere. Meals should be a surprise, and should show imagination."
-Edith Schaeffer,
Hidden Art

Simply Divine

Basque Bean Cassoulet

A traditional dish from the southwest of France

Soups & Stews

1	pound navy or pinto beans
4½	cups water
¼	pound salt pork or bacon
2	medium leeks, thinly sliced
2	cups chopped onions
1	(14-ounce) can chicken broth
1	medium onion stuffed with 6 whole cloves
5	carrots cut in 1-inch pieces
5	cloves garlic, minced
1	bay leaf
6	whole peppercorns
2	teaspoons Tabasco
1	teaspoon dried thyme leaves
1	teaspoon marjoram
1	(14½-ounce) can tomatoes, undrained and finely chopped
1	pound sweet or hot Italian sausage, cut into ½-inch pieces

In a large pot, combine beans and water. Soak 2 hours; do not drain. In a skillet, brown salt pork on all sides; remove. Add leeks and chopped onions; cook 10 minutes. Combine onion mixture with beans. Add broth, onion studded with cloves, carrots, garlic, bay leaf, peppercorns, and other seasonings. Bring to a boil; simmer covered 1 hour. Remove onion studded with cloves, bay leaf, and peppercorns. Stir in tomatoes and sausage. Cover and bake at 350° for 1 hour. Serves 8-10.

"The restaurant worked on the simple formula of removing the burden of decision from its customers. As in the station cafe at Bonnieux, you ate and drank what you were given. We had a crisp, oily salad and slices of pink country sausages, an aioli of snails and cod and hard-boiled eggs with garlic mayonnaise, creamy cheese from Fontvielle, and a homemade tart. It was the kind of meal that the French take for granted and tourists remember for years."

-Peter Mayle,
A Year in Provence

Simply Divine

Soups & Stews

Chunky Chicken Chili

1   onion, chopped
1-2 tablespoons butter
1-2 tablespoons oil
1½ pounds chicken breast, cut into bite-sized chunks
1   green bell pepper, chopped
1   red bell pepper, chopped
1   yellow bell pepper, chopped
1   (14½-ounce) can stewed tomatoes
1   (15½-ounce) can Mexican stewed tomatoes
1   (15-ounce) can dark red kidney beans, rinsed and drained
1   (15-ounce) can pinto beans, rinsed and drained
1   cup thick and chunky, mild, medium, or hot salsa
1   clove garlic, minced
1   tablespoon cumin
2-3 tablespoons chili powder
    grated cheddar or taco cheese
    sour cream

Sauté onion in butter and oil until tender. Add chicken and cook. Add peppers, tomatoes, beans, salsa, and seasonings. Simmer 30-45 minutes. Top with cheese and a dollop of sour cream.

"Let brotherly love continue. Be not forgetful to entertain strangers: for thereby some have entertained angels unawares."

-Hebrews 13:1-2.

"True hospitality is marked by an open response to the dignity of each and every person."

-Kathleen Norris,
Dakota

"To keep our table replenished, our doors open to those in need, requires faith."

-Isabel Anders,
Awaiting the Child

Cincinnati 5-Way Chili

Chili served with spaghetti, onions, cheese, ginger, and Tabasco

Soups & Stews

"This is the only way to eat chili."
-Ron David,
a native of Cincinnati.

2	pounds ground beef
¼	pound bacon, diced
1	large onion, chopped
4	cloves garlic, minced
2	teaspoons salt
	black pepper to taste
1	green bell pepper, chopped
¼	jalapeño pepper, seeded and chopped
4	tablespoons chili powder
½	teaspoon cumin
1	tablespoon oregano
1	teaspoon cocoa
1	(28-ounce) can tomatoes
1	(15-ounce) can chili hot beans, rinsed and drained
1	tablespoon Worcestershire sauce
1	cup beef broth

5-Way Ingredients:
   cooked spaghetti
   chopped onions
   grated cheese
   grated ginger
   Tabasco

"The most remarkable thing about my mother is that for thirty years she served the family nothing but leftovers. The original meal has never been found."
-Calvin Trillin.

In a large skillet, cook beef and bacon. Add onion and garlic; cook until tender. Drain grease. Add salt, black pepper, green and jalapeño peppers, seasonings, cocoa, tomatoes, beans, Worcestershire, and broth. Simmer 2 hours. Serve over spaghetti and top with onions, cheese, ginger, and Tabasco.

Soups & Stews

"Better a meal of vegetables where there is love
Than a fattened ox and hatred with it."
                                -Proverbs 15:17.

"O Lord that lends me life,
Lend me a heart replete with
    thankfulness."
                -William Shakespeare.

Three Bean Chili

Chili topped the way you like it

1	large onion, chopped
2	tablespoons vegetable oil
2	(14½-ounce) cans stewed tomatoes
1	(15-ounce) can pinto beans, drained and rinsed
1	(15-ounce) can kidney beans, drained and rinsed
1	(15-ounce) can black beans, drained and rinsed
1	medium green bell pepper, chopped
1	cup chicken broth
1-2	cups picante sauce, divided
1	teaspoon ground cumin
½	teaspoon salt
	shredded cheddar or Monterey Jack cheese (optional)
	chopped cilantro (optional)
	sour cream (optional)
	chopped green onions (optional)

In a large saucepan or Dutch oven, cook onion in oil until tender. Add tomatoes, beans, green pepper, broth, 1 cup picante sauce, cumin, and salt. Bring to a boil. Reduce heat and simmer uncovered 10 minutes, stirring occasionally. Ladle into bowls. Top as desired, using remaining picante sauce, cheese, cilantro, sour cream, or green onions. Serves 10.

Simply Divine

Seafood Chowder

Soups & Stews

1	pound halibut or other white fish
1	pound scallops, cut in bite-sized pieces
3-4	large potatoes, peeled and cut into ½-inch dice
1	cup butter
1	large onion, chopped
3	stalks celery, chopped
1	pound shrimp, peeled and deveined
¼	cup flour
2	(6-ounce) cans diced clams
2	cups milk, warmed
1	cup half-and-half, warmed
	salt
	pepper
	Tabasco

Tip:

When poaching food, keep the liquid just under the boiling point. The surface of the broth should quiver not bubble.

Poach halibut in enough water to cover fish; reserve liquid. Remove bones and flake fish. Poach scallops in enough water to cover; reserve liquid. In a saucepan, cover potatoes with water and boil until tender; reserve liquid. In a large pan, melt butter and sauté onion and celery. Add shrimp and cook until pink (about 3-4 minutes). Sprinkle in flour, stirring constantly. Add clams, fish, scallops, and poaching liquids. Stir. Add potatoes and cooking liquid, blending. Add milk and half-and-half, stirring well. Season to taste. Best if prepared a day ahead to allow flavors to blend. Serves 10.

Soups & Stews

Seafood Gumbo

3	cups water
1	whole stalk celery with leaves
¼	teaspoon Tabasco
2	teaspoons salt
2	tablespoons butter
1	clove garlic, minced
1	large onion, chopped
1	large green bell pepper, diced
2	cups canned tomatoes
2	cups okra, sliced
½	teaspoon black pepper
1	teaspoon sugar
2	pounds medium shrimp, shelled and deveined
2	teaspoons parsley
½	pint oysters
1	tablespoon prepared horseradish
1	pound crab meat

In a saucepan, combine water, celery, Tabasco, and salt. Simmer covered for 10 minutes. In a large skillet, melt butter. Add garlic, onion, and green pepper. Cook, covered, about 15 minutes, stirring frequently. Add tomatoes and okra. Simmer covered about 30 minutes. Add pepper, sugar, and shrimp. Simmer covered for 10 minutes. Add parsley and oysters and cook until oysters crinkle. Stir in celery liquid. Add horseradish and crabmeat. Stir. Serve in a bowl as gumbo or on a plate over a mound of white rice. Serves 10.

74 Simply Divine

Brunswick Stew

Brunswick Stew originated in 1828 in Brunswick County, Virginia, as a squirrel-meat and onion stew.

1	large hen or 2 broiler-fryers
2	pounds boneless beef
2	pounds boneless pork
4	(16-ounce) cans tomatoes, undrained
3	(16-ounce) cans cream style corn
2	(16-ounce) cans lima beans, drained
1	(14-ounce) bottle ketchup
1	cup cider vinegar
6	medium onions, chopped
½	cup Worcestershire sauce
	salt
	crushed crackers or toasted bread crumbs (optional)

Cover hen with water (about 3 quarts) and cook until tender. Reserve and refrigerate broth. Debone chicken. Cover beef and pork with water together in a pot and cook until tender. Chop poultry and meats, using a meat grinder or food processor. Set aside. De-fat chicken broth and place in stock pot. Add chopped poultry and meat, tomatoes, corn, beans, ketchup, vinegar, onions, Worcestershire, and salt. Bring to a boil, reduce heat, and simmer 1-1¼ hours. If stew is thin, thicken with crackers or crumbs. Serves 24.

Soups & Stews

Pilau, Fine for Camping Tours.

Take equal parts of venison, turkey, quail, duck and a small amount of middling meat; boil together; when thoroughly cooked remove all bones, skin and gristle. Mince the meat, season with butter, salt and small red peppers; add some well-cooked rice and cook all together till it is the consistency of Brunswick stew. A little allspice may be added if liked.

Gate City Cook Book

Soups & Stews

Crockpot Brunswick Stew

2	medium potatoes, peeled and diced
1	large onion, diced
1	(28-ounce) can tomatoes
1	(3-4 pound) fryer or roasting chicken, rinsed and patted dry
½	cup barbecue sauce
½	cup ketchup
	salt
	pepper
	Worcestershire sauce
2	(16-ounce) cans cream style corn

At night, put potatoes, onions, and tomatoes in the bottom of a crockpot. Place chicken on top. Cook overnight, about 8-10 hours. In the morning, remove and debone fryer. Put cooked chicken, barbecue sauce, ketchup, and seasonings (to taste) in the crockpot. Cook on low for 5-6 hours. About 1 hour before serving, add corn. Serves 8-10.

Hunter's Stew

This tasty recipe developed by Paul J. McNeal, Minister to Senior Adults, won the 1996 ChiliChill Out competition at SPdL.

Soups & Stews

1   pound venison sausage
1   (1.25-ounce) package chili seasoning
2   (8-ounce) cans tomato sauce
1   (14½-ounce) can whole tomatoes
1   (15-ounce) can kidney beans
1   small onion, chopped
     dash Tabasco
½   teaspoon seasoned salt
½   teaspoon lemon pepper

Variation:

In place of the venison, substitute ½ pound ground beef and ½ pound bulk pork sausage.

Brown meat and add chili seasoning. Stir in remaining ingredients. Bring to a boil. Cover and simmer for 10 minutes or until thoroughly heated. Serves 4.

Jim Denison's Mexican Stew

Tastes even better the second day

1-2 pounds ground meat
1   onion, chopped
1   package taco seasoning mix
1   (1-ounce) package ranch salad dressing mix
1   (15-ounce) can white hominy
1   (15-ounce) can yellow hominy or whole kernel corn
2   (14½-ounce) cans ranch style beans
2   (15½-ounce) cans Mexican-style stewed tomatoes or whole tomatoes

"My favorite thing is Mexican Stew. I like it because its hot and spiceyie."
    Craig Denison, age 8.

Brown the meat with the onion. Drain grease. Add mixes, hominy, beans, and tomatoes. Heat thoroughly and serve. Serves 4-6.

Simply Divine

Soups & Stews

T*ip*:

Today's cooks have more than a dozen varieties of oysters from which to choose, from the moderate size bluepoint, to the petite Olympia, to the sweet, tender belon oyster, which was once farmed only in France. Oyster selection affects flavor and texture of soup.

"O thou who clothest the lilies
And feedest the birds of the sky
Who leads the lambs to the pasture
And the hart to the waterside
And converted water into wine
Do thou come to our table
As guest and giver to dine."
    -Benedictine Blessing.

Oyster Stew

2	cups milk
1	tablespoon green onion, chopped fine
1	tablespoon parsley, minced
1/8	teaspoon nutmeg
1	celery stalk
1	pint fresh oysters with juice (do not use canned)
2	tablespoons butter
1	tablespoon flour
	salt
	pepper
	Worcestershire Sauce, Tabasco, or cayenne (optional)

Combine milk, onion, parsley, nutmeg, and celery in a pot together with oyster juice. Simmer for 15 minutes, stirring regularly. Remove celery rib. Add oysters and simmer 10 minutes. In a small pan, melt butter and stir in flour. Cook, stirring constantly, until the flour turns golden. Slowly add 1 cup liquid from the oyster mixture. Stir constantly. Cook until smooth and thick. Stir the thickening into the stew. Add seasonings to taste. Serves 2.

Salads

"I give you every seed-bearing plant on the face of the whole earth and every tree that has fruit with seed in it. They will be yours for food."

Genesis 1:29

Salads

GREEN SALADS

Mixed Greens with Roquefort and Dried Fruit Terrine	81
Bistro Oakleaf Salad	82
Baby Greens with Feta and Sugared Walnuts	83
Classic Caesar Salad	84
Caesar Salad with Blue Cheese Dressing	85
Spinach Salad	86
Strawberry Spinach Salad with Poppy Seed Dressing	87
Mandarin Green Salad with Slivered Almonds	88

SALAD DRESSINGS

Lemon Dressing	81
Garlic Croutons	82
Balsamic Vinaigrette	84
Herbal Vinegar	84
Honey-Mustard Salad Dressing	85
Berry Vinegar	85
Caramelized Pecans	87
Sugared Almonds	97
Creamy Citrus Dressing	101
Raspberry Vinaigrette	106

VEGETABLE SALADS

Summer Tomatoes	86
Bruschetta for Two	86
Fresh Tomatoes with Garlic and Mint	87
Mushroom and Parsley Salad	88
Coleslaw	89
Broccoli Coleslaw	89
Marinated Broccoli with Crumbled Feta	90
Broccoli Cauliflower Salad	91
Marinated Carrots	91
Tangy Congealed Asparagus	92

MAIN COURSE SALADS

Chicken Pasta Salad	92
Tomato Aspic with Crabmeat Salad	93
Chicken Almond Salad	94
Pineapple Chicken Salad with Ginger Dressing	95
Nutty Coconut Chicken Salad	96
Chinese Chicken Salad	97
Weezie's Rice Salad with Shrimp	98
Oriental Sesame Chicken	99

RICE, POTATO, AND BEAN SALADS

Artichoke Rice Salad	94
New Potato Salad	95
Potato Salad with Horseradish Dressing	96
Cornbread Salad	97
Garbanzo Bean Salad with Balsamic Vinegar	100

FRUIT SALADS

Apricot Freeze	100
Frozen Fruit Cups	101
Congealed Grapefruit Wedges	101
Frozen Queen Anne Salad	102
Apple Ambrosia	102
Strawberry Salad in a Pretzel Crust	103
Creamy Cranberry Salad	103
Pickled Peach Congealed Salad	104
Cherry Coke Salad	104
Congealed Citrus Buttermilk Salad	105
Cranberry Company Mold	105
Quick Cranberry Salad	105
Fruit Salad	106
Apple Salad with Honey Lime Dressing	106

HERITAGE RECIPES

Maraschino Cherry Salad	88
Cold Slaw	89
Chicken Salad	94
Potato Salad	95

Mixed Greens with Roquefort and Dried Fruit Terrine

Salads

½	pound Roquefort cheese at room temperature
6	tablespoons butter
½	cup chopped pecans
2	ounces chopped dried fruit
3	cups mixed greens, washed and dried
	lemon dressing

"Manners are a sensitive awareness of the feelings of others. If you have that awareness, you have good manners, no matter what fork you use."
-Emily Post.

Place cheese and butter in food processor. Process until smooth. Fold in pecans and dried fruit. Line a terrine mold or loaf pan with wax paper. Place cheese mixture in mold and press out all the air. Chill. Toss greens with dressing. Unmold terrine, cut into ¼-inch slices with hot knife, and place on top of greens. Serves 4-6.

Lemon Dressing

¼	cup lemon juice
2	tablespoons honey
½	cup olive oil
	pinch of basil
	pinch of tarragon
¼	teaspoon salt
	pepper to taste

Mix lemon juice and honey. Whisk oil into juice mixture. Add seasonings.

Simply Divine

Salads

"Let the salad-maker be a spendthrift for oil, a miser for vinegar, a statesman for salt, and a madman for mixing."

-Spanish proverb.

Garlic Croutons

3   tablespoons butter
3   tablespoons olive oil
3   cups stale bread cubes
2   large cloves garlic, minced
1   teaspoon chopped fresh parsley
1   teaspoon chopped fresh chives

In a large skillet heat butter and oil. Add bread cubes and cook over medium-high heat for 3-4 minutes, turning cubes constantly. Reduce heat; add garlic and herbs. Cook until golden, tossing frequently, about 20 minutes. Makes 3 cups.

Bistro Oakleaf Salad

Adapted from a European bistro salad

⅛   teaspoon salt
    freshly ground black pepper
2   teaspoons water
1   teaspoon minced shallots
4   teaspoons Dijon mustard
1   tablespoon red wine vinegar
½   cup vegetable oil
1   cup Garlic Croutons (see recipe)
2   heads bibb lettuce or red-tipped leaf lettuce, washed, dried, and torn
5   ounces red oakleaf lettuce, stems removed, washed and dried
½   cup shredded Gruyère cheese, separated

To make dressing, combine salt, pepper, water, shallots, mustard, vinegar, and oil in a jar. Close tightly and shake vigorously until the mixture becomes creamy. Pour dressing into a large bowl; add the lettuces and half the shredded cheese. Season with additional salt and pepper if desired. Mix thoroughly. Garnish with croutons and remaining cheese. Serves 4.

Baby Greens with Feta and Sugared Walnuts

Salads

2   cups walnut halves or pieces
1   cup packed brown sugar
1   tablespoon water
¼   cup olive oil or vegetable oil
3   tablespoons orange juice
2   tablespoons red wine vinegar or balsamic vinegar
1   teaspoon sugar
⅛   teaspoon dried basil, crushed
    dash salt
    dash pepper
6   cups torn baby greens
⅓   cup crumbled feta cheese (about 1½ ounces)

In a 1½-quart microwave-safe casserole, combine walnuts, brown sugar, and water, stirring to coat nuts. Microwave, uncovered, on high for 2 minutes. Stir well. Cook 3-5 more minutes or until sugar syrup coats nuts and nuts are toasted, stirring after every minute. Spread nuts on a baking sheet that has been lined with greased foil. Cool nuts completely and break apart. In a jar combine oil, juice, vinegar, sugar, and seasonings. Cover and shake. Chill. Divide baby greens among four serving plates. Sprinkle with nuts and feta cheese. Shake dressing and drizzle over salad. Serves 4.

Simply Divine

Salads

Classic Caesar Salad

1	large head of romaine lettuce, washed and dried
1-2	cloves garlic
2-3	anchovies
½	cup olive oil
	juice of ½ lemon
1	tablespoon apple cider vinegar
2	tablespoons wine vinegar
⅛	teaspoon dry mustard
⅛-¼	teaspoon freshly ground black pepper
⅓-½	cup Parmesan cheese
1	cup croutons

Break romaine lettuce into bite-sized pieces. Mash garlic and anchovies and blend well. Add olive oil to mixture, beating or stirring slowly until well blended. Add lemon juice, vinegars, dry mustard, pepper, and cheese. Stir until well blended. Pour over lettuce leaves and toss salad just before serving. Add croutons. Additional Parmesan cheese may be added to individual servings. Serves 6.

Herbal Vinegar

Great gift idea!

2	cups fresh herbs (basil, rosemary, chive, or dill flowers)
4	cups wine vinegar

Crush herbs gently and place in quart jar. Pour vinegar over herbs. Cover and let stand in dark place for 2-4 weeks. Stir occasionally with a wooden spoon. When flavor develops, strain out and discard herbs. Pour into decorative bottles, adding sprigs of fresh herbs. Cork tightly.

Balsamic Vinaigrette

1-2	teaspoons minced shallots
1	small clove garlic, minced
⅓	cup extra virgin olive oil
3	tablespoons balsamic vinegar
1	teaspoon chopped fresh tarragon
1	teaspoon chopped fresh basil
¼	teaspoon salt
	freshly ground black pepper to taste

Mix shallots and garlic. Combine with oil, vinegar, and seasonings in a bowl, and whisk until thoroughly mixed. Refrigerate up to a week. Serve at room temperature. Makes ½ cup.

Caesar Salad with Blue Cheese Dressing

Salads

1 clove garlic
½ cup vegetable oil or olive oil
1 tablespoon Worcestershire sauce
¼ cup lemon juice
½ cup Parmesan cheese or crumbled blue cheese
½ cup mayonnaise
1 teaspoon anchovy paste (optional)
   salt
   pepper
   romaine lettuce, washed and torn into bite-sized pieces
   croutons

Rub inside of large salad bowl with garlic; then mince garlic. Put oil, Worcestershire sauce, lemon juice, cheese, mayonnaise, anchovy paste, salt, and pepper in a blender and mix well, or put ingredients in a jar and shake well. Serve over lettuce and top with croutons.

Honey-Mustard Salad Dressing

¼ cup olive oil
2 tablespoons raspberry vinegar
1 tablespoon Dijon mustard
1½ tablespoons honey
⅛ teaspoon salt
¼ teaspoon black pepper
⅛ teaspoon nutmeg

Combine all ingredients in a jar. Shake well. Makes ½ cup.

Berry Vinegar

   fresh raspberries, strawberries, or blueberries
   white wine vinegar
   sugar

Fill a glass jar with whole berries. Cover with vinegar and seal. Let stand 1-2 weeks. Strain, reserving liquid. Add 1½ cups sugar to each cup of liquid. Simmer briefly until sugar is dissolved. Cool and bottle.

Salads

Tip:

When buying spinach in a bag, open the package as soon as you get home and discard any wet or rotting leaves.

Spinach Salad

1 cup vegetable oil
5 tablespoons red wine vinegar
4 tablespoons sour cream
1½ teaspoons salt
½ teaspoon dry mustard
2 tablespoons sugar
  coarsely ground black pepper
2 teaspoons chopped parsley
2 cloves garlic, crushed
2 (10-ounce) packages fresh spinach, washed and dried
4 hard cooked eggs, chopped
8 strips bacon, fried crisp and crumbled

In large bowl mix oil, vinegar, sour cream, and all seasonings together at least 6 hours before serving. Toss spinach with dressing before serving. Top with eggs and bacon. Serves 6-8.

Bruschetta for Two

2 large ripe Roma tomatoes, cut in ¼-inch dice
1 tablespoon extra virgin olive oil
1 large garlic clove, minced
2 teaspoons minced red onion
4 fresh basil leaves, snipped in strips, or
  ½ teaspoon dried basil
  salt
  freshly ground black pepper
1 small French baguette, sliced
2 tablespoons freshly grated Reggiano Parmigiano or other Parmesan cheese

In a small bowl combine tomatoes, oil, and seasonings. Cover and set aside for 1-2 hours. Grill or toast both sides of bread until golden. Top with tomato mixture and Parmesan. Serve immediately.

Summer Tomatoes

Sometimes the fresh, simple things are best

  beefsteak tomatoes, sliced thick
  extra virgin olive oil
  minced red onion
  chopped fresh basil
  freshly ground black pepper

Arrange tomato slices on large platter. Drizzle with olive oil. Sprinkle evenly with onion, basil, and pepper. Do not use salt as it makes the tomatoes juicy and masks the basil flavor.

Strawberry Spinach Salad with Poppy Seed Dressing

Especially pretty served in a glass bowl

¼	cup sugar
1	teaspoon dry mustard
1	teaspoon salt
⅓	cup vinegar
1-2	green onions, chopped
1	cup vegetable oil
1½	tablespoons poppy seeds
1	pound fresh spinach, cleaned and torn
2	cups thinly sliced celery
1	pint fresh strawberries, halved
1½	cups caramelized pecans

Combine sugar, mustard, salt, vinegar, and onions in food processor and blend to puree onions. With machine running, add oil in a slow, steady stream, blending until thick and smooth. Stir in poppy seeds. Refrigerate. Combine spinach, celery, strawberries, and pecans in a large bowl. Pour dressing over salad. Toss gently. Serves 4-6.

Salads

Caramelized Pecans

1-2	tablespoons butter
1	cup sugar
1½	cups pecan halves

Melt enough butter to coat a heavy skillet. Add sugar and pecans. Cook until browned. Transfer to wax paper to cool.

Fresh Tomatoes with Garlic and Mint

20-24	large mint leaves, chopped
2	cloves garlic, finely chopped
1	tablespoon salt
5	tablespoons vegetable oil
3	tablespoons vinegar
4-5	ripe tomatoes, sliced or quartered

Mash together mint, garlic, and salt. Add oil and vinegar; stir to mix. Pour over tomatoes and chill 6-8 hours or overnight.

Salads

Maraschino Cherry Salad.

Stuff maraschino cherries with blanched almonds; serve on leaves of heart lettuce with mayonnaise dressings.

Gate City Cook Book

Mandarin Green Salad with Slivered Almonds

	Mixture of greens, such as bibb, romaine, or spinach
1	cup diced celery
2	green onions, finely chopped
1	tablespoon minced parsley
1	cup Mandarin oranges, drained
½	cup slivered almonds, toasted
½	teaspoon salt
½	teaspoon Tabasco
2	teaspoons sugar
2	tablespoons tarragon vinegar
¼	cup vegetable oil

Mix together greens, celery, onions, parsley, oranges, and almonds. In separate bowl mix together salt, Tabasco, sugar, vinegar, and oil. Toss dressing with the salad just before serving. Serves 6-8.

Mushroom and Parsley Salad

Tip:

For a mild taste, use curly-leaf parsley. For a more intense flavor, use flat-leaf or Italian parsley.

1	pound mushrooms, sliced
½	pound Swiss or mozzarella cheese, cubed
	bunch of parsley, chopped
2	bunches green onions, chopped
1	package Italian dressing mix prepared according to package directions

Mix mushrooms, cheese, parsley, and onion. Add Italian dressing or use equivalent amount of Balsamic Vinaigrette on page 84. Marinate overnight in refrigerator.

88   Simply Divine

Coleslaw

1   medium head cabbage, shredded
1   small onion, minced
½   cup sweet pickle cubes
    grated carrots (optional)
    finely chopped green bell pepper (optional)
1   cup mayonnaise
¼   cup vinegar
¼   cup sugar
1   tablespoon salt
1   teaspoon dill seeds
1   teaspoon celery seeds
¼   teaspoon black pepper

Combine cabbage, onion, pickles, carrots, and green pepper in a large bowl. Set aside. Combine mayonnaise, vinegar, sugar, and seasonings. Add to cabbage mixture, stirring well. Chill several hours. Serves 12.

Salads

Cold Slaw.

Cut cabbage very fine, take one egg well beaten, one teaspoonful of sugar, salt and pepper, one teaspoonful of butter, half a cup of vinegar, cook to consistency of cream, pour on the cabbage and set aside to cool.

Gate City Cook Book

Broccoli Coleslaw

½   cup vegetable oil
⅓   cup sugar
⅔   cup red wine vinegar
1   package broccoli coleslaw
1   cup sunflower seeds
1   cup slivered almonds
1   bunch green onions, chopped
1   package ramen noodles, uncooked, beef flavor

Combine oil, sugar, vinegar, and seasoning from packaged noodles. Combine broccoli coleslaw, sunflower seeds, almonds, and onions. Mix with dressing. Add broken noodles just before serving. Serves 8.

Simply Divine

Salads

Tip:

To blanch means to plunge food briefly into boiling water, then quickly into cold water. Blanching enhances the color and flavor of vegetables. Fruits, such as tomatoes and peaches, are sometimes blanched to loosen their skins before peeling.

Marinated Broccoli with Crumbled Feta

1	large bunch of fresh broccoli, cut and blanched
⅓	cup vegetable oil
⅓	cup olive oil
¼	cup vinegar
1	teaspoon garlic salt
½	teaspoon dry mustard
1	teaspoon oregano
½	teaspoon thyme
½	teaspoon black pepper
	lettuce leaves
2-3	ounces feta cheese, crumbled
1	(6-ounce) can pitted ripe olives
1-2	tomatoes
1-2	hard cooked eggs (optional)

Arrange broccoli in 13x9-inch dish. Mix oils, vinegar, and all seasonings in a small bowl. Pour over broccoli. Cover and chill overnight. Turn at least once while marinating. To serve, drain broccoli well and place on lettuce leaves in flat serving dish. Top with cheese and olives. Surround with tomato wedges and sliced eggs. Serves 6.

Broccoli Cauliflower Salad

Great for picnics and family gatherings

1	bunch broccoli, cut into bite-sized pieces
1	head cauliflower, cut into bite-sized pieces
½	cup white raisins
½	cup peanuts or sunflower seeds
1	small red onion, sliced
½	cup mayonnaise
¼	cup sugar
¼	cup vinegar
4-6	slices of bacon, fried and crumbled

Mix broccoli, cauliflower, raisins, nuts, and onion in large salad bowl. In small bowl combine mayonnaise, sugar, and vinegar. Pour over vegetable mixture and mix to coat. Refrigerate several hours. Add bacon and serve. Serves 8-10.

Salads

Variation:

Omit the raisins and nuts and add ¼ pound grated Swiss cheese.

Marinated Carrots

1	can tomato soup
½	cup vegetable oil
1	cup sugar
¾	cup vinegar
1	teaspoon mustard
1	teaspoon Worcestershire sauce
	salt
	pepper
2-3	pounds carrots, sliced
	small onion, thinly sliced

Mix together soup, oil, sugar, vinegar, mustard, and seasonings. Boil or steam carrots in salted water until barely tender. Drain and cool. Alternately layer carrots and onion in large bowl. Pour soup mixture over vegetables and refrigerate several hours. Serves 20.

Tip:

When buying carrots, avoid those that are soft or cracked, two signs of old age.

Simply Divine   91

Salads

Tangy Congealed Asparagus

¾	cup sugar
½	cup vinegar
1	cup water
2	envelopes unflavored gelatin, softened in ½ cup cold water
2	tablespoons lemon juice
1	teaspoon salt
1	small onion, chopped
2	cups cut asparagus, cooked, or 2 (8½-ounce) cans asparagus
1	(2-ounce) jar pimiento
1	(5-ounce) can sliced water chestnuts
1	cup celery, chopped

Boil sugar and vinegar in 1 cup water. Add gelatin and cool until syrupy. Mix together lemon juice, salt, and vegetables. Add to gelatin mixture. Chill until firm. Serves 6.

Chicken Pasta Salad

12	ounces vermicelli, cooked
1½	cup bottled Italian dressing
¼	cup chopped parsley
1	tablespoon dried basil
15	mushrooms, sliced
½	cup snow peas or sugar snap peas, blanched
2-3	whole tomatoes, peeled and chopped
3	cups cooked chicken, cubed

Toss vermicelli with dressing, seasonings, vegetables, and chicken. Serves 6-10.

Tomato Aspic with Crabmeat Salad

Fresh avocados are delicious sliced around this dish

1½	envelopes unflavored gelatin
½	cup cold water
3½	cups crushed canned tomatoes
3	tablespoons grated onion
3	tablespoons grated green bell pepper
1	teaspoon Worcestershire sauce
2	dashes Tabasco
2	tablespoons fresh lemon juice
1½	teaspoons salt, or to taste
¼	teaspoon black pepper
3	cups fresh crabmeat, chilled
	mayonnaise
	lemon juice

Sprinkle gelatin over water in a small bowl. Heat tomatoes in a saucepan. Remove from heat and stir softened gelatin into the tomatoes. Add onion, green pepper, Worcestershire, Tabasco, lemon juice, salt, and pepper. Mix thoroughly and pour into a 6-cup ring mold. Refrigerate several hours or until thoroughly set. Loosen the aspic by placing the mold briefly in a pan of hot water. Turn it onto a serving platter. Refrigerate until it has set again. Toss crabmeat with mayonnaise and a bit of lemon juice and heap into the middle of the aspic ring. Serves 6-8.

Salads

"I like a cook who smiles out loud when he tastes his own work. Let God worry about your modesty. I want to see your enthusiasm."
  -Robert Farrar Capon.

Salads

Chicken Salad.

Put one large hen on to cook in boiling, salted water; when tender allow it to cook, cut in blocks, rejecting gristle and skin; chip fine four medium-sized heads of celery; add half a pint of capers, one-half pint of whipped cream, two teacups of mayonnaise; cut up ten olives. Mix all thoroughly, leaving mayonnaise and cream until just before serving. Keep cold and serve on lettuce leaves or in large, ripe tomatoes on lettuce leaves.

Gate City Cook Book

Variation:

To create an entrée, add chopped cooked chicken breast.

Chicken Almond Salad

4	cups cooked chicken, cut into bite-sized pieces
1	cup thinly sliced celery
1-2	tablespoons minced onion
1	tablespoon lemon juice
¾	cup mayonnaise
¼	cup heavy cream or half-and-half
1	teaspoon salt
½-1	teaspoon black pepper
¼-½	cup toasted almonds
	lettuce

Toss chicken and celery together. Mix onion, lemon juice, mayonnaise, and cream. Season with salt and pepper. Add to chicken and toss until chicken and celery are coated with dressing. Stir in almonds or reserve them for garnish. Chill before serving on bed of lettuce or other greens. Serve with Butter-Me-Nots on page 53. Serves 4-6.

Artichoke Rice Salad

Perfect for picnics or barbecues

1	package chicken-flavored rice mix
4	green onions, thinly sliced
⅓	green bell pepper, seeded and chopped
12	pimiento-stuffed olives, sliced
2	(6-ounce) jars marinated artichoke hearts
⅓	cup mayonnaise
¾	teaspoon curry, or more to taste

Cook rice as directed, omitting butter. Cool. Add onions, pepper, and olives. Drain artichoke hearts, reserving marinade. Cut artichoke hearts in half and add to salad. Combine reserved liquid with mayonnaise and curry and stir into salad. Chill overnight. Serves 8.

Pineapple Chicken Salad with Ginger Dressing

Salads

4	cups diced, cooked chicken
1	(20-ounce) can crushed pineapple, drained
2	tablespoons diced green onion
1	(6-ounce) can water chestnuts, drained and chopped
½	cup mayonnaise
½	cup sour cream
½	teaspoon salt
½	teaspoon ground ginger
¼	teaspoon black pepper
¼	cup slivered toasted almonds or pecans

Mix chicken, pineapple, onion, and water chestnuts. Chill. Mix mayonnaise, sour cream, seasonings, and almonds. Add desired amount to chicken mixture just before serving. Serves 6.

New Potato Salad

12	red potatoes
¼	cup chopped onion
¼	cup chopped celery
1	tablespoon parsley
5-6	slices bacon, cooked and crumbled
1½	tablespoons vinegar
½	teaspoon salt
¼	teaspoon black pepper
2	tablespoons vegetable oil
1	dill pickle, chopped
1	cup mayonnaise

Boil potatoes until done. Cut into bite-sized pieces. Add onion, celery, parsley, bacon, and vinegar. Sprinkle with salt and pepper and toss with oil. Add pickle and mayonnaise. Chill. Serves 8-10.

Potato Salad.

Boil five or six good-size Irish potatoes. When cold cut in pieces about the size of dice; to this add one bunch of celery, cut in the same size; one good-size onion chopped fine and two bell peppers cut in small pieces. Mix all together with French dressing, enough to moisten the mixture thoroughly; sprinkle in celery seeds and add more salt, if needed. Serve in white cabbage, after scooping out the center of cabbage enough to put in the salad. Put it in a dish of lettuce.
Gate City Cook Book

Simply Divine 95

Salads

Tip:

For juicy, tender meat, steam the chicken. Place pieces of chicken on a rack above simmering broth or herb-flavored water. Keeping the pot covered, allow about 45-60 minutes to cook the chicken.

Nutty Coconut Chicken Salad

A tropical salad with crunchy toasted topping

4	cups cooked chicken breast, cubed
2	cups chopped celery
2	cups grapes, halved
2	cups pecan pieces, divided
2	cups coconut, divided
1	(15-ounce) can pineapple tidbits, drained
1	cup sour cream
1	cup mayonnaise
¾	teaspoon salt

Mix together chicken, celery, grapes, 1 cup pecan pieces, 1 cup coconut, and pineapple. Toast 1 cup pecan pieces and 1 cup coconut. Mix together sour cream, mayonnaise, and salt. Stir into chicken mixture. Chill and serve topped with remaining toasted coconut and pecans. Serves 6-8.

Potato Salad with Horseradish Dressing

6-8	potatoes, boiled, peeled, and cubed
1	Vidalia onion, chopped
1	(8-ounce) carton sour cream
1½	cups mayonnaise
2	teaspoons parsley
1	teaspoon celery seed
1	teaspoon salt
1	teaspoon prepared horseradish

Mix all ingredients and let stand to allow flavors to blend. Serves 8-10.

Chinese Chicken Salad

Salads

3-4 cups mixed greens
1 cup diced celery
1 bunch green onions, sliced
1 (11-ounce) can Mandarin oranges, drained
¼ cup sugared, slivered almonds or pecans
 red grapes
1 tablespoon minced parsley
1 pound thinly-sliced chicken breast, stir-fried
½ teaspoon salt
¼ teaspoon Tabasco
¼ cup oil
2 tablespoons sugar
2 tablespoons red wine vinegar

Lay a base of mixed greens on 4 plates. Add celery, onions, oranges, almonds, grapes, and parsley to each plate. Top with chicken and sugared almonds (see recipe). Mix salt, Tabasco, oil, sugar, and vinegar in a jar and shake well. Pour over each salad when ready to serve. Serves 4.

Sugared Almonds

¼ cup sugar
2-3 tablespoons water
¼ cup almonds

Heat water and sugar over medium heat until thick. Stir in almonds; coat with syrup. Spread nuts on wax paper to cool.

Cornbread Salad

Serve with barbecue in a pretty dish, and garnish with extra tomatoes, green onions, and bacon

2 packages corn bread mix
3 medium tomatoes, diced
1 large green bell pepper, chopped
6-7 green onions, chopped
1¾ cups mayonnaise
4 slices bacon, fried and crumbled

Cook cornbread according to package directions. Crumble in a bowl and add all other ingredients. Mix well and refrigerate overnight. Serves 6.

Simply Divine

Salads

"My friend, Weezie Jackson, a member of Second-Ponce who passed away in 1996, called me one day and asked if I knew of any dish she could make for an open house for 100 people. So we made this great salad and had to mix it up in Weezie's kitchen sink. We lined the sink with a garbage bag since there wasn't a bowl big enough to hold it all! I took photos of the work in progress because most of her guests wouldn't believe Weezie made anything for 100 people since she wasn't much of a cook."

-Susan McKessy.

Weezie's Rice Salad with Shrimp

1	(6.9-ounce) box chicken-flavored rice vermicelli mix
1	(6.9-ounce) box wild rice-flavored vermicelli mix
1	Granny Smith apple, unpeeled and chopped

1-1½ cups snow peas or sugar snap peas

| 1 | (10-ounce) package frozen peas |

Italian-style bottled salad dressing
mustard-mayonnaise sauce
salt
pepper
chopped parsley
dill weed (optional)

| 1 | (6-ounce) can sliced water chestnuts, drained and chopped |
| 1 | (8-ounce) can pineapple tidbits, drained |

1-1½ pounds large shrimp, boiled and peeled

Cook both packages of vermicelli mix together according to directions, using ½ cup less water and half the margarine. Add apple, snow peas, and peas, to hot rice and set aside. Mix Italian dressing with mustard-mayonnaise sauce and seasonings to taste. Combine rice mixture, water chestnuts, and pineapple. Stir in dressing until well coated. Add shrimp and toss. Serve immediately or chill. Serves 10.

Oriental Sesame Chicken

Salads

- 1 package chicken-flavored ramen noodles, crushed
- ½ cup sesame seeds, toasted
- ¼ cup slivered almonds, toasted
- ¼ cup butter
- ½ cup vegetable oil
- 1 teaspoon sesame oil
- 1 tablespoon soy sauce
- ¼-⅓ cup sugar
- ¼ cup white vinegar
- ¼ teaspoon salt
- ¼ teaspoon black pepper
- 1 head napa cabbage
- 6 green onions
- 3-4 chicken breasts, cooked and chopped

T*ip*:

Napa cabbage is also called Peking, Chinese, or celery cabbage. Like celery, it has long stalks, but its crinkly green leaves resemble romaine lettuce. Often used in salads, napa cabbage is crisp with a mild, peppery flavor.

Brown noodles, sesame seeds, and almonds in butter with seasoning packet from noodles. Mix oils, soy sauce, sugar, vinegar, salt, and pepper for dressing. Chop cabbage and onions just before serving. Combine cabbage, onions, chicken, and noodle mixture. Add dressing. Serves 6-8.

Simply Divine

Salads

Garbanzo Bean Salad with Balsamic Vinegar

1	(14-ounce) can garbanzo beans, rinsed and drained
1	(14-ounce) can black beans, rinsed and drained
⅔	cup chopped red onion
¼	cup chopped fresh parsley
3	tablespoons olive oil
2	tablespoons balsamic vinegar or red wine vinegar
1-3	garlic cloves, finely chopped
	salt
	pepper
	lettuce leaves
	tomato

Combine all ingredients except lettuce and tomato in medium bowl. Toss to blend well. Cover and refrigerate for several hours. Let stand at room temperature 30 minutes before serving. Arrange salad on lettuce leaves and garnish with tomato. Serves 6-8.

Apricot Freeze

1	(17-ounce) can apricot halves, drained and chopped
2	(8-ounce) cartons orange yogurt, stirred well
½	cup sugar
⅓	cup chopped pecans
	lettuce leaves
	mayonnaise

Combine apricots, yogurt, sugar, and pecans. Line muffin pan with paper cupcake liners. Fill with mixture and freeze overnight. Remove paper liners to serve. Place on lettuce leaf and top with small amount of mayonnaise. Let stand at room temperature for 5-10 minutes before serving. Serves 10-12.

Frozen Fruit Cups

As good as dessert

2	cups sour cream
2	tablespoons lemon juice
¾	cup sugar
⅛	teaspoon salt
1	(8¼-ounce) can crushed pineapple, undrained
¼-½	cup chopped maraschino cherries
3	bananas, peeled and cubed
¼	cup chopped pecans
2-3	drops red food coloring

Combine all ingredients. Line 24 muffin tins with paper cupcake liners. Fill with fruit mixture. Cover. Freeze for up to a month. Remove liners before serving.

Congealed Grapefruit Wedges

Spectacular presentation

2	medium-large grapefruit
1	(6-ounce) package lemon jello
¾	cup boiling water
1	kiwi, peeled and sliced

Cut grapefruit in half. Remove segments and juice; discard membrane. Reserve shells. Measure segments and juice to make 3 cups. Mix jello with water. Cool and add grapefruit mixture. Fill shells with mixture and chill until firm. To serve, halve shells; garnish with Creamy Citrus Dressing (see recipe) and kiwi. Serves 8.

Salads

Tip:

Garnish with mint and edible flowers, such as violets, violas, pansies, honeysuckle, geraniums, and apple, peach, or chamomile blossoms.

Creamy Citrus Dressing

3	scant tablespoons sugar
1	tablespoon flour
1	egg yolk
	juice of 1 lemon
⅓	cup pineapple juice
4	marshmallows
⅓	cup chopped nuts
⅓	pint heavy cream, whipped

Place sugar, flour, egg yolk, and juices in a double boiler and cook until thick. Add marshmallows and nuts; stir. When cool, add whipped cream.

Simply Divine 101

Salads

Tip:

If you cannot find Queen or Royal Anne cherries, use another sweet cherry, such as Bing or Lambert cherries.

Frozen Queen Anne Salad

1 cup canned pineapple tidbits, well drained
1 cup Queen Anne cherries or dark sweet cherries, drained
¼ pound marshmallows, cut into small pieces
¼ pound blanched almonds

Mix fruit, marshmallows, and almonds, and chill in refrigerator while making dressing.

Dressing
4 egg yolks
4 tablespoons sugar
4 tablespoons tarragon vinegar
1 (3-ounce) package cream cheese
1 pint heavy cream, whipped

Beat egg yolks, sugar, and vinegar until creamy, and cook gently in double boiler until thick. Remove from stove and add cream cheese. Gently add whipped cream to cooled cream cheese mixture, reserving a small amount for garnish. Add cold fruit mixture. Pour into 13x9-inch pan and freeze at least 3 hours. Garnish. Serves 18.

Apple Ambrosia

According to Greek mythology, ambrosia was the food of the gods.

Variation:

In place of canned fruit, use 2 cups fresh pineapple.

3 large crisp apples, peeled and grated
1 (6-ounce) can coconut
1 (6-ounce) can frozen orange juice concentrate
1 (15-ounce) can crushed pineapple
9-12 ounces water

Mix together apples, coconut, orange juice, pineapple, and water. Refrigerate for several hours or overnight. Serves 8.

Simply Divine

Strawberry Salad in a Pretzel Crust

Salads

2   cups pretzels, broken into small pieces
¾   cup melted butter
1   cup plus 3 tablespoons sugar, divided
1   (8-ounce) package cream cheese
1   (10-ounce) carton whipped topping
1   (6-ounce) package strawberry jello
1½ cups hot water
2   (10-ounce) packages frozen strawberries
    fresh strawberries

Mix pretzels, butter, and 3 tablespoons sugar. Line bottom of 13x9-inch pan with mixture and bake at 400° for 8 minutes. Remove from oven and pat down. Cool. Beat cream cheese and 1 cup of sugar. Stir in whipped topping and spread on crust. Dissolve jello in hot water and stir in frozen berries. Cool until partially set. Spoon over cream cheese mixture and refrigerate overnight. Garnish with fresh strawberries. Serves 15-18.

Creamy Cranberry Salad

1   (6-ounce) package raspberry jello
1½ cups boiling water
1   (8-ounce) package cream cheese, softened
1   (20-ounce) can crushed pineapple, drained, juice reserved
1   can whole cranberry sauce
½   cup chopped nuts

Dissolve jello in boiling water; cool. Mix cream cheese with a small amount of pineapple juice. Add pineapple, cranberry sauce, and nuts. Add to gelatin mixture. Pour into 9-inch square dish. Chill until firm. Serves 9.

Simply Divine

Salads

Variation:

In place of ginger marmalade, use ½ cup orange marmalade plus minced crystallized ginger to taste.

Pickled Peach Congealed Salad

1   (29-ounce) jar pickled peaches, 1 cup liquid reserved
½   cup orange juice
½   cup water
2   teaspoons lemon juice
1   envelope unflavored gelatin, softened in ¼ cup cold water
1   (3-ounce) package lemon or orange jello
1   (8-ounce) can crushed pineapple
1   cup preserved ginger marmalade
½   teaspoon salt
½   cup chopped pecans

Slice or chop peaches; set aside. Combine peach liquid, orange juice, water, and lemon juice. Bring to a boil. Remove from heat and add softened gelatin and jello. Stir until dissolved. Add peaches, pineapple, marmalade, salt, and pecans. Chill in small ring mold until firm. Serves 6-8.

Cherry Coke Salad

Visitors like to take this recipe home as a souvenir of Atlanta.

1   (16-ounce) can pitted dark sweet cherries
1   (3-ounce) package cherry jello
1   cup Coca-Cola®
2   tablespoons fresh lemon juice
1   (3-ounce) package cream cheese
½   cup chopped pecans or walnuts

Drain cherries, reserving juice. Boil ¾ cup of the juice and add jello. Stir until dissolved. Stir in Coca-Cola® and lemon juice. Chill until it starts to stiffen. Cut cheese into very small pieces. Fold cheese, nuts, and whole cherries into mixture. Spoon into one-quart mold. Chill until firm. Serves 6.

Congealed Citrus Buttermilk Salad

Salads

1   (6-ounce) package orange jello
1   (20-ounce) can crushed pineapple
2   tablespoons sugar
2   cups buttermilk
1   (12-ounce) container whipped topping
½-1 cup chopped pecans (optional)

Mix jello, pineapple, and sugar together in a saucepan. Heat until jello is dissolved. Cool completely and add buttermilk. Refrigerate until mixture begins to thicken. Fold in whipped topping and nuts. Pour into 13x9-inch dish. Refrigerate until firm. Cut into squares and serve. Serves 15-18.

Cranberry Company Mold

1   pound fresh cranberries, ground in blender
1¼ cups sugar
1   (6-ounce) package orange jello
1   package unflavored gelatin
1   small can crushed pineapple
¼   cup orange juice
1   tablespoon grated orange zest
½   cup chopped apple
½   cup chopped celery
½   cup chopped pecans

Combine cranberries with sugar; stir well and let stand for a couple of hours. Mix jello according to package directions. Remove from heat and stir in unflavored gelatin. Cool until slightly jelled. Add cranberry mixture, pineapple, orange juice, zest, apple, celery, and pecans. Stir well and congeal. Serves 8.

Quick Cranberry Salad

½   envelope unflavored gelatin
1   (3-ounce) package cherry jello
1   cup boiling water
1   (14-ounce) container cranberry-orange relish
1   (8-ounce) can crushed pineapple
½   cup chopped celery
1   cup pecans

Dissolve gelatin and jello in water. Cool until syrupy and add relish, pineapple, celery, and pecans. Pour into mold and refrigerate until firm.

Salads

Raspberry Vinaigrette

½   cup salad oil
½   cup raspberry vinegar
¼   teaspoon salt
    freshly ground black pepper
1   tablespoon sour cream or
    crème fraîche
1-2 teaspoons sugar
Whisk ingredients together.

Fruit Salad

2   red apples, cored and chopped
2   green apples, cored and chopped
    lemon juice
2   cups blueberries
2   kiwi, peeled and sliced
1   cup green seedless grapes
1   cup red seedless grapes
1   pint strawberries, halved
    Raspberry Vinaigrette

Prepare apples, sprinkling generously with lemon juice to prevent discoloration. Stir mixture, drain on paper towel, and place in large bowl. Add remaining fruit to apple mixture. Pour Raspberry Vinaigrette (see recipe) over fruit. Allow flavors to blend before serving.

Apple Salad with Honey Lime Dressing

4   tart red apples
3   tablespoons honey
⅓   cup fresh lime juice
¼   cup chopped crystallized ginger
½   cup raisins
½   cup chopped walnuts
½   cup chopped celery

Peel 2 apples; then core all 4 apples and cut into julienne strips. Combine honey and lime juice. Pour over apples, mixing well. Add ginger, raisins, nuts, and celery. Toss lightly and serve.

Meat & Game

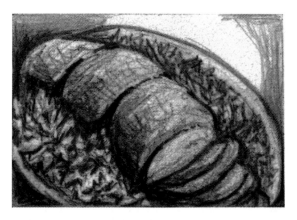

"I know that there is nothing better for men than to be happy and do good while they live. That every man may eat and drink, and find satisfaction in all his toil—this is the gift of God."

Ecclesiastes 3:12-13

Meat & Game

BEEF
Rib Roast and Yorkshire Pudding 109
Beef Tenderloin in a Blanket of Herbs ... 110
Old Joe's "Lundun Broyll" Pot Roast 113
Granny's Pot Roast 114
Fabulous Fajitas 116
Sweet and Sour Beef 117
Apple-Glazed Brisket 118
Family Stroganoff 119
Braised Beef à la Hendrix 120
Grilled Flank Steak 120
Kebabs 124
Not a Traditional Meat Loaf 126
Super Supper Nachos 126
Fiesta Cornbread 127
Cheesy Pizza Loaf 128
Rotini and Beef Bake 128
Homemade Spaghetti Sauce 129
Stuffed Shells Florentine 130
Spaghetti Pie 131
Swedish Meat Balls and Gravy 132
Stuffed Eggplant 134

LAMB
Rack of Lamb with Pan Sauce 111
Broiled Lamb Chops 114

PORK
Pork Roast with Figs and Veggies 110
Braised Pork with Spiced Cranberries ... 112
Pork Loin with Garlic and Onion 112
Ham Loaves with Mustard Glaze 121
Pork Chops with Seasoned Rice 122
Savory Grilled Pork Chops 124
Barbecued Ribs 125
Italian Pinwheel Loaf 133

VEAL
Stuffed Breast of Veal 115
Vermicelli Crowned with
    Veal Parmigiana 123

GAME
Baked Venison Loaves 135
Roast Venison 136
Anointed Quail 136
Baptized Quail 137
Pheasant in Seasoned Sauce 137
Crawford Farms Quail with
    Black-Eyed Pea Relish 138

SAUCES AND RELISHES
Jim McCranie's Barbecue Sauce 125
Horseradish Sauce 134
Apple Chutney 135
Gingersnap Gravy 136
Black-Eyed Pea Relish 138
Sassy Sauerkraut 139
Hot and Vinegar-y Barbecue
    and Basting Sauces 140
New South Tomato Ketchup 141
Georgia Barbecue Sauce 142

MARINADES
"Lundun Broyll" Marinade 113
Marinade 124
Citrus Marinade 142

HERITAGE RECIPES
Mint Sauce 111
Veal or Poultry Stuffing 115
To Boil a Ham 122
Love in Disguise 123
Beef Hash 133
Peach Pickles 135
Sauce for Barbecue 142

Rib Roast and Yorkshire Pudding

Very easy, very impressive

1 beef rib roast, 3 ribs or more
  pepper
  salt

Preheat oven to 450°. Wipe the meat with a damp cloth and season with pepper. (Do not salt.) Put meat in an open roaster, fat side up. Place roast in oven and sear for a few minutes. Reduce heat to 350° and begin basting with pan juices. For a rare roast, allow 18-20 minutes per pound. For a medium roast, allow 25 minutes per pound. For a well-done roast, allow 30 minutes per pound. Carve and salt. Serve with Yorkshire Pudding and Franconia Potatoes (see recipes). Serves 4-6.

Yorkshire Pudding
6-8 tablespoons roast beef pan drippings
1 cup flour
½ teaspoon salt
2 eggs
1 cup milk
1 tablespoon snipped chives

Have all ingredients except pan drippings at room temperature. Spoon 1-2 teaspoons pan drippings into each cup of a 12-cup muffin tin. Place tin in oven to keep hot while preparing batter. In a mixing bowl, combine flour and salt. In a separate bowl, beat eggs and milk. Make a well in the center of the flour and pour in the egg mixture. Beat ingredients together. Spoon batter into muffin cups until about half-filled. Sprinkle chives on top. Bake at 450° until puffy and golden, about 15-20 minutes. Makes 12.

Meat & Game

Franconia Potatoes

6 medium potatoes, peeled
  salt

Place potatoes in pot of salted water. Bring to boil; cook 2-3 minutes. Drain and season. About 40 minutes before roast is finished, remove the rack under the meat. Place potatoes in pan around roast; baste with drippings. Roast potatoes until golden brown and tender, turning them occasionally to brown evenly. Serves 6.

Simply Divine 109

Meat & Game

"A dinner invitation, once accepted, is a sacred obligation. If you die before the dinner takes place, your executor must attend."
—Ward McAllister.

Tip:
Because all beef tenderloins have about the same diameter, they will have the same cooking time, regardless of weight.

Beef Tenderloin in a Blanket of Herbs

A *perfect result every time*

1   beef tenderloin, 3 pounds
     fresh minced garlic
     dried thyme
     freshly ground black pepper
     fresh chopped parsley
     butter, softened

Fold small end of fillet under and tie with string. Sprinkle beef generously with garlic and herbs; rub in. Pat on butter. Refrigerate overnight. Before roasting, let meat stand at room temperature for 1 hour. Place on rack in roasting pan; roast at 400° for 30-35 minutes for rare to medium rare. Let stand 15-20 minutes for meat tissues to reabsorb juice before slicing. Serve with Parmesan Potato Bake on page 204. Serves 10.

Pork Roast with Figs and Veggies

Mouthwatering aroma

1   pound carrots, peeled and cut in 1½-inch pieces
2   pounds Red Bliss potatoes, unpeeled
2   large onions, sliced
1   boneless pork butt or pork shoulder roast, 4-5 pounds
6   whole fresh figs or 4-6 tablespoons fig preserves

In a large roaster, place carrots, potatoes, and onions. On top of vegetables, place roast. Top roast with fresh figs or preserves. Cover and bake at 325° for 3½-4 hours. Serves 6-8.

110   **Simply Divine**

Rack of Lamb with Pan Sauce

For a memorable meal, serve with garlic mashed potatoes, steamed snow peas, and roasted portobello mushrooms.

2	tablespoons vegetable oil
¼	teaspoon salt
¼	teaspoon black pepper
¼	teaspoon oregano
⅛	teaspoon garlic powder
2	racks of lamb, 1½-2 pounds each
½	cup chopped parsley
1	cup red wine
½	cup butter

Combine oil, salt, pepper, oregano, and garlic. Brush on lamb. Place meat, bone ends up, in a shallow roasting pan. Insert meat thermometer. Bake uncovered at 400° until done (about 35 minutes or 140°-rare; 55 minutes or 160°-medium; 70 minutes or 170°-well done). Transfer lamb to a warm serving platter, reserving pan drippings. Sprinkle lamb with parsley and let stand 10 minutes before slicing. Add wine to drippings in roasting pan. Cook over low heat, stirring with a wooden spoon to loosen drippings. Add butter and simmer 4-5 minutes before serving with meat. Serves 6.

Meat & Game

This is an excerpt from a Heritage Recipe for roast leg of lamb:

Mint Sauce.

Two tablespoonfuls finely chopped mint (green), one dessert spoonful of moist sugar, three or four tablespoonfuls of vinegar. Put the mint into a basin, add the sugar and pour over a little warm water, sufficient to dissolve the sugar; cover and let cook, then add the vinegar; stir well and pour into a sauce pan.

Gate City Cook Book

Simply Divine 111

Meat & Game

Variation:

Pork may also be cooked in a covered roaster at 325° for 2½-3½ hours.

Braised Pork with Spiced Cranberries

1	boneless pork roast, 3-4 pounds
	salt
	freshly ground black pepper
¼	cup honey
1	tablespoon fresh orange juice
1	teaspoon grated orange zest
⅛	teaspoon ground cloves
⅛	teaspoon ground allspice
1	(16-ounce) can whole berry cranberry sauce

Sprinkle roast with salt and pepper. Place meat in slow cooker. Mix remaining ingredients together and pour over the roast. Cover and cook on low for 8-10 hours. Serves 6.

Pork Loin with Garlic and Onion

Slow cooked and savory

1	pork loin roast, 4-5 pounds
	salt
	pepper
1-2	cloves garlic, slivered
1	onion, sliced
2	bay leaves (optional)
1	cup hot water
2	tablespoons soy sauce

Rub roast with salt and pepper. Make slits in meat and insert slivers of garlic. Put half of the sliced onion in the bottom of a slow cooker. Add roast, remaining onion, and bay leaves. Mix water and soy sauce; pour over roast. Cover and cook on low 10 hours.

Simply Divine

Old Joe's "Lundun Broyll" Pot Roast

Meat & Game

1 pot roast, 1¼-inch to 1½-inches thick
"Lundun Broyll" marinade (see recipe)

With a fork, pierce meat on all sides. Marinate roast in "Lundun Broyll" marinade for at least 2 hours, turning the roast frequently to insure that the marinade seeps into the meat. Grill on hot coals, preferably charcoal, basting with additional marinade. Turn frequently to prevent burning. Grill until done. Slice meat on the diagonal.

Tip:

Try "Lundun Broyll" Marinade on other cuts of meat, such as round and flank steak. Allow the steak to marinate 2-24 hours; cook rare so the meat does not become tough.

"Lundun Broyll" Marinade
¼ cup cider vinegar
¼ cup vegetable oil
¼ cup Worcestershire sauce
¼ cup soy sauce
¼ teaspoon dry mustard
½ teaspoon minced garlic
½ teaspoon salt
½ teaspoon black pepper
½ teaspoon Tabasco
1 medium onion, peeled and quartered

In a blender or food processor, puree all ingredients.

Simply Divine

Meat & Game

Granny's Pot Roast

1   chuck roast, about 4 pounds
½   package onion soup mix
3   cloves garlic
3   bay leaves
      salt
      pepper
1   (14-ounce) can tomato juice
5   carrots, thinly sliced
¼   cup raisins
1   (10-ounce) package frozen peas

In a large oven-proof skillet, sear meat. Pour off fat. Sprinkle meat with soup mix and seasonings; add tomato juice. Cover; cook in oven at 250° for 3 hours or until meat is tender. Add carrots and raisins. Cook 15 minutes. Add peas; cook 10 minutes until vegetables are tender. Serves 6-8.

Broiled Lamb Chops

An easy dish for special occasions

Tip:

Chops may also be grilled.

2   tablespoons vegetable oil
1½   teaspoons ground ginger
½   teaspoon salt
½   teaspoon garlic powder
6   loin lamb chops

Combine oil and seasonings. Place chops on greased rack of broiling pan. Brush top side with oil mixture. Broil 5 minutes, turn, and baste with remaining oil. Broil 5 minutes or until done. Serves 3-6.

114   Simply Divine

Stuffed Breast of Veal

- 1   cup uncooked long-grain rice
- 2   cups salted water
- 2   eggs, beaten
- 2   tablespoons chopped parsley
- ½   cup raisins
- ½   cup grated Romano cheese
- 2   cloves garlic, minced
     salt
     pepper
- 1   breast of veal, about 4-5 pounds, with pocket cut for stuffing
- 2   tablespoons olive oil
- 1   tablespoon fresh or 1 teaspoon dried rosemary

Cook rice in water until tender and fluffy, about 20 minutes. Stir in eggs, parsley, raisins, cheese, garlic, salt, and pepper. Place mixture in breast pocket and skewer with sturdy toothpicks. Place veal on a rack, bone side down, in roasting pan. Brush top with oil; sprinkle with rosemary, salt, and pepper. Place in oven. Bake at 450° for 20 minutes. Reduce heat to 350°. Loosely cover roast with aluminum foil. Bake until tender, about 2 hours. Remove veal from oven; let stand 15 minutes before carving. Serves 4-5. Note: Place any surplus rice mixture in a small greased baking dish and bake covered during last 20-30 minutes. Serve with veal.

Meat & Game

Variation:

Experiment with the rices. Try a wild rice mix or pecan rice.

Veal or Poultry Stuffing.

Three cups stale bread crumbs, one teaspoonful of salt, one-half teaspoonful of white pepper, two tablespoonfuls of chopped parsley, one cup finely chopped suet or butter, one egg. Sage or onions may be added if liked.

Gate City Cook Book

Meat & Game

Variation:

Sprinkle boneless chicken breasts with salt and ground cumin. Then marinate in lime juice and pepper and proceed according to directions.

Fabulous Fajitas

     juice of 2-3 limes
1-1½ teaspoons salt
½   teaspoon black pepper
1   flank or skirt steak, about 1 pound
4   flour tortillas

Toppings
    diced tomato
    chopped green onion
    guacamole
    sour cream
    picante or taco sauce
    grated cheese
    chopped cilantro

Combine lime juice, salt, and pepper in a heavy-duty zip-top plastic bag. Place steak in bag and seal tightly. Turn bag to coat meat evenly. Refrigerate 6 to 8 hours. Grill steak to desired doneness (about 5 to 6 minutes per side) and slice diagonally. Wrap tortillas in aluminum foil and heat at 325° for 15 minutes. To create fajitas, wrap tortillas around steak along with any combination of toppings. Serves 4.

Sweet and Sour Beef

For a winning combination, serve this tangy dish over hot rice.

Meat & Game

1½	pounds sirloin, ½ inch thick, cut into cubes
1	small onion, chopped
3	tablespoons oil
	salt
	pepper
½	cup sugar
½	teaspoon ground ginger
½	cup cider vinegar
	juice from (8¼-ounce can) pineapple chunks, fruit reserved
1	tablespoon soy sauce
3	tablespoons corn starch dissolved in ½ cup water
1	medium green bell pepper sliced in thin strips
½	pint-sized package cherry tomatoes

Brown sirloin and onion in oil. Add salt and pepper. Mix together sugar, ginger, vinegar, pineapple juice, and soy sauce. Add to meat. Bring to a boil. Reduce heat and simmer 30 minutes until cubes are tender. Add cornstarch; cook until thickened. Add pineapple chunks and green pepper strips. Cook 10 minutes. Just before serving, add tomatoes. Serves 6-8.

Simply Divine

Meat & Game

Tip:

There are two cuts of brisket available at the market: the leaner, more expensive, flat cut and the more flavorful point cut which boasts more fat.

Apple-Glazed Brisket

Tender, flavorful meat

1	beef brisket, 4-5 pounds
1	medium onion, quartered
2	large cloves garlic, halved
10	whole cloves
	water
1	(10-ounce) jar apple jelly
1/3	cup beef broth
3	tablespoons Dijon or spicy brown mustard
3	tablespoons minced green onions
1½	teaspoons salt
3/4	teaspoon cracked black peppercorns
3/4	teaspoon curry powder
	parsley sprigs
	tomato roses

Place brisket, onion, garlic, and cloves in large Dutch oven. Add water to cover. Bring to a boil. Reduce heat. Cover and simmer for 2½ to 3 hours or until tender. Drain meat, cover, and refrigerate up to 24 hours. To prepare glaze, combine apple jelly, broth, mustard, onions, and seasonings in small saucepan. Heat until jelly melts, stirring occasionally. Place brisket in shallow roasting pan, brush with glaze, and put in the oven. Cook at 325° for 45 minutes, basting frequently with glaze. Place glazed brisket on a serving platter and carve into thin slices. Garnish with parsley sprigs and tomato roses. Serves 8.

Family Stroganoff

1   lean round, top, or sirloin steak, 1-1½ pounds
    flour
¼   cup butter
1   (4-ounce) can sliced mushrooms, drained
½   teaspoon minced garlic
½   teaspoon salt
⅛   teaspoon black pepper
2   tablespoons chopped onion
1-2 cups water
1-2 beef bouillon cubes or 1-2 teaspoons beef bouillon
    granules
1   cup sour cream
8   ounces medium egg noodles

Cut steak into thin, bite-sized pieces. Dust with flour. In a large skillet, brown meat in butter. Add mushrooms, garlic, seasonings, and chopped onion; stir. Add water and bouillon to meat; stir until bouillon dissolves. Cover and simmer 1-2 hours, stirring occasionally. Add additional water as needed to make gravy. Just before serving, remove pan from heat; add sour cream, stirring lightly. Serve over noodles. Serves 4.

Meat & Game

"Two elements enter into successful and happy gatherings at table. The food, whether simple or elaborate, must be carefully prepared; willingly prepared; imaginatively prepared. And the guests--friends, family or strangers--must be conscious of their welcome. Formal dinners of ill-assorted folk invited for the sole purpose of repaying social obligations are an abomination. The breaking together of bread, the sharing of salt, is too ancient a symbol of friendliness to be profaned. At the moment of dining, the assembled group stands for a little while as a safe unit, under a safe roof, against the perils and enmities of the world. The group will break up and scatter, later. For this short time, let them eat, drink and be merry."
-Marjorie Kinnan Rawlings,
Cross Creek Cookery

Meat & Game

"This dish is so simple even a man can fix it."

-Vernon J. Hendrix, M.D.,
author, Bible teacher,
falconer, traveler,
and cook.

Braised Beef à la Hendrix

2   pounds lean beef stew meat
2   tablespoons Worcestershire sauce
1   tablespoon lime or lemon juice
    garlic salt
¾   cup beef broth or red wine
    pinch of rosemary (optional)
    black pepper (optional)

Marinate meat in Worcestershire, lime juice, and garlic salt for four hours. Put meat and marinade in crockpot. Add broth and seasonings. Cook on low for 10 hours. Serve with rice or noodles. Serves 4-6.

Grilled Flank Steak

T*ip*:

Always refrigerate meat if it is marinating for longer than one hour.

1   flank steak, 1-1½ pounds
½   cup vegetable oil
3-4   tablespoons vinegar
3-4   tablespoons lemon juice
2   tablespoons Worcestershire sauce
2   tablespoons soy sauce
1½   tablespoons chopped parsley
1½   teaspoons salt
½   teaspoon garlic salt
2   teaspoons dry mustard
1   teaspoon freshly ground pepper

Place steak in a shallow container. Combine remaining ingredients; pour over meat. Cover, chill, and marinate 2 hours or longer, turning steak often. Remove meat from marinade; grill over hot coals, about 10-12 minutes on each side, or to desired degree of doneness. Serves 4.

Ham Loaves with Mustard Glaze

Meat & Game

- 2 pounds ground ham
- ½ pound sausage
- ¼ cup cracker crumbs
- 1½ tablespoons chopped onion
- 1 egg, beaten
- 1½ tablespoons chopped parsley
- 1½ tablespoons chopped green bell pepper
- salt
- pepper
- 1½ teaspoons dry mustard
- dash thyme
- 1 tablespoon brown sugar
- ¾ cup apple juice
- 1-2 tablespoons flour

Glaze
- 1 cup brown sugar
- 1 teaspoon prepared mustard
- 3 tablespoons tarragon vinegar

Mix meats with crumbs, onion, egg, parsley, green pepper, seasonings, brown sugar, and apple juice. Shape into 12 small loaves. Place in shallow baking pan; sprinkle with flour. Bake at 400° for 30 minutes. Pour off grease. Mix glaze. Brush tops of loaves with glaze; bake 15 minutes. Lower heat to 350°. Glaze again; bake 15 minutes, watching so glaze does not scorch pan. Serve with Spinach with Artichokes on page 189. Serves 8-12.

"For holiday ham, you get some meat. Sometimes mommy puts some stuff on there—some raisins and stuff like that. You put it on the pan on the stove and you cook it for 6 to 10 minutes, I think at 3 or 4 degrees. You can have hamburgers, green beans, mashed potatoes and corn. I think that's it."

Jack Weber, age 5½.

Tip:

To vary the taste of the glaze, use light brown sugar for a delicate taste or dark brown sugar for a more intense flavor.

Simply Divine

Meat & Game

To Boil a Ham.

A blade of mace, a few cloves, a sprig of thyme and two bay leaves. Soak a ham well in a large quantity of water for twenty-four hours, then trim and scrape very clean; put into a large stew pan with more than sufficient water to cover it; put in mace, cloves, thyme and bay leaves. Boil four or five hours according to weight; when done let it become cold in liquor in which it was boiled, then remove rind carefully without injuring the fat; press cloth over it to absorb as much of the grease as possible. It is always improved by setting into the oven for nearly an hour, till much of the fat dries out, and it also makes it more tender. Shake some bread raspings over the fat; serve cold, garnished with parsley.

Gate City Cook Book

Pork Chops with Seasoned Rice

6	thick, boneless pork loin chops with fat trimmed
2	tablespoons shortening
1½	cups rice, uncooked
3⅓	cups broth
	salt
	pepper
½	teaspoon marjoram
½	teaspoon thyme
1	medium onion, cut into 6 slices
1	large tomato, cut into 6 slices
½	green bell pepper, cut into 6 rings
8-12	fresh mushrooms, sliced

In a skillet, brown chops in shortening. Remove chops; set aside. Grease a 2-quart casserole and spread rice over the bottom. Add broth to pan drippings; bring to boil. Evenly pour half the broth over the rice. Arrange chops on top of rice and sprinkle with seasonings. On each chop, place one slice of onion, tomato, and green pepper, seasoning to taste. Distribute mushrooms evenly around chops. Add remaining broth. Cover with foil. Bake at 350° for 50-60 minutes, until rice absorbs all liquid. Serves 6.

Simply Divine

Vermicelli Crowned with Veal Parmigiana

A grand presentation

1	cup grated Parmesan cheese, divided
¼	cup dry, unseasoned bread crumbs
½	teaspoon oregano
¼	teaspoon black pepper
6	veal cutlets, ¼ inch thick
¼	cup flour
2	eggs, lightly beaten
2-3	tablespoons olive oil
1	(2½-ounce) jar sliced mushrooms, drained
1	(28-ounce) jar spaghetti sauce
8	ounces vermicelli or spaghetti
1-2	tablespoons butter
1	cup shredded mozzarella cheese

In a shallow dish, combine ½ cup Parmesan cheese, bread crumbs, oregano, and pepper. Dust both sides of each cutlet with flour, dip in egg, and coat with crumb mixture. In large skillet, heat oil. Fry cutlets until golden brown, about 6-7 minutes. Remove meat from skillet and arrange in ungreased 13x9-inch baking dish. Sprinkle with mushrooms and add spaghetti sauce. Bake at 350° for 25-30 minutes or until bubbly. Cook pasta. Drain; toss with butter. Arrange hot pasta evenly in a large, round serving dish. Sprinkle outer edges with remaining Parmesan cheese. Remove cutlets from oven. Arrange hot meat and sauce in center of pasta, leaving a 1-inch border of pasta showing. Sprinkle cutlets with mozzarella. Serves 6.

Meat & Game

While veal is considered a delicacy today, turn-of-the-century Southern cooks prized organ meats. The Gate City Cook Book included recipes for Creamed Brains, Brain Fritters, Calf's or Hog's Head, Braised Sweetbreads, and the following gem:

"Love in Disguise."

Calf's heart stuffed, surrounded with chopped meat, seasoned well, rolled in powdered vermicelli. Baked in moderate oven. Serve hot with own gravy.

Gate City Cook Book

Meat & Game

Savory Grilled Pork Chops

If Moses had ever tasted these, he might have argued with God about the value of pigs!

4   pork chops, ¾-1 inch thick, trimmed of fat
¼   cup teriyaki
       garlic juice or garlic powder
1-2 teaspoons crab boil

Place chops in container. Mix teriyaki with garlic juice. Pour over chops. Sprinkle liberally with crab boil. Marinate, covered, for 1 hour or more, turning chops once and resprinkling with crab boil. Grill over moderately-hot heat for 10-12 minutes per side. When turning meat, baste with remaining marinade. Do not overcook. Serves 4.

Kebabs

Variation:

Along with the meat, marinate chunks of vegetables, such as sweet onions, bell peppers, mushrooms, and cherry tomatoes.

2-3 pounds beef cubes

Marinade

1   clove garlic, sliced
1   cup vegetable oil
½   cup vinegar
1   teaspoon salt
¼   teaspoon black pepper
2   teaspoons dry mustard
2   teaspoons Worcestershire sauce
      dash cayenne
      drop of Tabasco

Place meat in a large zip-top plastic bag. Mix marinade and pour over meat. Close bag. Marinate overnight. Remove meat and thread on skewers. Grill over hot coals until done. Serves 4-6.

Barbecued Ribs

Cook them and they will come!

Meat & Game

	salt
	pepper
2	whole slabs (small to medium-sized) lean pork spareribs or meaty baby back ribs
	Jim McCranie's Barbecue Sauce (see recipe)

Salt and pepper both sides of meat. Using a grill with a cover, place meat over medium charcoal fire. Turn ribs every 5 to 10 minutes, keeping meat covered during most of cooking. (Slow, covered cooking helps tenderize meat.) When ribs begin to brown around 30 to 45 minutes, baste with sauce. Turn meat often, basting at each turning until ribs are done, about 45 additional minutes. Serves 4-6.

Jim McCranie's Barbecue Sauce

1	cup ketchup
½	cup cider vinegar
	juice of 2 lemons
3	tablespoons Worcestershire sauce
2	tablespoons yellow mustard
3	tablespoons honey

Mix ingredients thoroughly.

"To test for doneness, cut end rib from slab and eat quickly before others see you. This is my son Jason's favorite part of the process."
—Jim McCranie, seasoned griller.

"To lick greasy fingers or to wipe them on your coat is impolite. It is better to use the tablecloth or the serviette."
—Erasmus, On Civility in Children, published 1530

"Dear Miss Manners:
Who says there is a 'right' way of doing things and a 'wrong'?

Gentle Reader:
Miss Manners does. You want to make something of it?"
—Judith Martin, Miss Manners

Simply Divine

Meat & Game

Variation:

Serve as a dip or appetizer with white or blue corn chips.

Super Supper Nachos

1   pound ground beef
1   large onion, diced
    salt
    pepper
    chili powder
1   (15-ounce) can refried beans
2   (4-ounce) cans chopped green chilies
3   cups shredded cheddar cheese
    ripe olives
    sour cream
    salsa

Brown ground beef and onion in large skillet. Drain fat. Flavor meat with seasonings to taste. Spread refried beans in bottom of 13x9-inch baking dish. Top evenly with meat mixture. Sprinkle chilies over top. Cover evenly with cheese. Bake uncovered at 400° for 15 minutes. Remove from oven and garnish with olives, sour cream, and salsa. Serve with tortilla chips. Serves 6-8.

Not a Traditional Meat Loaf

Variation:

Bake meatloaf in a greased ring mold or muffin tins.

Tip:

When mixing a meatloaf, use a light touch and a two- or three-tined fork.

1   pound ground beef
1½   cups fresh bread crumbs
1   cup cottage cheese
1   egg
¼   cup minced onion
2   teaspoons seasoned salt
½   cup ketchup

Mix together meat, crumbs, cottage cheese, egg, onion, and salt. In an 8x8-inch baking dish, evenly spread the meat. Pour ketchup over meat; or use New South Tomato Ketchup on page 141. Bake at 350° for 35-45 minutes. Serves 4.

Simply Divine

Fiesta Cornbread

Cooked to perfection in an iron skillet

Meat & Game

1	pound ground beef
2½	cups plain cornmeal
2	eggs, beaten
⅔	cup vegetable oil
1	(15-ounce) can cream style corn
1	cup sour cream
1	teaspoon salt
1	tablespoon baking powder
½-1	teaspoon cayenne pepper
1	(4-ounce) can green chilies, chopped (optional)
2	cups grated Mexican blend cheese

Brown beef. Set aside. Combine cornmeal, eggs, oil, corn, sour cream, salt, baking powder, and cayenne. Spread half the mixture in the bottom of a greased 10-inch skillet. Cover with beef, chilies, and cheese. Top with remaining mixture. Bake at 350° for 1 hour. Serves 6-8.

Tip:

An iron skillet is basic equipment in the Southern kitchen. To re-season an iron pan, wash, dry, and coat it with unsalted shortening or vegetable oil. Place the skillet in the oven and bake at 350° for one to two hours.

Simply Divine

Meat & Game

Cheesy Pizza Loaf

Children love the pizza taste.

½   cup chopped onion
1   (6-ounce) can tomato paste
1   cup water
2   teaspoons salt
1½ pounds ground beef
1   egg
1   cup bread crumbs
1   teaspoon oregano
     mozzarella slices

In a pan, combine onion, tomato paste, and water. Heat mixture; simmer 20 minutes. Mix together salt, beef, egg, bread crumbs, and oregano. Add ½ cup of simmered sauce; blend well. Place meat in 9x5-inch loaf pan. Bake at 375° for 1 hour. Pour remaining sauce over loaf and top with mozzarella cheese. Bake 15 minutes or until cheese melts and sauce is bubbly. Serves 4-6.

Rotini and Beef Bake

"My favorite food is funicelli with bolognase sauce. It contains funicelli (a twisty Pasta) and a regular spegehtti sauce with sausage AND hamburger called Bolognese."
— Robert Cruz, age 11.

1   pound ground beef
1   cup chopped onions
¼   teaspoon chili powder
1   (8-ounce) can tomato sauce
1   (16-ounce) package rotini, cooked and drained
1   (16-ounce) can kidney beans, drained
½   teaspoon salt
½   teaspoon black pepper
2   cups shredded cheese

Lightly brown beef and onions. Add chili powder and tomato sauce. Cook over medium heat for 15 minutes. Add rotini, beans, and seasonings. Mix well. Place in large, greased baking dish. Top with cheese. Bake uncovered at 375° for 20 minutes. Serves 6-8.

Homemade Spaghetti Sauce

Double the recipe and freeze half.

2   pounds ground round or chuck steak
4   medium onions, chopped
4   medium green bell peppers, chopped
6   stalks celery, chopped
2   cloves garlic, crushed
2   (28-ounce) cans crushed tomatoes
2   teaspoons salt
1   teaspoon black pepper
2   teaspoons Worcestershire sauce
2   tablespoons chili powder
4   teaspoons sugar

In a Dutch oven, brown meat, onions, green peppers, celery, and garlic. Add remaining ingredients, blending well. Simmer 2 hours, stirring often to prevent sticking. Freeze or refrigerate until needed. Serve over pasta. Serves 8.

Meat & Game

"My favorite food is Patti's, my stepgrandma's, spagetti. What she does is goes out and picks tomatoes from a picking feild and brings them home and makes hand made spagetti sauce with the tomatoes. Then she chops up hand picked mushrooms from the feild and puts them in the sauce. She goes to a store that sells noodles shipped from itally. She spends hours fixing me spagetti every night when I visit her. I even make her put her sauce in jars and I take it home."
      Monica Terry, age 11.

Tip:

Match sauces to pasta. Heavy sauces, like Homemade Spaghetti Sauce, go well with thick spaghettis, large shells, and broad noodles. Lighter sauces are better matched with thin or delicate pastas, such as angel hair.

Simply Divine

Meat & Game

Variation:

Replace the meat with 1 cup shredded carrots for a vegetarian meal.

Tip:

If you don't have ricotta, substitute cottage cheese pureed in a food processor or the drier textured pot cheese. Ricotta is preferred because of its sweet taste.

Stuffed Shells Florentine

1	(12-ounce) package jumbo shells or (8-ounce) package manicotti
1	(15-ounce) container ricotta cheese
2	cups shredded mozzarella cheese
1	egg
½	teaspoon salt
½	teaspoon black pepper
1	pound ground beef or turkey
1	(10-ounce) package frozen spinach, thawed and squeezed
3	cups spaghetti sauce, divided
1	cup grated Parmesan cheese

Boil shells according to package directions. Drain. In a small bowl, mix ricotta and mozzarella cheeses, egg, salt, and pepper. Set aside. Brown meat; drain. Add meat and spinach to cheeses. Mix well. Pour 2 cups spaghetti sauce into bottom of a greased 13x9-inch baking dish. Arrange shells in a single layer and fill with cheese. Pour remaining sauce over shells. Top with Parmesan cheese. Bake at 350° for 30 minutes or until bubbly. Serves 6.

Spaghetti Pie

6	ounces spaghetti
2	tablespoons butter
⅓	cup grated Parmesan cheese
2	eggs, beaten
1	cup cottage cheese
1	pound ground beef or sausage
½	cup chopped onion
¼	cup chopped green bell pepper
1	cup chopped canned tomatoes with juice
1	(6-ounce) can tomato paste
1	teaspoon sugar
1	teaspoon dried oregano
½	teaspoon garlic salt
½	cup shredded mozzarella cheese

Cook spaghetti according to package directions. Drain and stir in butter. Add Parmesan cheese and eggs, blending well. In a greased 10-inch pie pan, shape spaghetti mixture into a "crust" and cover evenly with cottage cheese. In a skillet, cook meat, onion, and green pepper until vegetables are tender and meat is browned. Drain grease. Stir in tomatoes, tomato paste, sugar, oregano, and garlic salt. Heat through. Spread meat over cottage cheese. Bake uncovered at 350° for 20 minutes. Sprinkle mozzarella on top; bake until cheese melts. Serves 6.

Meat & Game

"Spaghetti, I like this because it tastes good and it smells good. Buy noodels & boil them. Buy sauce & put it on the noodels."

Emily Deeter, age 9¾.

Meat & Game

"Let your conversation be always full of grace, seasoned with salt, so that you may know how to answer everyone."

-Colossians 4:6

Swedish Meat Balls and Gravy

Meat balls spiced with ginger and nutmeg

½	cup chopped onion
3	tablespoons butter, divided
¾	pound ground beef
½	pound ground veal
¼	pound ground pork
1½	cups bread crumbs, soaked in 1 cup light cream
¼	cup chopped parsley
1	egg
1½	teaspoons salt
¼	teaspoon ground ginger
¼	teaspoon nutmeg
	dash of pepper

Gravy

2	tablespoons flour
¾	cup condensed beef broth
¼	cup cold water
½	teaspoon instant coffee granules (optional)

Sauté onion in 1 tablespoon butter. Combine onion, meats, bread crumbs, parsley, egg, and seasonings until well mixed. Form 1½-inch balls. Brown in remaining butter, shaking skillet often to keep meatballs round. Remove meatballs from skillet and drain on paper towels.

To prepare gravy, mix flour into pan drippings. Add broth, water, and instant coffee. Stir well. Add meatballs and cook slowly 30 minutes. Serve over rice or noodles. Serves 8-10.

Italian Pinwheel Loaf

Variation on a meatloaf

1	cup soft bread crumbs
⅓	cup minced onion
1	teaspoon salt
⅛	teaspoon black pepper
¼	cup milk
1	egg, slightly beaten
½	pound ground beef
½	pound sweet or hot Italian sausage, casing removed
¼	cup minced Italian parsley
½	cup shredded mozzarella cheese
1	(4-ounce) can mushrooms stems and pieces, drained

In a large mixing bowl, combine bread crumbs, onion, salt, pepper, milk, and egg. Mix thoroughly. Crumble meats into the bread crumb mixture, mixing gently. Spread mixture on waxed paper and shape into a flattened rectangle. Sprinkle top with parsley, cheese, and mushrooms to within ½ inch of the border. Roll up, jelly roll fashion. Place in a 9x5-inch loaf pan, sealing edges. Bake at 350° for 45 minutes. Let stand a few minutes before slicing. Serves 4.

Meat & Game

Beef Hash (Very Fine).

Take any cold beef, grind in meat grinder, mix with chopped Irish potatoes, celery, onion and season with salt, pepper, sage and a sprinkle of red pepper; put in baking pan. Boil Irish potatoes lightly, season with salt, pepper and run through a potato masher; cover the steak as much as half an inch thick with this and sprinkle bread crumbs over the top, run in oven and brown.

Gate City Cook Book

Simply Divine 133

Meat & Game

Variation:

Use zucchini instead of eggplant. Trim the ends of the zucchini and cook in a pot of boiling water for 3 minutes. Halve and scoop out the pulp. Fill zucchini with meat mixture and place in an oiled, shallow baking dish large enough to hold the vegetables in one layer. Fill and bake.

Tip:

When buying eggplant, look for a firm, heavy, smooth-skinned fruit with no soft or bruised spots.

Stuffed Eggplant

Eggplant is a fruit, a very large berry.

2	eggplants, small to medium
1	large onion, chopped
1	medium tomato, chopped
3	cloves garlic, chopped
1-2	tablespoons olive or vegetable oil
1	pound ground beef or lamb, browned and drained
¼	cup parsley
1	teaspoon salt
½	teaspoon black pepper
½	teaspoon oregano
1	cup water
¼	cup shredded cheddar cheese

Cut eggplant in half lengthwise. Remove pulp, leaving a ¼-inch shell; set shells aside. Cut pulp into ½-inch cubes. Sauté pulp, onion, tomato, and garlic in oil. Add meat, parsley, and seasonings. Stuff shells with mixture; place in a 13x9-inch baking dish. Pour water around shells. Cover tightly with aluminum foil and bake at 350° for 30 minutes. Top each eggplant with cheese. Bake uncovered for 5 minutes or until cheese melts. Serve with Corn Pudding. See recipe on page 188. Serves 4.

Tip:

Use leftover horseradish to perk up the flavor of soups, mayonnaise, and mustards.

Horseradish Sauce

Horseradish was one of the five bitter herbs used during Passover.

½	cup low-fat mayonnaise
¼-½	cup skim milk
1-2	tablespoons (or more) prepared horseradish
1	tablespoon Dijon mustard
¼	teaspoon paprika

Combine ingredients, blending well. Serve with beef, pork, or seafood. Serves 4-6.

Simply Divine

Baked Venison Loaves

A *tasty, low-fat dish*

Meat & Game

3   egg whites or 2 whole eggs
½   cup milk
1   teaspoon salt
½   teaspoon black pepper
1   tablespoon Worcestershire sauce
1½   cups bread crumbs
½   cup finely chopped onion
2   pounds ground venison or ground turkey

Beat eggs, milk, salt, pepper, and Worcestershire. Stir in bread crumbs; let stand for 5 minutes. Add onions and venison, mixing well. Shape into 8 flattened ovals and place on a broiler pan coated with nonstick cooking spray. Bake at 350° for 40 minutes or until browned. Serves 8.

Variation:

Make loaves using 1½ pounds venison and ½ pound ground sausage.

Apple Chutney

Great with pork, turkey, or chicken

3½   cups apple butter
2   (14-ounce) jars mincemeat
1   (10-ounce) jar sweet pickle relish, undrained
¼   cup dry minced onion
¼   teaspoon Tabasco

Combine all ingredients, blending well. Place in small jars. Store in refrigerator up to 4 weeks. Fills 8 half-pint containers.

There were so many recipes for pickled fruits and vegetables in the Gate City Cook Book *that pickles were a separate category.*

Peach Pickles.

Seven pounds fruit, three pounds sugar, one quart vinegar. Boil sugar and vinegar together until thick; drop in peaches and boil until tender. Boil down juice if not thick.
    Gate City Cook Book

Simply Divine   135

Meat & Game

Gingersnap Gravy

3   tablespoons bacon drippings
2-3 tablespoons flour
1½ cups marinade
3   gingersnaps, crushed
½   cup currant jelly

To make gravy, heat bacon drippings in skillet. Blend in flour. Gradually add marinade, gingersnaps, and jelly. Stir until thickened. Serves 6.

Roast Venison

1   venison roast, 4-5 pounds
1   cup wine vinegar
1   cup cold water
1   onion, sliced
1   bay leaf
2   whole cloves
1   clove garlic, minced
1   tablespoon salt
1   teaspoon black pepper
¾   cup flour
½   cup bacon drippings
3   strips bacon or salt pork, ¼ inch thick

Place roast in a container. Combine vinegar, water, onion, and seasonings; pour over meat. Marinate 3 days, turning occasionally. Remove venison; reserve marinade. Dry roast with paper towels. Pat flour into meat; brown on all sides in sizzling hot bacon drippings. Place strips of bacon over roast and secure with string or toothpicks. Insert meat thermometer so that tip is in the thickest part and not touching bone. Roast in shallow pan at 450° for 20 minutes, basting with ½ cup marinade. Reduce heat to 350°. Continue roasting until thermometer reaches 140°, about 1¾-2 hours. Serve with Gingersnap Gravy (see recipe).

Anointed Quail

Quick, easy, elegant

4   dressed quail, 4 ounces each
    olive oil
1   tablespoon butter

Gently rub quail with oil. Place birds in shallow pan with butter. Bake at 450° for 10 minutes; reduce temperature to 300° and cook 15-18 minutes or until browned. Serve on a bed of wild rice with asparagus tips and Apple Chutney on page 135. Serves 2.

Tip:

For added flavor, tuck a sprig of parsley or celery leaves in the cavity of the quail. Remove flavorings before serving.

136   Simply Divine

Pheasant in Seasoned Sauce

Moist, tender

Meat & Game

1   pheasant, cut into pieces
    flour
    salt
    pepper
    vegetable oil

Sauce
1   (10¾-ounce) can mushroom soup
1½   cups chicken broth
½   cup heavy cream or plain yogurt
½   teaspoon poultry seasoning
1   tablespoon fresh minced parsley (optional)

Dredge pheasant in flour seasoned with salt and pepper. Brown meat in oil. Place pieces in casserole. Mix sauce, blending well, and pour over meat. Bake at 325° for 1 hour. Serves 4.

Baptized Quail

8   quail
    Italian salad dressing
2   small onions, quartered, or 8 jalapeño peppers
8   strips bacon

Baptize quail in Italian dressing; marinate 4-8 hours. Remove from marinade. Stuff birds with onion or jalapeños. Bard bird with bacon, securing it with string or toothpicks. Grill until evenly browned, about 20 minutes, taking care that dripping bacon grease does not cause flaming which can burn quail. Serve immediately. Serves 4.

Tip:

Barding is tying bacon or fatback around game or other lean meat to prevent it from drying out during grilling or roasting. The fat bastes the meat as it cooks and should be removed before serving.

Simply Divine   137

Meat & Game

"This recipe is from Crawford Farms, my childhood home, where quail are plentiful. The mustard-based sauce is typical of South Carolina barbecue sauces."

-Jim Crawford.

Jim, a long-time member of EEE Sunday School Class, is an accomplished cook. When he's not cooking, he is editor of Guide to Georgia, the oldest tourism magazine in the state.

Crawford Farms Quail with Black-Eyed Pea Relish

½   pound spicy bulk sausage
½   cup minced sweet onion
1   Granny Smith apple, peeled, cored, and minced
¼   cup grainy mustard
¼   cup fresh lemon juice
3   garlic cloves, minced
2   tablespoons teriyaki
2   tablespoons minced fresh thyme
2   teaspoons freshly cracked pepper
1   teaspoon minced lemon zest
½   teaspoon salt
½   cup peanut oil
12   partially deboned quail (check with butcher)
     Black-Eyed Pea Relish

In a medium skillet, cook sausage and onion over moderately high heat, crumbling the meat. Drain fat. Stir in apple. Refrigerate 5 minutes. In a food processor, combine mustard, lemon juice, garlic, teriyaki, and seasonings. With processor running, slowly add oil to thicken sauce. Stuff quail with sausage mixture; place birds in baking dish. Pour mustard sauce evenly over quail; marinate 1-2 hours. Place birds without touching on a broiling pan. Roast at 500° for about 20 minutes, rotating pan to brown evenly. Spoon Black-Eyed Pea Relish on 6 dinner plates. Top each portion with 2 quail and serve. Serves 6.

Black-Eyed Pea Relish
1   cup dried black-eyed peas
1   small sweet potato, peeled and cut in ½ inch dice
     salt
¼   cup extra virgin olive oil
4   medium sweet onions, minced

(Continued on next page)

(Continued)

Meat & Game

- ¼ cup minced red bell pepper
- ¼ cup minced Italian parsley
- 2 tablespoons minced fresh basil
- 2 tablespoons minced chives
- 2 tablespoons raspberry vinegar
- freshly cracked black pepper

In a bowl, cover the black-eyed peas with boiling water; soak 1 hour. Drain and rinse. Place peas in a saucepan; add water to cover by 1 inch. Add sweet potato and salt; bring to boil. Reduce heat; simmer gently until vegetables are tender, about 1 hour. Drain; set aside. In a large skillet, heat oil over moderate heat. Add onions and cook, stirring until onions are transparent, about 7 minutes. Cool. Stir in red bell pepper, herbs, and vinegar. Add cooked peas. Season with black pepper. Serve at room temperature. Makes about 3 cups.

Sassy Sauerkraut

Perfect for a picnic or barbecue

- ¾ cup sugar
- ¾ cup white vinegar
- 1 (14-ounce) can sauerkraut, rinsed and drained
- 1 (16-ounce) can bean sprouts, drained
- ½ cup onion, chopped
- ½ cup green bell pepper, chopped
- ½ cup celery, chopped
- 1 (2-ounce) jar pimientos

In a small saucepan, dissolve sugar in vinegar; boil 5 minutes. Combine vegetables. Pour vinegar syrup over. Mix, cool, and refrigerate. Serve as a relish with meat or as a salad.

Tip:

Because Sassy Sauerkraut has no mayonnaise, it travels well to picnics or barbecues where food cannot be adequately refrigerated.

Simply Divine   139

Meat & Game

"Real barbecuin' is done on low heat and takes a lot of time and a lot of turnin'. Chicken takes a whole pitcher of sweet ice tea, and a mess of ribs takes most of the afternoon. Use [this sauce] when barbecuing ribs, chicken, or thin pork chops and they'll be good enough to make a puppy pull a freight train!"

-Joe Perry.

Hot and Vinegar-y Barbecue and Basting Sauces

This recipe was tested at the first barbecue jointly held by the men of Martin Street Church of God and SPdL in the spring of 1996.

Barbecue Sauce
1   medium onion, finely chopped
2   tablespoons margarine
1¼   cups ketchup
½   cup apple cider vinegar
½   cup water
3   tablespoons Worcestershire sauce
¼   cup honey
½   teaspoon minced garlic
½   teaspoon dry mustard
½   teaspoon chili powder
2   teaspoons salt
2½   teaspoons black pepper
2½   teaspoons Tabasco
½   teaspoon cayenne pepper

Sauté onion in margarine until very tender. Add ketchup, vinegar, water, and Worcestershire sauce; cover and simmer briefly. Stir in honey, garlic, and other seasonings. Cover and simmer for 30 minutes. Let stand until cool. Use during the first half of the barbecuing process.

Basting Sauce
1½   cups water
2   cups apple cider vinegar
2   tablespoons Worcestershire sauce
1   tablespoon vegetable oil
1   tablespoon Tabasco
1   teaspoon dry mustard
1   teaspoon chili powder
1   teaspoon black pepper

(Continued on next page)

(Continued)

Meat & Game

Simmer water, vinegar, Worcestershire, and oil. Add Tabasco and remaining seasonings. Bring to near boil. Cover, cut burner off, and let stand until cool. (Re-warm before using.) During the last half of barbecuing, decrease the heat. Slowly blend Barbecue Sauce with the Basting Sauce. Baste food liberally, allowing it to get on and into the meat.

New South Tomato Ketchup

In the Old South, a cook's reputation was often established by ketchup made from mushrooms, walnuts, or tomatoes.

1	(28-ounce) can crushed tomatoes
¼	cup finely chopped onion
¼	cup finely chopped green or yellow bell pepper
¼	cup balsamic vinegar
1	plump clove garlic, minced
1	small bay leaf
⅛	teaspoon allspice
⅛	teaspoon ground cloves
⅛	teaspoon dried mustard
¼	teaspoon freshly ground black pepper
¼	teaspoon celery seed
½-¾	teaspoon salt

Tip:

To prepare ketchup in a slow cooker, cook on low for 6-12 hours. If a thicker sauce is desired, remove cover and cook on high until sauce is reduced. Recipe may be doubled.

In a medium saucepan, combine all ingredients. Bring to boil over medium heat; stir to prevent scorching. Reduce heat; simmer uncovered until ketchup is thick and reduced by half, about 35-40 minutes. Cool. Remove bay leaf. For a smoother sauce, process in blender. Store in airtight container; refrigerate. Wait 24 hours before serving. Flavor improves with age. Refrigerated ketchup keeps about 2 weeks. Makes 1¾ cups.

Simply Divine 141

Meat & Game

Sauce for Barbecue.

One gallon good vinegar, two pounds good butter, one large bottle Lea & Perrin's sauce, half dozen lemons, half dozen onions, lot of dry pepper. Slice onions and lemons and put half of above in iron pot and boil until onions are done. Then baste with a mop the meat as it is being cooked. When first pot gives out, use the balance. About three hours before the meat is done is long enough to baste with above. Up to then the meat must be basted with salt water. It takes experience to learn how to do this, so if you fail, try it again. Above is enough for two small carcasses.

Gate City Cook Book

Georgia Barbecue Sauce

1½ cups ketchup
1 cup cider vinegar
⅓ cup vegetable oil
⅓ cup Worcestershire sauce
½ cup firmly packed brown sugar
3 tablespoons yellow mustard
2-3 cloves garlic, minced
1 lemon, cut in half

In a saucepan, combine ketchup, vinegar, oil, Worcestershire, sugar, mustard, and garlic. Squeeze lemon juice into sauce and add 1 lemon half. Heat slowly about 10 minutes, to just under the boiling point. Use sparingly as a basting sauce for pork, ham, ribs, or chicken. Heat additional sauce and serve with food. Makes 3 cups.

Citrus Marinade

1 cup vegetable oil
¾ cup lemon juice
1 (12-ounce) can frozen orange juice concentrate
¾ cup white vinegar
2-3 teaspoons dried oregano
2-3 teaspoons dried basil
1 teaspoon garlic salt

Mix ingredients, blending well. Excellent when used to marinate or baste chicken or fish. Makes about 4 cups.

Poultry & Seafood

"I stand at the door and knock. If anyone hears my voice and opens the door, I will go in and eat with him, and he with me."

Revelation 3:20

Poultry & Seafood

POULTRY

Roasted Sticky Chicken 145
No-Fat Fried Chicken 145
Chicken Dijon 146
Lean and Spicy Chicken 146
Royal Chicken with Chilies 147
Chicken Breasts Stuffed
 with Apples and Gouda 148
Buffet Chicken Breasts 149
Chicken Italiano 150
Chicken Cheese Quartet 151
Chicken Bundles 152
Creole Pasta 153
Hickory Smoked
 Chicken and Artichoke Pasta 154
Chicken Pie in Puff Pastry 155
Rock of Ages Pot Pie 156
Chicken Olé 156
Braised Chicken with Mushrooms 157
Saucy Chicken and Asparagus 158
Chicken with Figs 159
Apple Chicken Curry 160
Chicken with Wild Rice 161
Chicken Enchiladas 162
Cornish Hens with Seasoned Stuffing.... 163
Red Raisin Sauce 163
Chicken Salad Gratinée 164
Foiled Turkey Breast 164

FISH

Orange Roughy with Star Fruit Salsa 165
Poached Salmon Steaks
 with Cucumber Dill Sauce 166
Nut-Crusted White Fish 167
Catfish Crisp 168
Blackened Tuna 169
Spicy Cajun Seasoning 169

SEAFOOD

Shrimp and Linguine 169
Crawfish Fettuccine 170
Shrimp Jubilee 171
Southwest Crab Cakes 171
Shrimp Creole 172
Shrimp with Grits 173
Cheese Grits 173
Seagoing Shrimp 173
Barbecued Shrimp 174
Florida Paella 175
Shellfish with Wild Rice 176

HERITAGE RECIPES

Chicken Croquettes 151
Boiled Shad with White Sauce 166
Tartare Sauce 168
Oysters in Ramekins 170
Shrimp Pie 176

Roasted Sticky Chicken

Roast two or three at a time.

Poultry & Seafood

"Poultry is for the cook what canvas is for the painter."
—Brillat-Savarin

2	teaspoons salt
1	teaspoon paprika
¾	teaspoon cayenne pepper
½	teaspoon onion powder
½	teaspoon thyme
¼	teaspoon garlic powder
¼	teaspoon black pepper
¼	teaspoon white pepper
1	(3-3½ pound) chicken
1	cup coarsely chopped onions

In a small bowl combine seasonings. Rub mixture inside and outside chicken, patting it in well. Place bird in plastic bag, seal, and refrigerate overnight. When ready to roast, stuff cavity with onions. Roast uncovered at 250° about 5 hours, basting occasionally with pan juices. Bird is done when skin turns golden brown and pan juices start to caramelize. Serve with Bistro Oakleaf Salad on page 82. Serves 3-4.

No-Fat Fried Chicken

4	chicken breasts with bone
	plain or seasoned salt to taste

Place bone side of breasts in a cold 12-inch nonstick skillet. Turn heat to medium and cover tightly. (As heat rises, breasts release enough moisture to prevent sticking.) After 15 minutes, turn breasts to skin side and salt bone side. When skin is nicely browned, turn breasts again, lowering heat to lowest setting. Continue to cook until meat is so tender it lifts easily from bone. If desired, use drippings to make cream gravy. Serves 4.

Variation:

Marinate chicken in Citrus Marinade (see recipe page 142) for three hours.

Poultry & Seafood

Chicken Dijon

4	boneless chicken breasts
½	cup flour seasoned with salt and pepper
3	tablespoons butter, divided
1	tablespoon oil
	Dijon mustard
1	onion, chopped
½	cup sliced mushrooms
2	tablespoons parsley
	salt
	pepper
1	cup heavy whipping cream

Dredge chicken in flour. In a skillet brown breasts in 2 tablespoons butter and 1 tablespoon oil. Remove and spread generously with mustard. Place chicken in baking dish. Sauté onion in pan used for chicken. Add 1 tablespoon butter and sauté mushrooms. Add seasonings. Distribute mixture around chicken. Pour cream over and bake at 350° for 35 minutes. Serves 4.

Lean and Spicy Chicken

1	tablespoon olive oil
1	teaspoon crushed garlic
4	large boneless chicken breasts
1-2	teaspoons crab boil
	lemon-pepper seasoning

Mix oil with garlic; brush over chicken. Generously sprinkle both sides of breasts with crab boil and lemon-pepper seasoning. Marinate 1 hour. Grill over medium-high heat for 4-5 minutes per side. Do not overcook. Serves 4.

Royal Chicken with Chilies

For a crowd, double or triple the recipe.

¼	cup olive oil
6	boneless chicken breasts
1	(7-ounce) can whole green chilies, cut into ½-inch strips
1	cup heavy whipping cream
1	tablespoon chopped parsley
1	teaspoon black pepper
⅛	teaspoon salt
¾	cup shredded Swiss cheese
	cooked rice

Heat oil in large skillet over medium-high heat. Add chicken; brown lightly on both sides. Transfer chicken to baking dish. Arrange chilies over chicken. In a separate bowl whisk cream and seasonings. Pour cream mixture over chicken; sprinkle with cheese. Bake at 325° for 45 minutes or until chicken is tender. Spoon rice onto plates; top with chicken and sauce. Serves 6.

Poultry & Seafood

Tip:

Four types of cream — half-and-half, light (coffee) cream, light whipping cream, and heavy whipping cream — are frequently used to enrich sauces. What each cream adds is fat. Half-and-half is 10½-18% fat; light cream is 18-30% fat. Light whipping cream is 30-36% fat; heavy whipping cream is 36-40% fat. The higher the fat content, the smoother the texture of the sauce.

Simply Divine

Poultry & Seafood

Variation:

Creamy, aged Gouda is similar in flavor to white cheddar, which may also be used.

Chicken Breasts Stuffed with Apples and Gouda

4	boneless chicken breasts
1	Granny Smith apple, thinly sliced
4	slices Gouda cheese
¼	cup flour
	salt
	freshly ground black pepper
2	tablespoons butter, divided
1	small onion, finely chopped
	sprig of fresh thyme
1	bay leaf
1	cup apple juice
1	cup chicken broth
1½	teaspoons cornstarch

Butterfly breasts. Between opened halves, place 2 slices of apple and 1 slice of cheese. Close halves. Secure open edge with sturdy toothpicks. Combine flour, salt, and pepper. Dredge chicken, shaking off excess flour. Heat 1 tablespoon butter in large skillet. Add chicken; cook 3-5 minutes on each side. Remove chicken to baking dish. Cover and heat in 325° oven for 15-20 minutes. In same skillet melt remaining butter; add onion, thyme, and bay leaf. Cook until onion is soft, about 3-5 minutes. Add apple juice; stir to loosen pan drippings. Over medium-high heat, reduce sauce by half. Combine chicken broth and cornstarch. Whisk into apple juice. Bring to boil; simmer about 2 minutes or until thickened. Pour sauce over chicken or serve separately. Serves 4.

Buffet Chicken Breasts

A *do-ahead preparation*

12	boneless chicken breasts
1	cup sour cream
¼	cup lemon juice
4	teaspoons Worcestershire sauce
4	teaspoons celery salt
2	teaspoons paprika
2	cloves garlic, minced
4	teaspoons salt
½	teaspoon black pepper
1¾	cups dry bread crumbs
½-1	cup butter, melted

Place breasts in large pan. Mix sour cream with seasonings. Pour over chicken, immersing pieces. Cover; refrigerate overnight. When ready to cook, remove chicken from mixture and roll in crumbs. Place in 15x10-inch shallow baking pan. Drizzle ⅔ of butter over pieces. Bake at 350° for 45 minutes. Drizzle remaining butter over chicken. Bake 10-15 minutes. Serves 12.

Poultry & Seafood

Tip:

To make dried bread crumbs, place single layers of sliced bread on a baking sheet. Bake at 300° until browned. Cool slices; grind in a food processor until desired texture. Place in an airtight container and store in a dry, cool area.

"We are all in rehearsal for that great banquet to come, the Supper of the Lamb. Through our simple choices of unity over division, kindness over bitterness, prayer over anger, we do help to usher in the kingdom, prepare the way, call attention to the Good News. Eating and drinking together has everything to do with joy, with the destiny for which we were created, as Jesus has reminded us again and again."

-Isabel Anders,
Awaiting the Child

Simply Divine

Poultry & Seafood

*"May my food my body maintain,
may my body my soul sustain,
may my soul in deed and word
give thanks for all things to the Lord."*
            -Isak Dinesen,
         "Babette's Feast"

Chicken Italiano

Your guests will applaud these stuffed, breaded chicken breasts served with a versatile herb sauce.

2	(15-ounce) cans Italian tomato sauce
4	teaspoons marjoram or basil
4	teaspoons thyme
4	teaspoons oregano
4	teaspoons garlic powder
¼	cup olive oil, divided
8	boneless chicken breasts
	salt
2	large tomatoes, diced
½	cup mushrooms, sliced
1	cup shredded cheddar cheese
2	eggs, lightly beaten
1½	cups Italian seasoned bread crumbs

Combine sauce with seasonings and 2 tablespoons oil. Simmer. With a mallet, pound breasts flat and sprinkle with salt. Place tomatoes, mushrooms, and cheese in center of breasts; fold over and seal edges with sturdy toothpicks. Dip breasts in egg; coat in bread crumbs. In a skillet cook breasts in remaining oil, about 5 minutes each side. Arrange in baking dish and bake at 375° for 15 minutes. Pour sauce over and serve. Serves 8.

Simply Divine

Chicken Cheese Quartet

Delicious and surprisingly low-fat!

½   cup part-skim ricotta cheese
¼   cup shredded part-skim mozzarella cheese
2   tablespoons grated Parmesan cheese
1   cup chopped cooked spinach, drained well
4   (4-ounce) chicken cutlets pounded ¼-inch thick
1   teaspoon butter

Sauce
¾   cup skim milk
½   cup reduced-sodium chicken broth
1   tablespoon cornstarch
1   teaspoon butter
¾   cup shredded reduced-fat cheddar cheese

In a small bowl combine cheeses and spinach. Mix well. Spread ¼ of mixture over each cutlet. Starting at short end, tightly roll cutlets, jelly roll style. Secure end with toothpicks. In nonstick skillet, melt butter over medium-high heat. Add cutlets; cook, turning often until browned, about 2 minutes. Place in 13x9-inch baking dish.

To prepare sauce, blend milk, chicken broth, and cornstarch. In the skillet used for chicken, melt butter over medium heat. Add milk mixture; cook, stirring until it thickens. Remove from heat. Stir in cheddar. Pour over cutlets. Bake at 400° for 15 minutes until chicken is done and sauce is bubbly.

Poultry & Seafood

This is the recipe of Mrs. S. R. Dull, who published the popular cookbook, Southern Cooking, *in 1928. Her cookbook was affectionately nicknamed "the Southern bride's Bible."*

Chicken Croquettes.

One chicken about three and a half pounds, boil and put through a meat chopper, make a cream dressing, using two tablespoonfuls of butter, two tablespoonfuls CAPITOLA flour (heaping), put in a sauce pan and let melt till hot and smooth, add one and a half cups of hot sweet milk, pour on chicken, season with chopped parsley, pepper, salt and lemon peel (grated), make into shapes, crumb, dip in egg crumb again and fry in hot lard or oil till a pretty brown. Serve hot.

Gate City Cook Book

Simply Divine   151

Poultry & Seafood

"Lord Jesus, be our holy guest,
Our morning joy, our evening rest;
And with this food impart
Thy love and peace to every heart.
Amen."

-Park McGinty.

Chicken Bundles

A *tasty way to wrap up dinner!*

1	(8-ounce) package cream cheese, softened
¼	cup milk
1	teaspoon dill weed
½	teaspoon salt
½	teaspoon black pepper
4	cups cubed cooked chicken
½	cup chopped celery
4	green onions with tops, thinly slivered
3	(8-ounce) tubes crescent rolls
¼	cup butter or margarine, melted
¼	cup seasoned bread crumbs

In a small bowl, beat cream cheese, milk, dill weed, salt, and pepper until smooth. Stir in chicken, celery, and onions. Unroll crescent roll dough; separate into 12 rectangles, 4 from each tube. Press perforations together. Spoon ⅓ cup of chicken mixture into center of each rectangle. Bring edges up to center and pinch to seal. Brush with butter and sprinkle with bread crumbs. Bake at 350° for 15-20 minutes or until golden brown.

Creole Pasta

Poultry & Seafood

- 2 boneless chicken breasts cut into thin strips
- 2 teaspoons Creole seasoning
- 2 tablespoons butter or margarine
- 8 slices each green and red bell peppers
- 4 large fresh mushrooms, sliced
- 1 green onion, chopped
- 1-2 cups heavy whipping cream
- ¼ teaspoon dried basil
- ¼ teaspoon lemon-pepper seasoning
- ¼ teaspoon salt
- ⅛ teaspoon garlic powder
- ⅛ teaspoon black pepper
- 4 ounces linguine, cooked and drained
  freshly grated Reggiano Parmigiano or other Parmesan cheese

Coat both sides of chicken with Creole seasoning. Set aside for flavors to develop. In large skillet over medium heat, sauté chicken in butter until tender, about 5-7 minutes. Add peppers, mushrooms, and onion. Cook and stir for 2-3 minutes. Reduce heat. Add cream and seasonings; heat, stirring well. Serve over linguine. Sprinkle with Parmesan cheese. Serves 2.

Variation:

For a spicier taste, use Cajun seasoning.

Simply Divine

Poultry & Seafood

"I like my moms noodles. They have chicken and brocli in it and I love the way it tastes. It tastes salty and good. I love it."
Ansley Stephens, age 9½.

Hickory Smoked Chicken and Artichoke Pasta

2	cups hickory chips
4	boneless chicken breasts
1	(3-ounce) package sun-dried tomatoes
1	cup boiling water
1	pound linguine
½	cup butter
2	cups heavy whipping cream
1	cup grated Parmesan cheese
½	teaspoon white pepper
1	(14-ounce) can artichoke hearts, drained and quartered
1	(1¾-ounce) bottle pine nuts, toasted

Soak hickory chips in water for 2-4 hours. Drain; place in aluminum pie pan with holes poked in bottom. Place pie pan over hot coals in grill until smoking heavily. Grill chicken breasts until done. Remove, cool, and slice thinly. Pour boiling water over sun-dried tomatoes. Soak ½ hour; drain. Cook pasta according to directions. Drain; set aside. In large skillet melt butter. Add cream, Parmesan, and pepper. Pour over linguine, adding chicken, artichoke hearts, and tomatoes. Top with pine nuts. Toss well. Serves 8.

Chicken Pie in Puff Pastry

Poultry & Seafood

Six individual pot pies

1	cup chopped onion
1	cup chopped celery
1	cup chopped carrot
¼	cup plus 2 tablespoons butter, melted
1	cup frozen peas
¼	cup plus 2 tablespoons flour
2	cups chicken broth
1	cup plus 1 tablespoon half-and-half, divided
1	teaspoon salt
¼	teaspoon black pepper
4	cups diced cooked chicken
2	(17¼-ounce) packages frozen puff pastry, thawed
1	egg yolk

Sauté onion, celery, and carrot in butter in a large skillet for 10 minutes. Stir in peas and flour; cook 1 minute, stirring constantly. Gradually add chicken broth and 1 cup half-and-half. Cook over medium heat, stirring until mixture thickens and bubbles. Stir in salt, pepper, and chicken. Ladle chicken mixture into 6 (10-ounce) ovenproof soup bowls, filling to within ¾-inch of rim. Set bowls aside. Roll pastry sheets to ⅛-inch thickness. Cut 6 circles from pastry, ½ inch larger than soup bowls. Reserve remaining pastry to make decorative designs for pie tops if desired. Combine egg yolk and 1 tablespoon half-and-half, stirring well. Brush one side of each circle with egg mixture. Place pastry circles, brushed side down, over each bowl, folding edges under and pressing firmly to side of bowl to seal. Top pies with decorative designs. Brush with remaining egg mixture. Place pies on baking pan. Bake at 400° for 15-20 minutes or until tops are puffed and browned. Serve immediately. Serves 6.

Poultry & Seafood

Tip:

Make two at a time. Enjoy one; freeze the other. You will always have one on hand for a friend or neighbor.

Rock of Ages Pot Pie

Frozen, it's as heavy as a rock and keeps for ages.

3	cups cooked diced chicken
1	(29-ounce) can mixed vegetables or 3 (10-ounce) boxes frozen mixed vegetables, cooked and drained
1	(10½-ounce) can potato soup
2	teaspoons rosemary
1	teaspoon celery seed
	salt
	pepper
	garlic powder
2	(9-inch) deep-dish pie crusts

Mix chicken, vegetables, soup, and seasonings. Fit 1 pie crust into bottom of pie pan. Place chicken mixture in crust; top with remaining crust. Prick top with a fork. Bake at 350° for 45 minutes. Serves 4-6.

Chicken Olé

1	tablespoon oil
1	pound boneless chicken breast, cubed
1	small onion, chopped
1	small green bell pepper, chopped
1	(16-ounce) can corn, drained
1	cup chicken broth
1	cup thick and chunky salsa
1½	cups quick-cooking rice
½	cup shredded cheddar cheese

Heat oil in skillet over medium-high heat. Add chicken, onion, and green pepper, stirring until chicken is cooked. Add corn, broth, and salsa. Bring to boil. Stir in rice; cover. Remove from heat. Let stand 5 minutes. Fluff with fork. Sprinkle with cheese. Cover and let stand until cheese melts. Serves 4.

Braised Chicken with Mushrooms

Slow-cooked company chicken

6	boneless chicken breasts
	salt
	pepper
1	chicken bouillon cube dissolved in ½ cup boiling water
1	(10½-ounce) can mushroom soup
1	(4-ounce) can sliced mushrooms, drained
1	cup sour cream mixed with ¼ cup flour
1-2	tablespoons chopped parsley (optional)

Sprinkle chicken with salt and pepper. Place in slow cooker. Mix bouillon, soup, mushrooms, and sour cream. Pour over chicken. Cook on low 6-8 hours. (High: 2½-3½ hours with sour cream added during last 30 minutes.) Serve with rice or noodles. Sprinkle with chopped parsley. Serves 4.

Poultry & Seafood

Variation:

Experiment by adding seasonings, such as garlic, lemon juice, or rosemary.

"Food cannot take care of spiritual, psychological and emotional problems, but the feeling of being loved and cared for, the actual comfort of the beauty and flavour of food, the increase of blood sugar and physical well-being, help one to go on during the next hours better equipped to meet the problems."

-Edith Schaeffer,
Hidden Art

Poultry & Seafood

Saucy Chicken and Asparagus

1   (10-ounce) package frozen asparagus or ¾ pound fresh
½   cup flour
⅛   teaspoon salt
⅛   teaspoon black pepper
⅛   teaspoon paprika
6   boneless chicken breasts
¼   butter or margarine

Sauce
1   (10¾-ounce) can mushroom soup
1   cup heavy whipping cream or half-and-half
¼   teaspoon salt
⅛   teaspoon Tabasco
¼   cup grated Parmesan cheese

Cook asparagus. Drain and arrange in greased 13x9-inch baking dish. Combine flour and seasonings; dredge chicken in flour. Melt butter in skillet. Cook chicken until golden brown on both sides. Drain. Arrange chicken breasts on top of asparagus.

Combine soup, heavy cream, salt, and hot sauce. Spoon over chicken; sprinkle with cheese. Bake uncovered at 400° about 20 minutes.

Chicken with Figs

A *tantalizing blend of flavors*

1	(3½-pound) chicken cut into pieces
¾	teaspoon black peppercorns
¾	teaspoon cumin seeds, toasted
1¼	teaspoons coriander seeds
½	teaspoon salt
1	cup thinly sliced onion
20	whole garlic cloves, peeled
1	bay leaf
18	fresh Black Mission figs
1	cup ruby port
	zest of 1 lemon
½	cup coarsely chopped parsley

Arrange chicken pieces in 13x9-inch baking dish. In a spice grinder, crush peppercorns, cumin, and coriander. Place spices in bowl; add salt and mix. Sprinkle spice mixture over chicken, pressing it in. Scatter onion, garlic, bay leaf, and figs among chicken. Add port. Sprinkle zest evenly on top. Cover dish with foil. Bake at 350° for 50 minutes. Uncover and continue baking until chicken is tender, about 15-20 minutes. Sprinkle with parsley. Serves 4.

Poultry & Seafood

***Ti**p:*

If a head of garlic sprouts, separate the cloves and plant them. Soon you will have garlic chives which are perfect for seasoning fish, potatoes, cream soups, and sauces.

"Friendship is unnecessary, like philosophy, like art, like the universe itself (for God did not need to create). It has no survival value; rather it is one of those things which give value to survival."

—C.S. Lewis.

Simply Divine

Poultry & Seafood

Tip:

Curry powder is a blend of ground herbs, seeds, and spices. Commercially prepared curry powders quickly lose their pungency and should be replaced about every two months.

Apple Chicken Curry

A *fun dinner for family or company*

2	tablespoons butter
1½	cups chopped pared apple
½	cup chopped onion
1	clove garlic, minced
2	tablespoons flour
2-3	teaspoons curry powder
1	teaspoon salt
2	cups milk
2	cups cooked cubed chicken
	steamed rice

Condiments (optional)
    raisins
    coconut
    diced bananas
    chopped hard cooked eggs
    chutney
    chopped peanuts
    crumbled bacon
    chopped mango

In a skillet melt butter. Add apple, onion, and garlic. Cook 5 minutes over medium heat. Stir in flour, curry, and salt. Slowly blend in milk. Cook, stirring until thick. Add chicken and heat through. Serve over rice with condiments. Serves 6.

Chicken with Wild Rice

Poultry & Seafood

- 1 (6-ounce) box long-grain and wild rice mix
- ½ cup chopped onion
- ½ cup butter or margarine
- ¼ cup flour
  chicken broth
- 1 (6-ounce) can drained sliced mushrooms, liquid reserved
- 1½ cups skim milk
- 3 cups cooked diced chicken
- 2 tablespoons snipped parsley
- 1½ teaspoons salt
- ¼ teaspoon black pepper
- ½ cup toasted slivered almonds

Cook rice according to instructions on box. Set aside. Sauté onion in butter until tender. Remove from heat; stir in flour. Add enough chicken broth to mushroom liquid to measure 1½ cups. Gradually stir broth into flour mixture. Add milk; cook and stir until thick. Add rice, mushrooms, chicken, parsley, and seasonings. Mix well. Place in 13x9-inch baking dish; sprinkle with almonds. Bake at 350° for 30 minutes. Serves 6.

Variation:

In place of mushrooms, substitute 1 (2-ounce) jar of drained pimientos.

Poultry & Seafood

Chicken Enchiladas

2	boneless poached or grilled chicken breasts
¾	teaspoon salt, divided
1	cup chopped onion
1	clove garlic, minced
2	tablespoons butter
1	(16-ounce) can tomatoes, sliced
1	(8-ounce) can tomato sauce
¼	cup green chilies, chopped
1	teaspoon sugar
½	teaspoon ground cumin
½	teaspoon oregano
½	teaspoon basil
12	frozen tortillas, thawed
2½	cups Monterey Jack cheese, grated
¾	cup sour cream

Cut or shred chicken. Sprinkle with ¼ teaspoon salt. Set aside. In a saucepan, sauté onion and garlic in butter until tender. Add tomatoes, tomato sauce, chilies, sugar, and seasonings. Bring to boil. Reduce heat; simmer covered for 20 minutes. Remove from heat. Dip each tortilla in tomato mixture to soften. Place 2 tablespoons chicken and 2 tablespoons cheese on each tortilla. Roll up and place seam-side down in a 13x9-inch baking dish. Blend sour cream into remaining sauce; pour over tortillas. Sprinkle with remaining cheese. Cover and bake at 350° for 40 minutes or until hot and bubbly. Serves 6.

Cornish Hens with Seasoned Stuffing

Poultry & Seafood

4	Cornish hens
	salt
	pepper
2	cups seasoned croutons
½	cup wheat germ
½	cup finely chopped celery with leaves
½	cup chicken broth
6	tablespoons melted butter, divided
1	teaspoon sugar

Lightly season body cavity of hens. Twist wing tips up and back under each hen, tucking neck skin under wings to secure. In a large bowl, combine croutons, wheat germ, celery, broth, 2 tablespoons melted butter, sugar, salt, and pepper. Lightly spoon mixture into cavities. Tie legs together. Brush hens with 2 tablespoons melted butter. Place hens, breast side up, on rack in shallow roasting pan. Bake at 425° for 1 hour, basting occasionally with remaining butter until leg moves easily up and down. During last 15 minutes of roasting, cut strings from legs and brush birds with Red Raisin Sauce (see recipe). Serve with remaining sauce. Serves 4.

Red Raisin Sauce

1	(10-ounce) jar red currant jelly
½	cup raisins
¼	cup butter
2	teaspoons lemon juice
¼	teaspoon allspice

In a saucepan over medium-low heat, heat jelly, raisins, butter, lemon juice, and allspice, stirring until mixture is hot and well blended. Makes about 1¾ cups sauce.

Poultry & Seafood

Chicken Salad Gratinée

4	cups cooked chicken, cut into chunks
¾	cup mayonnaise
2	tablespoons lemon juice
1	teaspoon salt
½	teaspoon seasoned salt flavor enhancer
2	cups chopped celery
1	teaspoon chopped onion
2	tablespoons chopped pimientos
2	hard cooked eggs, chopped
1	(10¾-ounce) can cream of chicken soup
1½	cups grated sharp cheddar cheese
⅔	cup almonds, toasted and finely chopped
1½	cups crushed potato chips

Combine chicken, mayonnaise, seasonings, vegetables, eggs, and soup. Put in 13x9-inch baking dish. Top with cheese. Refrigerate overnight. Before baking, sprinkle with almonds and chips. Bake at 400° for 20-25 minutes. Serves 8.

Foiled Turkey Breast

Bake it frozen!

"Thanksgiving dinner's sad
and thankless
Christmas dinner's dark and blue
When you stop and try to see it
From the turkey's point of view."
-Shel Silverstein,
Where the Sidewalk Ends

2-4	tablespoons butter, softened
½	teaspoon salt
¼	teaspoon cracked black pepper
	choice of paprika, thyme, rosemary, or tarragon
1	whole frozen turkey breast, 5-7 pounds
	heavy foil

Make a paste of butter and seasonings. Spread over top of breast. Center bird on foil and wrap securely, double folding top and side seams. Bake at 400° for 3 hours. Remove from oven. Carefully open the top of foil; fold back. Spoon juices over breast and return to oven for 30 minutes until brown. Cool slightly before slicing. Serve with Red Raisin Sauce on page 163. Serves 6.

Orange Roughy with Star Fruit Salsa

A *delicious fish with a sensational salsa*

Poultry & Seafood

Star Fruit Salsa
- 2 medium star fruit, thinly sliced
- 1 cup fresh strawberries, sliced
- ½ cup minced onion
- 1 tablespoon chopped jalapeño pepper
- 1 tablespoon minced fresh cilantro
- 1 teaspoon grated lime zest
- 1 tablespoon lime juice
- ¼ teaspoon ground coriander
- ⅛ teaspoon cayenne pepper

Combine salsa ingredients. Cover; chill 2 hours

- 2 tablespoons lime juice
- 2 teaspoons butter, melted
- 6 (4-ounce) orange roughy fillets
  fresh cilantro sprigs (optional)

To prepare fish, combine lime juice and butter. Stir well. Place fillets on rack of broiler pan coated with cooking spray and brush with lime mixture. Broil 5½ inches from heat for 10 minutes or until fish flakes easily when tested with a fork. Do not overcook. To serve, spoon salsa over fillets. Garnish with cilantro sprigs. Serves 6.

Tip:

Star fruit is also sold under the names "carambola" or "Chinese star fruit." The oval shaped, tropical fruit has five ribs, is golden yellow, and tastes like a plum. When cut crosswise, the pieces resemble a star. The fruit is available late summer to midwinter. When buying, look for evenly colored carambola, though green tinged fruit will ripen at room temperature. Store ripe fruit in a tightly wrapped plastic bag in the refrigerator.

Poultry & Seafood

Boiled Shad with White Sauce.

Boil the shad thoroughly in a pan constructed for this purpose, costing two dollars and a half, the fish will slide out of the pan without touching, then dress the fish with parsley and cream sauce.

Gate City Cook Book

Poached Salmon Steaks with Cucumber Dill Sauce

Serve hot or cold.

2	salmon steaks, ¾-1 inch thick
¼	cup lemon juice
¼	cup white wine
¼	teaspoon chicken bouillon granules
⅛	teaspoon onion salt
2	cups hot, steamed spinach
	lemon slices (optional)
	parsley sprigs (optional)

Place salmon steaks flat in a pan just large enough to hold them. In small saucepan, combine lemon juice, wine, bouillon granules, and onion salt. Heat to boiling. Pour over salmon, cover, and poach 8-10 minutes, just until salmon flakes. Do not overcook. Place salmon on hot platter lined with spinach. Garnish with lemon slices and parsley. Serve with Cucumber Dill Sauce. Serves 2.

Cucumber Dill Sauce

½	medium cucumber
⅔	cup sour cream or plain yogurt
2	teaspoons chopped chives or chopped green onion tops
2	teaspoons snipped parsley
1	teaspoon lemon juice
¼	teaspoon dill weed
	salt
	pepper

Peel cucumber, remove seeds, and chop finely. Add sour cream and seasonings. Serve cold or warm.

Nut-Crusted White Fish

3	tablespoons pine nuts
½	cup seasoned bread crumbs
¼	cup pitted Kalamata or ripe olives
1	teaspoon minced shallots
1	teaspoon minced garlic
1	teaspoon parsley
½	teaspoon grated lemon zest
1	teaspoon minced fresh tarragon
2	tablespoons olive oil
	salt
	freshly ground black pepper
4	fillets halibut, flounder, cod, or other firm white fish, 5-6 ounces each
	juice of 1 lemon
¼	cup dry white wine

In food processor, chop pine nuts fairly fine; mix with bread crumbs. Set aside. On a cutting board, finely chop olives, shallots, garlic, zest, and tarragon; place in bowl. Add olive oil and seasonings. Stir to make spreadable paste. Preheat oven to 450°. Lightly oil a baking dish just large enough to hold fish. Spread each side of fillet with about 2 teaspoons of paste. Lightly pat one-fourth of crumb mixture on top of each fillet. Place in baking dish, crumb side up. Carefully pour lemon juice and wine around fish to a depth of at least ⅛ inch. Bake uncovered until fish flakes when tested with a fork, about 6-10 minutes. Serves 4.

Poultry & Seafood

Tip:

Pine nuts are sold under the names "Indian nut," "piñon," "pignoli," and "pignolia." The Chinese pine nut has a strong flavor and is usually sold in Asian markets. The higher-priced Mediterranean or Italian pine nut has a lighter, more delicate flavor.

Poultry & Seafood

Tip:

Channel catfish is considered the best eating.

Tartare Sauce.

Half a pint of mayonnaise, three olives, six cucumbers, one small onion, chopped fine; add to this half cup of cider vinegar; mix well.
　　　　　Gate City Cook Book

Catfish Crisp

Fillets which are crispy on the outside, moist on the inside

2	large fresh catfish fillets
4	tablespoons lemon juice
4	tablespoons water
1	tablespoon plus 2 teaspoons seafood or Cajun seasoning, divided
½	cup freshly toasted bread crumbs
2-3	tablespoons finely chopped parsley
3	tablespoons minced green onions
1	tablespoon olive oil

Fit fillets snuggly in a glass baking dish. Mix lemon juice and water; pour over fish. Marinate 1 hour, turning fillets occasionally. Remove fish; sprinkle both sides with ½ teaspoon of seafood seasoning, gently patting it into fillet. In a bowl, combine remaining seasoning, bread crumbs, parsley, and onions. Add oil and stir until crumbs are moist. Coat fillets with crumb mixture, pressing gently on each side. Shake off excess. Place fillets in nonstick baking pan and cook at 450° for 6 minutes, turn, and cook for 6 minutes. Turn again and cook 4 minutes. Do not overcook. Serves 2.

Blackened Tuna

A *hot skillet combined with a spicy seasoning gives this fish its extra crispy crust.*

2   (4-ounce) fillets of tuna, halibut, or snapper
4   teaspoons butter or margarine
    lemon slices

Roll fillets in Spicy Cajun Seasoning (see recipe), rubbing spices into flesh. Melt butter in nonstick skillet over medium-high heat. Quickly add fillets before butter burns. Turn heat to high and cook fish for 2-3 minutes on one side until charred. Carefully turn fish over. Cook second side for 2-3 minutes. Reduce heat to low, cover, and cook an additional 5 minutes until fish flakes when tested with a fork. Garnish with lemon slices. Serves 2.

Shrimp and Linguine

Linguine, the Italian word for "little tongues," is often called "flat spaghetti."

8   ounces linguine
4   cloves garlic, minced
¼   cup olive oil
1   pound shrimp, peeled
1   (14-ounce) can artichoke hearts, quartered
4   tomatoes, chopped
1   teaspoon oregano
2   tablespoons lemon juice
1   cup feta cheese, crumbled

In lightly salted water, cook linguine al dente; drain. While pasta is cooking, sauté garlic in olive oil. Add shrimp. Sauté 2-3 minutes. Add remaining ingredients. Stir; heat through. Add to linguine; mix lightly. Serve warm. Serves 4.

Poultry & Seafood

Tip:

To create classic blackened fish, use a cast-iron skillet heated until the bottom of the pan is ash white in color.

Spicy Cajun Seasoning

2   minced cloves garlic
1   teaspoon onion powder
1   teaspoon paprika
½   teaspoon thyme
½   teaspoon oregano
1   teaspoon coarsely ground black pepper
½-1   teaspoon cayenne pepper
½   teaspoon chili powder

Combine seasonings.

"I like Pasta because my dad makes it homeade, and it is really good."
                    Lauren Reid, age 12.

Simply Divine   169

Poultry & Seafood

Seafood recipes abounded in the Gate City Cook Book, but it was oysters, not shrimp, that took center stage. In addition to the following recipe, the editor included Croquettes of Oysters, Oyster Patties, Oyster Short Cake, Oyster Cocktail, Potato Oyster Balls, and Celeried Oysters.

Oysters in Ramekins.

Put as many layers of oysters and cracker crumbs as you wish, highly seasoned with paprika, salt and butter, cover the last layer with cracker crumbs, butter and bake lightly in ramekins.

              Gate City Cook Book

Crawfish Fettuccine

12	ounces cooked fettuccine, drained
1	tablespoon minced garlic
2	cups chopped onions
1	cup chopped celery
1	cup chopped green bell peppers
1-2	tablespoons olive oil
2	pounds crawfish tails
½	cup tomatoes with chilies
2	cups half-and-half
8	ounces processed cheese loaf
	Creole seasoning
	flour
	water
½	cup chopped green onions
	freshly grated Parmesan cheese

Place pasta in large baking dish. Sauté garlic, onions, celery, and green peppers in oil until tender. Add crawfish; cook 5 minutes over medium-high heat. Add tomatoes with chilies, half-and-half, and processed cheese loaf. Cook until cheese is melted, stirring occasionally to prevent mixture from scorching. Season generously with Creole seasoning. If mixture is thin, thicken with a paste of flour and water. Add green onion, pour over pasta, and mix together. Cover with Parmesan. Bake at 350° for 20 minutes. Serve with additional Parmesan cheese. Serves 4.

Shrimp Jubilee

2   quarts water plus 1 tablespoon olive oil
1-2 tablespoons fresh basil, chopped
1   teaspoon dried thyme
1   teaspoon dried oregano
½   bunch broccoli, chopped coarsely
3   tomatoes, chopped
2   carrots, peeled and chopped
½   green bell pepper, seeded and chopped
8   ounces angel hair pasta
6   tablespoons butter or margarine, melted
4   ounces feta cheese crumbled
½-¾ cup Parmesan cheese
1-1¼ pounds medium shrimp, cooked, peeled, and deveined

Bring water to boil. Add herbs, vegetables, and pasta. Cook 5-7 minutes until pasta is done. Strain mixture; place in bowl. Add butter, cheeses, and shrimp; toss well. Serve immediately. Serves 6-8.

Southwest Crab Cakes

A *shortcut to good eating*

2   crab cakes, purchased from grocery or market
2   tablespoons Parmesan cheese
1-2 tablespoons olive oil
2   cloves garlic, crushed
1   (15-ounce) can black beans, drained
2   stalks celery, chopped
½   red bell pepper, julienned
2   tablespoons salsa

Coat crab cakes in Parmesan. Sauté garlic in oil. Add crab cakes; cook over medium heat, about 8 minutes per side. In separate pan, combine beans, celery, and bell pepper; warm. Spread bean mixture on plate. Place crab cake in center. Top with 1 tablespoon salsa. Serves 2.

Poultry & Seafood

Variation:

Add raw walnuts and raisins to taste.

Simply Divine

Poultry & Seafood

Tip:

At the heart of Creole (and Cajun) cooking is the "holy trinity" of chopped green pepper, onion, and celery. For the best results, use the freshest vegetables available.

Shrimp Creole

½ cup chopped green bell pepper
½ cup chopped onion
½ cup chopped celery
2 cloves garlic, minced
2 (14½-ounce) cans whole tomatoes, undrained and chopped
1 (8-ounce) can tomato sauce
1 teaspoon sugar
½ teaspoon salt
½ teaspoon chili powder
1 tablespoon Worcestershire sauce
½ teaspoon hot sauce
2 teaspoons cornstarch
1 tablespoon water
1½ pounds medium shrimp, peeled and deveined
3 cups long-grain rice, cooked without salt or fat

Coat Dutch oven with cooking spray; place over medium-high heat until hot. Add green pepper, onion, celery, and garlic; sauté 5 minutes or until vegetables are tender. Add tomatoes, tomato sauce, sugar, salt, chili powder, Worcestershire, and hot sauce. Stir well. Cook uncovered over medium heat for 15 minutes, stirring occasionally. Cover, reduce heat, and simmer 45 minutes. In a small bowl, combine cornstarch with water, blending well. Add to tomato mixture, stirring constantly. Add shrimp; simmer 5 minutes or until shrimp are cooked. Serve over rice. Serves 6.

Simply Divine

Shrimp with Grits

A *traditional Low Country dish*

Poultry & Seafood

6	strips bacon
2	cups mushrooms, sliced
1	cup green onions, chopped
1	garlic clove, minced
4	teaspoons lemon juice
	dash Tabasco
2	tablespoons parsley
	salt
	pepper
1	pound shrimp, peeled
	half-and-half (optional)
	cheese grits, prepared for 2

Fry bacon and crumble. Drain skillet, reserving 4 tablespoons grease. Sauté mushrooms, onions, and flavorings in grease. Add shrimp; cook until pink. To thicken sauce or enhance its richness, add half-and-half. Serve over cheese grits. Top with bacon. Serves 2.

Cheese Grits

1	cup quick grits
1	teaspoon salt
4	cups boiling water
1-1½	cups shredded cheese

Stir the grits slowly into the salted water. Reduce heat, cover, and cook about 20 minutes, stirring often. Stir in cheese and cook until smooth. Serves 2-4.

Seagoing Shrimp

A *secret ingredient gives the effect of shrimp swimming in seaweed.*

6	cups water
¼	cup sliced onion
	juice of 1 lemon
1	clove garlic, crushed
1	bay leaf
1	tablespoon salt
1	(14-ounce) can sauerkraut, rinsed
¼	cup green bell pepper, julienned
1	pound shrimp, peeled

Bring water, onion, lemon juice, garlic, bay leaf, and salt to gentle boil. Simmer 5 minutes. Discard onion, garlic, and bay leaf. Add sauerkraut and peppers; bring to boil. Add shrimp and cook 5 minutes or until pink. Drain and serve. Serves 3.

Variation:

To enhance the flavor of both sauerkraut and shrimp, add 1 teaspoon caraway seed to the seasonings. Be sure to remove the seeds before adding the sauerkraut, as extended simmering makes caraway seeds bitter.

Simply Divine

Poultry & Seafood

Barbecued Shrimp

Serve with French bread to sop the sauce.

8   pounds large shrimp, unpeeled

Sauce
1   cup butter
1   cup olive oil
8   ounces chili sauce
3   tablespoons Worcestershire
2   lemons, sliced
4   cloves garlic, chopped
3   tablespoons lemon juice
1   tablespoon parsley, chopped
2   teaspoons paprika
2   teaspoons oregano
2   teaspoons cayenne pepper
1   teaspoon Tabasco
3   tablespoons liquid hickory smoke seasoning
    salt
    pepper

Clean shrimp; spread in large shallow pan. In a saucepan, gently heat sauce ingredients, blending well. Pour over shrimp. Refrigerate. Baste and turn shrimp every 30 minutes for several hours. Bake at 300° for 30 minutes, turning shrimp at 10-minute intervals. Serves 6-8.

Florida Paella

Delicious with a simple green salad and crusty French bread

⅓	cup chopped onion
¾	cup chopped celery
1	clove garlic, crushed
	chopped bell pepper as desired
2	tablespoons oil
2	cups long-grain white rice or yellow rice
4	cups hot chicken broth
1	pound fresh shrimp, peeled and deveined
1	can minced clams, drained
2	cups diced cooked chicken
	lobster, crabmeat, chopped ham, sliced Polish or chorizo sausage (optional)
1½	teaspoons salt
½	teaspoon black pepper
1	teaspoon cumin seed
1	teaspoon oregano
	grated Parmesan cheese
	pitted ripe olives and/or stuffed green olives
1	(4-ounce) jar pimiento, drained
1	(10-ounce) box frozen peas, thawed
1	(4-ounce) can sliced mushrooms or sautéed fresh mushrooms
	chopped fresh parsley

Sauté onion, celery, garlic, and bell pepper in oil. Remove vegetables. In same pan, sauté rice until golden. Place rice, sautéed vegetables, and broth in large casserole. Add shrimp, clams, chicken, optional shellfish and meats, and seasonings. Mix lightly. Bake covered at 350° for 40-50 minutes until liquid is absorbed and rice is fluffy. Add Parmesan cheese, olives, pimientos, peas, and mushrooms. Toss lightly. Cover; return to oven for 10 minutes. If paella is dry, add water or broth. Sprinkle with additional Parmesan cheese and parsley. Serves 8.

Poultry & Seafood

"This is my Aunt Julia's South Florida version of a favorite Spanish dish. Make this paella as simple or as elaborate as you wish."
-Catherine Capps

Tip:

As long as you keep the proportions of liquid and rice the same, you may add or subtract ingredients to suit your taste and budget.

Poultry & Seafood

Shrimp Pie.

One or two cans of shrimp, or same amount of fresh shrimp, cover bottom of pan with slices of bread, cover bread with shrimp, then salt and pepper slightly, using black pepper, then dot shrimp with butter, mix a tablespoonful of Worcestershire sauce (Lea & Perrin's) in a cup of cream, and pour over shrimp and bread. Then add another layer of shrimp and bread as before, with salt, pepper and butter as before, and so on until shrimp is used up. Let last layer be of bread. Then fill pan with cream or rich milk, put in oven and cook slowly until bread on top is toasted light brown. Then serve. This receipt will also do for crabs, using crab meat instead of shrimp.

    Gate City Cook Book

Shellfish with Wild Rice

1	cup celery, diced
1	Bermuda onion, diced
1	green bell pepper, diced
3	tablespoons butter, divided
1	tablespoon olive oil
1	pound sliced mushrooms
¾	pound cooked shrimp
½	pound cooked crabmeat
1	pound cooked lobster meat
1½	cups cooked wild rice
1	tablespoon Worcestershire sauce
1½	cups mayonnaise
1	teaspoon curry
	salt
	pepper
	bread crumbs

Sauté celery, onion, and green pepper in 1 tablespoon butter and 1 tablespoon oil. In a separate pan, sauté mushrooms in 2 tablespoons butter. Combine vegetables and mushrooms. Add shellfish, wild rice, Worcestershire, mayonnaise, and seasonings. Mix gently. Place in a buttered 13x9-inch baking dish; top with bread crumbs. Bake at 325° for 45 minutes. Serves 8-10.

Vegetables & Side Dishes

"Give thanks to the Lord, for he is good...who gives food to every creature."

Psalm 136:1, 25

Vegetables & Side Dishes

VEGETABLES

Claire's Crudités	179
Oven-Roasted Vegetables	180
Vegetarian Medley	181
Baked Vegetable Quartet	181
Fruit and Vegetable Medley	181
Awesome Asparagus Casserole	182
Asparagus As Is	182
Asparagus Stir-Fry	183
Basic Broccoli	184
Cheesy Broccoli and Rice	184
Broccoli Bake	185
Easy Broccoli Soufflé	185
Piquant Green Beans	186
Pseudo-Southern Green Beans	186
Fresh Carrot Puree	187
Cauliflower Bake	187
Cauliflower à la Polonaise	188
Corn Pudding	188
Vidalia Pie	189
Spinach with Artichokes	189
Creamed Spinach au Gratin	190
Steamed Balsamic Spinach	191
Squash Deluxe	191
Posh Squash	191
Microwaved Spaghetti Squash	192
Warmly Dressed Winter Squash	193
Stuffed Zucchini	193
Mushroom-Stuffed Tomatoes	194
Fried Green Tomatoes	195
Tomato Pie	195
Celery Amandine	210

POTATOES

Parmesan Potato Bake	204
Unfried Fries	204
Mediterranean Potatoes	205
Stuffed Baked Potatoes	206
Sweet Potato Supreme	206
Potato Croquettes	207
Yam and Cranberry Bake	207
Creamy Potato Puff	207

SIDES

New Orleans Red Beans and Rice	196
Mexican Black Beans on Rice	197
Vegetarian Pasta with Chunky Tomato Sauce	198
Sofia's Sauce for Pasta or Potatoes	199
Classic Pesto Primavera	200
Confetti Rice	201
Risotto aux Légumes	202
Peppery Grits	203
Macaroni and Cheese Mold	204
Country Chicken Dressing	210
Cornbread Dressing Gone Wild	211
Quick Cornbread Dressing	212

FRUIT SIDES

Cranberry Apple Crunch	208
Scalloped Pineapple	208
Hot Mixed Fruit	209
Curried Fruit	209

HERITAGE RECIPES

Scalloped Onions	189
Baked Tomatoes	194
Baked Beans	197
Caramel Potatoes	207
Turkey Dressing	212

Claire's Crudités

Chilled on a large glass tray, the colorful vegetables are ready for the buffet when guests arrive. Crudités on individual platters are often an entrée item in Europe.

Vegetables & Side Dishes

4	dozen slender asparagus spears, thick ends removed
1	broccoflower, broken in bunches of several florets each
4	small zucchini, sliced in ¼-inch rounds
1	(8-ounce) package button mushrooms
1	(1 pint) package cherry tomatoes
1	cucumber, peeled and sliced
1	green bell pepper
1	yellow bell pepper
1	bunch small red radishes

Marinade

½	cup olive oil
¾	cup red wine vinegar
1	garlic clove, minced
1	tablespoon grated onion
1-2	teaspoons lemon juice
2	teaspoons salt
½	teaspoon coarsely ground pepper
2	tablespoons sugar
	sprinkling of dry mustard, dill weed, basil, oregano, rosemary

Steam asparagus, broccoflower, and zucchini separately until just fork tender; drain in colander and plunge into ice water to cool. Drop mushrooms into boiling water for 1 minute; drain on paper towels. If cherry tomatoes are as large as a walnut, peel and slice in half.

Combine marinade ingredients in a saucepan, bring to a boil, and simmer 5 minutes. Cool before pouring over vegetables in separate containers or zip-top plastic bags. Marinate in refrigerator for 12 hours or more. To serve, arrange separately on a large platter in varying color groups. Add thinly sliced circles of unmarinated red and green peppers and whole radishes. Serves 12.

"To capture the rapture of an evening in Provence, begin with a regional hors d'oeuvre, Chèvre Persillade (page 20). Roast a lovely leg of lamb and serve with crudités and a risotto. Depend on a good French bakery for an accompanying olive bread and colorful fruit tarts."
-Claire Willingham.
Claire is the chairman of the Heritage Committee at Second-Ponce.

Simply Divine

Vegetables & Side Dishes

Oven-Roasted Vegetables

The aroma while roasting is wonderful. Vary vegetables as desired for color and texture.

10	small new potatoes, unpeeled
8	ounces cut and peeled baby carrots
1	small onion, peeled and cut into wedges
¼	cup olive oil
3	tablespoons lemon juice
3	cloves garlic, minced
1	tablespoon snipped fresh rosemary or oregano
1	teaspoon salt (optional)
½	teaspoon black pepper
2	cups eggplant or zucchini slices
1	medium red or green bell pepper, cut into ½-inch slices

Use potatoes whole if they are tiny, or quarter larger ones. Place potatoes, carrots, and onion in a 13x9-inch baking pan. Combine olive oil, lemon juice, garlic, rosemary or oregano, salt, and pepper. Drizzle over vegetables and toss to coat. Roast uncovered at 450° for 30 minutes, stirring occasionally. Cut eggplant or zucchini lengthwise into quarters, then into ½-inch slices. Add eggplant or zucchini and pepper to roasted vegetables. Toss to combine. Roast another 15-30 minutes at 450°, adding oil if vegetables become dry. Serves 4-6.

Vegetarian Medley

Vegetables of choice could be substituted, such as petite lima beans, green beans, peas.

1	(16-ounce) package mixed frozen vegetables
1	cup chopped celery
1	cup chopped onions
½	cup butter or margarine, divided
1	cup cubed cheddar cheese
1	cup mayonnaise
1	(8-ounce) can sliced water chestnuts, drained
1	(4-ounce) pack saltines, crushed

Cook vegetables by package directions and drain. Sauté celery and onions in 2 tablespoons butter. Combine vegetables, celery and onions, cheese, mayonnaise, and water chestnuts in a 2½-quart casserole. Melt remaining butter, add crushed saltines, and spread evenly on top. Bake at 375° for 30 minutes. Serves 8-10.

Baked Vegetable Quartet

1-2	medium onions, peeled and sliced
1	tablespoon butter or margarine
8	small to medium zucchini, sliced
8	small to medium yellow squash, sliced
2	(14½-ounce) cans stewed tomatoes, including juice
½	teaspoon oregano
½	teaspoon salt (optional)
¼	teaspoon black pepper
5	ounces sharp cheddar cheese, sliced

In large skillet or saucepan, sauté onions in butter over medium heat. Add zucchini, squash, tomatoes, and seasonings; lower heat and cook until vegetables are just fork tender. Pour into 3-quart ungreased casserole and cover top with cheese. Bake at 350° for 30 minutes. Serves 8-10.

Vegetables & Side Dishes

Fruit and Vegetable Medley

2	cups sliced onions
1	cup diced carrots
1	cup diced apples
	sprinkling of salt and pepper
¼	cup water
2	tablespoons butter
	chopped parsley

Layer onions, carrots, and apples in a baking dish, sprinkling each layer with salt and pepper. Add water, dot with butter, cover, and bake at 350° for 1 hour. Sprinkle with parsley. Serves 4.

Vegetables & Side Dishes

"This is excellent served at a buffet with a ham and a squash casserole. It's been a Christmas tradition at my house for years."

-Carol Warren.

Awesome Asparagus Casserole

3   (1 pound, 3-ounce) cans extra large asparagus
1   (10¾-ounce) can cream of mushroom soup
1   cup grated sharp cheddar cheese
1   teaspoon lemon juice
1   cup saltine cracker crumbs

Gradually blend ½ cup liquid from asparagus into mushroom soup, adding cheese and lemon juice until smooth; set aside. In a buttered 9x9x2-inch glass casserole dish, spread a layer of cracker crumbs, then a layer of drained asparagus, then soup mixture. Repeat. Top with a layer of cracker crumbs. Bake at 350° for 30 minutes. Serves 6.

Asparagus As Is

With so many options for fixing it fancy, asparagus can be overlooked for its simple beauty.

Variation:

Sprinkle asparagus with finely grated Parmesan cheese. Or sauté a few green onions and sliced mushrooms in butter and add toasted almonds.

2   pounds fresh asparagus, firm and bright green with tight tips
3   tablespoons olive oil
    salt and pepper to taste

Break off thick ends of stalks; if stems seem tough, peel the outer skin from lower portion of stalks. Put olive oil in a 13x9-inch glass baking dish. Arrange the asparagus in a single layer, turning to coat in oil. Sprinkle lightly with salt and pepper. Roast at 475° about 6 minutes, until just tender. Serves 4-5.

Asparagus Stir-Fry

For variety, substitute fresh broccoli florets for asparagus; or add coarsely chopped mushrooms or thinly sliced carrots.

Vegetables & Side Dishes

3	tablespoons soy sauce
2	tablespoons cornstarch
1½	cups water or vegetable stock
1	teaspoon vegetable oil
½	teaspoon ground ginger
1-2	garlic cloves, minced
	sprinkle of black pepper
2	tablespoons extra virgin olive oil
½-1	pound fresh asparagus (small to medium), cut in 2-inch lengths
½	cup very young Vidalia onions, chopped
½-1	red bell pepper, chopped
½-1	green bell pepper, chopped
½-¾	cup almonds or cashew nuts
2-4	cups hot cooked rice

Combine soy sauce and cornstarch. Stir in water, oil, ginger, garlic, and pepper. Set aside. In a wok or large skillet, heat oil. Stir-fry asparagus until barely tender. Add onions and peppers, and continue to stir-fry until crisp tender. Stir the sauce mixture and add, stirring until thickened and bubbly. Reduce heat; fold in nuts. Cover and cook 1 minute, until nuts are heated through. Spoon over rice. Serve with a salad and Kebabs on page 124. Serves 2-4.

Vegetables & Side Dishes

Tip:

Roasting vegetables helps them retain flavor, color, and nutritional value. It is an ideal preparation for a crowd because the vegetables can be prepared in advance and put into the oven just before serving.

Basic Broccoli

4	large stems of broccoli, cut into smaller crowns
¼	cup olive oil
1	teaspoon minced garlic
¼	teaspoon salt
¼	teaspoon black pepper

For a crunchy texture, toss broccoli with olive oil and seasonings. Spread in single layer in baking dish and roast at 475° for 10-12 minutes. For a more tender texture, place broccoli in pot with stems down, and add water to ¼-inch depth. Bring to a boil, reduce heat, cover, and steam for 6 minutes. Drain and toss gently with seasonings. Serves 8.

"This makes a delicious entrée with the addition of cooked shrimp. Stir the shellfish in gently just before topping with the croutons."

-Joan Johnson.

Cheesy Broccoli and Rice

3	cups cooked rice
2	(10-ounce) packages frozen chopped broccoli
3	tablespoons butter, divided
1	medium onion, chopped
3-4	stalks celery, chopped
1	(1-pound) jar processed cheese spread
1	cup croutons

While rice is cooking, cook broccoli until fork tender. Sauté chopped onion and celery in 2 tablespoons butter and set aside. Place hot rice and hot broccoli in 2-quart baking dish, and immediately stir in softened cheese spread. Add onions and celery, and mix thoroughly. Bake covered at 325° for 30 minutes. Sauté croutons in remaining tablespoon of butter. Uncover and sprinkle croutons on top. Bake uncovered for 15 minutes. Serves 6-7.

Broccoli Bake

Vegetables & Side Dishes

2 (10-ounce) packages frozen chopped broccoli
1 (10¾-ounce) can cream of mushroom soup
1½ cups shredded cheddar cheese
½ cup sour cream
1 egg, beaten
1 tablespoon horseradish sauce
1 cup cracker crumbs
¼ cup butter, melted

Cook broccoli until just tender; drain well and set aside. Thoroughly mix soup, cheese, sour cream, egg, and horseradish sauce. Fold in broccoli. Put in greased 2-quart casserole. Mix butter with crumbs; use as topping on broccoli mixture. Bake at 350° for 25 minutes. Serves 6-8.

Tip:

Studies have shown that eating certain vegetables helps reduce or prevent disease. Among the "top twelve" beneficial vegetables are: broccoli, Brussels sprouts, cabbage, cauliflower, horseradish, kale, kohlrabi, mustard greens, radish, rutabaga, turnip, and watercress.

Easy Broccoli Soufflé

2 (10-ounce) packages frozen chopped broccoli
1 cup mayonnaise
1 tablespoon butter or margarine, melted
1 tablespoon self-rising flour
3 eggs
¼ cup milk
½-1 teaspoon salt
¼ teaspoon black pepper
   sprinkling of Parmesan cheese

Cook broccoli and drain. Process mayonnaise, butter, flour, eggs, milk, and seasonings in blender until thoroughly mixed. Combine broccoli with blended ingredients. Pour into buttered soufflé dish, and sprinkle with Parmesan cheese. Bake at 350° for 30 minutes. Serves 8.

Simply Divine

Vegetables & Side Dishes

Piquant Green Beans

3 (9-ounce) packages green beans or 2 pounds fresh green beans
2 slices bacon
½ cup diced onion
1 tablespoon flour
¼ cup wine vinegar
2 tablespoons sugar
1 teaspoon salt
½ teaspoon black pepper

Cook beans until just fork tender and set aside. In a large skillet fry bacon until crisp, remove, and crumble. Sauté onion in the drippings, add flour, and blend until smooth. Slowly add vinegar, sugar, salt, and pepper. Reduce heat and simmer until thickened, stirring constantly. Add green beans; toss to coat. Cover and heat through. Remove to serving bowl and sprinkle with crumbled bacon. Serves 8.

Pseudo-Southern Green Beans

Quick and easy, yet they taste like slowly cooked fresh beans, Southern style.

4 (14½-ounce) cans whole green beans, drained
1 clove garlic, minced
½ cup butter, melted
¼-½ cup brown sugar
4 strips bacon

Spread green beans in 13x9-inch casserole. Combine garlic, butter, and brown sugar and pour over beans. Place bacon strips across the top. Bake at 350° on center rack of oven for 40 minutes, until bacon is crisp. Serves 6-8.

Fresh Carrot Puree

Beautiful, smooth, and colorful

4	pounds carrots, peeled and cooked until tender
½	cup unsalted butter, melted
1½	cups chicken broth, warmed
½	cup fresh orange juice
½	teaspoon orange zest
1	teaspoon ground cardamom
1½	teaspoons salt
¼	teaspoon cayenne pepper

Mix all ingredients together. Puree in a food processor until smooth. Bake covered at 350° for 25 minutes until steaming hot. Top with Crème Fraîche on page 269. Serves 8-10.

Cauliflower Bake

1	large cauliflower, separated into florets
¼	cup butter or margarine, melted
1	medium onion, chopped
½	cup chopped green bell pepper
1	cup crumbs of round buttery crackers
1	tablespoon sugar
½	teaspoon salt
½	teaspoon black pepper
1½	cups (6 ounces) shredded cheddar cheese, divided
1	(14½-ounce) can diced tomatoes, undrained

Steam cauliflower in lightly salted water until just tender, and set aside. In a large skillet, sauté onion and green pepper in butter; add cracker crumbs and seasonings. Gently stir in cauliflower, 1 cup of the cheese, and tomatoes. Spoon into lightly greased 13x9-inch baking dish. Bake at 350° for 35 minutes. Remove to sprinkle with remaining ½ cup cheese, and bake additional 5 minutes. Serves 6.

Vegetables & Side Dishes

Tip:

Many health-conscious chefs are replacing heavy sauces with low-fat, fresh-tasting vegetable purees. The purees, made from asparagus, beets, peppers, peas, carrots, and other vegetables, may be used to surround entrées with contrasting color.

Variation:

Serve in ramekins and garnish with chives, or use as a sauce with white fish, pork, or other mild foods.

Vegetables & Side Dishes

"Butter should not be spared in dressing plain vegetables. Without enough of it, vegetables betray themselves too painfully as roots and herbs. A cream sauce, or thin cream and butter, is often a delightful addition to carrots, lima beans, cauliflower, kohl-rabi and the like, but it is kind only to serve it to the thin."
-Marjorie Kinnan Rawlings,
Cross Creek Cookery

Cauliflower à la Polonaise

3   onions, chopped
3   bell peppers (green, red, and yellow), chopped
2   garlic cloves, minced
½   cup butter, divided
2   (14½-ounce) cans diced tomatoes, drained
1   large cauliflower, separated into small florets
4   tablespoons flour
2   cups milk
    salt to taste
12 eggs, hard cooked and sliced
¼   cup cracker meal
    sprinkling of paprika

Sauté onions, peppers, and garlic in ¼ cup butter; add tomatoes and set aside. Cook cauliflower in salted water until crisp tender. Make a cream sauce with remaining ¼ cup butter, flour, and milk; salt to taste. In 13x9-inch casserole, layer tomato mixture, cauliflower, cream sauce, and eggs. Repeat. Sprinkle with cracker meal and paprika. Bake at 350° for 30 minutes, until bubbly and light brown. Can be made ahead and refrigerated before baking, but should not be frozen. Serves 10-12.

Corn Pudding

1   (14¾-ounce) can cream style corn
½   cup milk
1   egg, beaten
2   tablespoons flour
3   tablespoons butter, melted
2   tablespoons sugar
    sprinkling of nutmeg

Combine corn, milk, egg, flour, butter, and sugar. Pour mixture into a greased 1½-quart baking dish. Sprinkle with nutmeg. Bake at 350° for 1 hour or until custard is set. Serves 3-4.

Vidalia Pie

Vegetables & Side Dishes

1½ cups crushed saltines
6   tablespoons margarine, divided
2½ cups thinly sliced Vidalia or other sweet onions
2   eggs, beaten
¾   cup milk
    salt and pepper to taste
1   cup shredded sharp cheddar cheese

Melt 4 tablespoons margarine, and stir in crushed saltines. Use mixture to line 10-inch buttered pie pan. Melt remaining 2 tablespoons margarine and sauté onions until tender, not brown. Turn into the lined pie pan. Mix eggs, milk, salt, and pepper; pour over onions. Sprinkle with cheese. Bake at 350° about 45 minutes, or until inserted knife comes out clean. Serves 8.

Scalloped Onions.

Put onions to boil in cold water with a little salt; cook till half done, then pour this water off and put on hot water and cook until done, drain. Place in dish and pour the following dressing over them: One cup of milk, one tablespoonful of butter, one tablespoonful of CAPITOLA flour, pepper and salt to taste; cook until thick. Grate toasted bread and sprinkle over all; dot with butter and brown in stove.

    Gate City Cook Book

Spinach with Artichokes

When loving church friends rally to the needs of families stressed by illness or bereavement, casseroles are especially helpful.

2   (10-ounce) packages chopped spinach
¼   cup margarine, melted
1   (8-ounce) package cream cheese, softened
1   teaspoon lemon juice
1   (14-ounce) can artichoke hearts, quartered
    bread or cracker crumbs to cover, dotted with butter
    sprinkling of Parmesan cheese (optional)

Cook spinach by package directions and drain well. While hot, add margarine, cream cheese, and lemon juice, blending until smooth. Space artichoke hearts evenly in a greased 2-quart casserole, then spread on spinach mixture. Cover with crumbs and dot with butter, adding Parmesan cheese if desired. Bake at 350° for 30 minutes. Serves 6-8.

Simply Divine

Vegetables & Side Dishes

Creamed Spinach au Gratin

A *slightly assertive side dish*

2	(10-ounce) packages frozen chopped spinach
3	tablespoons butter
2	tablespoons chopped onion
2	tablespoons flour
½	cup cream or half-and-half
½	cup spinach liquid
½	teaspoon celery salt
½	teaspoon garlic salt
1	teaspoon Worcestershire sauce
	pinch of cayenne pepper (optional)
6	ounces Monterey Jack cheese with jalapeños, cut into pieces
	buttered bread crumbs

Cook spinach by package directions and drain, reserving liquid. Melt butter in saucepan over low heat. Sauté onion, add flour, and blend until smooth. Gradually add cream and liquid, stirring constantly to avoid lumps. When smooth and thick, add seasonings and cheese. Stir until melted. Combine with spinach, and spoon into buttered casserole. Top with buttered bread crumbs, and bake at 350° until lightly browned. May be refrigerated or frozen before baking. Serves 5-6.

Steamed Balsamic Spinach

Vegetables & Side Dishes

2   pounds fresh spinach
1   tablespoon butter
1   tablespoon balsamic vinegar
    freshly ground black pepper

Wash spinach, removing stems. Lift from water into non-aluminum saucepan. Cover and cook over high heat until hot, about 3 minutes. Remove lid to stir spinach. Recover and reduce heat, cooking 4-5 additional minutes until spinach is wilted and bright green. Drain excess moisture, and toss with butter, vinegar, and pepper. Serves 4-6.

Tip:

Flavorful balsamic vinegar is made from the juice of the white Trebbiano grape. It is dark in color and has an intense, sweet-tart taste. Use it to flavor vinaigrettes and roasted vegetables. Or sprinkle it over lightly-sugared fresh fruit.

Squash Deluxe

Every Southern cook has a favorite squash casserole.

1   pound yellow crookneck squash, sliced thin
1   medium onion, finely chopped
2   tablespoons butter or margarine
4   tablespoons finely chopped green bell pepper
1   teaspoon seasoned salt
¼   teaspoon black pepper
1   egg, well beaten
½   cup heavy cream
¼   cup sauterne or other white wine
⅓   cup grated sharp cheddar cheese
     buttered bread crumbs

Cook squash in small amount of boiling salted water until barely tender. Drain well, mash coarsely, and set aside. Sauté onion in butter, adding green pepper, until both are soft; stir in seasonings and squash, then egg, cream, and wine. Turn into greased 2-quart casserole. Bake at 350° for total time of 30-35 minutes, until just set in the center. Sprinkle cheese over the top, then bread crumbs, for the last 10 minutes of baking. Serves 4-5.

Posh Squash

2   pounds yellow squash, sliced
1   small onion, chopped
1   cup mayonnaise
1   cup Parmesan cheese
2   eggs, beaten
½   teaspoon salt
¼   teaspoon black pepper
½   cup soft bread crumbs
1   tablespoon melted butter

Cook squash and onion in salted water until tender. Drain and set aside. Mix mayonnaise, cheese, eggs, and seasonings. Gently stir in squash. Turn into greased casserole. Top with bread crumbs and butter. Bake at 350° for 30 minutes. Serves 6.

Simply Divine

Vegetables & Side Dishes

Microwaved Spaghetti Squash

1	spaghetti squash, 3-4 pounds
4	ripe tomatoes
1	tablespoon olive oil
¼	cup chopped green onion
1-2	cloves garlic, minced
1	teaspoon salt
	freshly ground black pepper, to taste
½-¾	cup shredded mozzarella cheese
¼	cup Parmesan cheese
	sprinkling of additional Parmesan cheese

Cut squash lengthwise and remove seeds. Place cut side down with ¼ cup water in glass baking pan, and cover with clear plastic wrap. Microwave 10 minutes on high, turning once, until skin is tender; let stand 5 minutes. Pull out strands of pulp with fork and set aside, discarding skin. Cut X's on bottoms of tomatoes, and stand them in small glass pan. Microwave 4 minutes on high, let stand 1 minute, then peel, core, chop, and drain. Set aside. Microwave olive oil 1 minute on high, stir in onions and garlic, and continue to microwave 3-4 additional minutes. Combine strands of squash with tomatoes, sautéed onions and garlic, salt, and pepper, and toss together. Turn into 2-quart glass baking dish, top with mozzarella and ¼ cup Parmesan cheese, and microwave on high for 4 minutes. Serve with additional Parmesan cheese. Serves 4-6.

Warmly Dressed Winter Squash

Vegetables & Side Dishes

"My son-in-law liked this squash so much that he ate it peeling and all!"
-Vicki Whitman.

2	medium acorn squash or other winter squash
2	crisp apples, cored and chopped
½	cup chopped walnuts
½	cup raisins
4	tablespoons brown sugar
2	tablespoons melted butter

Cut the squash in halves, discarding seeds. Cook in buttered baking dish at 350° for 30 minutes. Combine apples, walnuts, raisins, and brown sugar; spoon into baked squash, and drizzle with butter. Bake an additional 25-30 minutes, until tender. Serves 4.

Stuffed Zucchini

6	medium zucchini, washed
3	cups round buttery crackers, crushed
2	tablespoons Parmesan cheese, divided
1	small onion, minced and sautéed
3	tablespoons minced parsley
1	teaspoon salt
⅛	teaspoon black pepper
2	eggs, beaten
1	tablespoon butter or margarine

Boil zucchini for 5 minutes. Cut in half lengthwise and remove pulp. Place in greased baking pan. Combine pulp, crackers, 1 tablespoon Parmesan cheese, onion, parsley, seasonings, and eggs. Mix well and fill zucchini shells. Dot with butter and sprinkle remaining cheese on top. Bake at 350° for 25-30 minutes. Serves 6.

Vegetables & Side Dishes

Baked Tomatoes.

Select as many tomatoes as you need, cut off the stem end and remove the pulp. Fill with macaroni which has been boiled, grated cheese and a little of the juice of the tomatoes; season with pepper and salt. Add a small lump of butter to each tomato. Bake in a moderate oven half an hour.

Gate City Cook Book

Mushroom-Stuffed Tomatoes

2	medium tomatoes
2	large fresh shiitake mushrooms, chopped
1½	teaspoons lemon juice
1	tablespoon unsalted butter, melted
1	shallot, minced
1	tablespoon chopped fresh basil
1	teaspoon chopped fresh parsley
½	teaspoon sugar
4	teaspoons heavy cream
1	egg yolk
	salt
	freshly ground black pepper
2	tablespoons freshly grated Parmesan cheese

Cut tomatoes in half crosswise. Gently squeeze out seeds and discard. Scoop out pulp; chop it and reserve. Sprinkle each half with salt and turn upside down to stand 30 minutes. Sprinkle mushrooms with lemon juice, and sauté in butter over medium heat for 1 minute. Add shallot and continue to sauté until golden, about 5 minutes. Stir in tomato pulp, herbs, and sugar. Cook until the mixture thickens, about 10 minutes. Reduce heat to low. Lightly beat together cream and egg yolk, and stir into thickened mixture. When warmed through, season with salt and pepper to taste. Place tomato halves in shallow baking pan; fill each with mushroom mixture and sprinkle with cheese. Bake at 400° about 20 minutes, until lightly browned. Serves 4.

Fried Green Tomatoes

A good side dish for breakfast or supper

Vegetables & Side Dishes

4	green tomatoes, firm to medium soft
1	egg, beaten
1	cup dried bread crumbs
⅓	cup margarine
	sprinkling of salt and pepper
	sour cream (optional)

Cut tomatoes into ¾-inch slices. Dip them into egg, then turn in crumbs. Melt margarine in large skillet and fry coated slices, turning once, until golden brown. Season to taste and garnish with sour cream. Serves 6.

Tomato Pie

Excellent side dish with any meat

1	(9-inch) deep-dish pie crust
2-3	large tomatoes
	sprinkling of salt and pepper
1	tablespoon snipped fresh basil
1	tablespoon snipped fresh chives
2-3	green onions, chopped and sautéed
1	cup mayonnaise
1	cup grated sharp cheddar cheese

Variation:

In place of cheddar, use mozzarella, or mix up a topping of bread crumbs and Parmesan cheese.

Bake pie crust by directions until lightly done. Coarsely chop tomatoes and drain well on paper towels. Fill pie crust with tomatoes. Sprinkle with salt, pepper, herbs, and sautéed onions. Mix mayonnaise and grated cheese, and spread over tomatoes. Bake at 350° for 30 minutes. Serves 6.

Vegetables & Side Dishes

New Orleans Red Beans and Rice

Add salad and bread for a full, balanced meal.

8	cups water
1	pound dried red beans, washed
1	cup chopped celery
1	cup chopped onion
1½	cloves garlic, minced
1	pound smoked ham, cubed
1	pound smoked sausage, sliced
2	teaspoons garlic salt
¼-½	teaspoon Tabasco
1	teaspoon Worcestershire sauce
2	bay leaves
	salt to taste
	coarsely ground black pepper to taste
2	tablespoons cornstarch, blended into 1 cup water
¼	cup chopped parsley
4	cups cooked rice

In large pot combine all ingredients except cornstarch, parsley, and rice. Cook approximately 2½ hours, until beans are soft. Slowly add cornstarch, stirring while the mixture thickens. Remove bay leaves and add parsley. Serve over hot, fluffy rice. Serves 6-8.

Mexican Black Beans on Rice

Vegetables & Side Dishes

1   cup chopped onion
½   cup chopped green bell pepper
2   teaspoons olive oil
1   (15-ounce) can black beans, rinsed and drained
½   teaspoon ground cumin
¼   teaspoon ground red pepper
⅛   teaspoon dried coriander
     salt to taste
¾   cup chopped fresh tomatoes
2   cups cooked long-grain rice

Sauté onion and green pepper in olive oil until tender. Stir in beans and seasonings; cook at medium-high for 3 minutes. Add tomatoes and continue cooking until heated through, about 3 additional minutes. Serve on a bed of fluffy rice. Serves 8.

Baked Beans.

One quart navy beans, two-thirds cup molasses, dime's worth of salt pork, one tablespoonful salt, pepper to taste, one-half teaspoonful mustard. Soak beans over night in cold water. Parboil them in salted water, very slowly, four hours. Put in bean pot alternately, a layer of beans, pork, molasses, with the pepper and mustard. Bake slowly five hours.

Gate City Cook Book

Simply Divine

Vegetables & Side Dishes

Vegetarian Pasta with Chunky Tomato Sauce

Crisp-tender vegetables are added to a basic Italian tomato sauce just before serving over pasta.

Variation:

In place of vegetables, substitute artichoke hearts, ripe olives, capers, chopped Italian parsley, and additional garlic.

Chunky Tomato Sauce

¼	cup olive oil
1	large onion, diced
2	cloves garlic, minced
2	(14½-ounce) cans diced tomatoes
1	(6-ounce) can tomato paste
1	tablespoon red wine vinegar
1	tablespoon honey
1	teaspoon grated lemon zest
1	teaspoon salt
⅛	teaspoon black pepper
1	teaspoon oregano
1	teaspoon marjoram
½	teaspoon thyme
1	bay leaf
	pinch of ground cloves
2	broccoli crowns
1-2	cups cauliflower florets
2	zucchini, sliced
½	red bell pepper, sliced in bite-size strips
1	(8-ounce) can sliced water chestnuts, drained
1	(4½-ounce) jar button mushrooms, including juice
4-6	basil leaves, snipped
1	(16-ounce) package spaghetti or other pasta of choice
	Parmesan cheese

For tomato sauce, heat olive oil in large pot; sauté onion and garlic until transparent. Add tomatoes, paste, vinegar, honey, zest, and seasonings. Bring to a boil, reduce heat, and simmer 30 minutes, stirring occasionally. Remove bay leaf.

(Continued on next page)

Vegetables & Side Dishes

(Continued)
Prepare vegetables, using florets and peeled tender stems of broccoli. Steam broccoli, cauliflower, zucchini, and red pepper in minimum amount of water until fork tender. Stir vegetables and basil into tomato sauce. Heat through; do not overcook. If additional liquid is needed, use broth from vegetables.

Cook pasta by package directions, and top with vegetables in sauce. Sprinkle Parmesan cheese as desired. Serves 12.

Sofia's Sauce for Pasta or Potatoes

½	cup butter or substitute, softened
½	cup Parmesan and Romano cheese
2	cups sour cream, regular or nonfat
⅓	cup peeled and chopped cucumber
¼	cup snipped chives
1	teaspoon salt (optional)
1	(16-ounce) package plain pasta or spinach rotini, or 6 baking potatoes
1	large tomato
1	(3-ounce) jar olives, ripe or stuffed green additional Parmesan cheese

"I always arrange my food with flair even if I'm only dining alone. Food is fun, a chance to be creative."
—**Sofia Bauerle.** Sofia is a former ballerina who paints, sculpts, weaves baskets, and exercises regularly at the Family Life Center.

Cream together butter and cheese, adding sour cream to blend smoothly. Stir in cucumber, chives, and salt. Refrigerate until ready to serve. Cook pasta by package directions, or bake potatoes until fluffy soft. Spoon sauce on top and garnish with chopped tomatoes, olives, and a sprinkling of additional Parmesan cheese if desired. Serves 6.

Vegetables & Side Dishes

Variation:

For a delicious entrée, substitute Romano for the Parmesan cheese, and add chopped chicken breast or shrimp.

Classic Pesto Primavera

1   cup sliced carrots
1¼   cups sun-dried tomatoes, cut in fourths
1   (16-ounce) package linguine
3   quarts water
2   yellow squash, cut into thin strips
1   red bell pepper, cut into thin strips
⅓   cup pesto

Pesto
3   cloves garlic, minced
        pinch of salt
¼   cup olive oil
2   cups firmly packed fresh basil leaves
¼   cup pine nuts
½   cup freshly grated Parmesan cheese

Topping
2   tablespoons pine nuts, toasted

Add carrots, dried tomatoes, and linguine to boiling water and cook 8 minutes. Add squash and red pepper, and cook 2 additional minutes. Drain well and stir in ⅓ cup pesto. Sprinkle with toasted pine nuts and serve immediately. Serves 8.

To make pesto, combine garlic, salt, and oil in food processor or blender. Process until smooth. Add basil and ¼ cup pine nuts. Continue to process, scraping down sides if necessary, until smooth. Transfer to a bowl, and stir in Parmesan cheese.

Confetti Rice

A *colorful side dish with pork, beef, or chicken*

Vegetables & Side Dishes

- 2 (14½-ounce) cans chicken broth
- 2 cups long-grain white rice, uncooked
- 2 tablespoons butter
- ½ cup seeded and chopped green bell pepper
- ½ cup seeded and chopped yellow bell pepper
- ½ cup chopped green onions
- ¾ cup chopped celery
- 1 teaspoon instant minced garlic
- 1 (6-ounce) jar sliced mushrooms, drained
- 2 tablespoons diced pimiento
- ½ teaspoon ground thyme
- ½ teaspoon salt
-   sprinkling of coarse ground black pepper
- 1-2 dashes hot pepper sauce

Bring chicken broth to boil in large cooking pot. Turn off heat, stir in rice and butter. Add vegetables and seasonings. Pour into greased 3-quart baking dish. Cover and bake at 350° for 35 minutes. Serves 8-10.

Vegetables & Side Dishes

"In Pioneer countries hospitality is a necessity of life not to the travellers alone but to the settlers. A visitor is a friend, he brings news, good or bad, which is bread to the hungry minds in lonely places. A real friend who comes to the house is a heavenly messenger, who brings the panis angelorum."

-Isak Dinesen,
Out of Africa

Risotto aux Légumes

Braised rice with vegetables, served creamy rather than fluffy. The short, rounded kernels of Italian-grown Arborio rice yield the starch necessary for risotto's classic texture.

½	cup plus 2 tablespoons butter
1¼	cups chopped onion
1¼	cups chopped celery
1¼	cups chopped carrots
1	(12-ounce) box Arborio rice
5	cups chicken stock
½	teaspoon salt
½	teaspoon coarse black pepper
1¾	cups frozen green peas
⅓	cup chopped fresh parsley
1¼	cups Parmesan cheese, divided

Melt butter in large cooking pot and sauté onion, celery, and carrots. Add rice and continue to sauté slowly, stirring gently, until it turns a milky color. Add hot chicken stock, salt, and pepper. Reduce heat, cover, and simmer 18 minutes, until liquid is absorbed but mixture is still creamy. Gently stir in frozen peas, parsley, and 1 cup of the Parmesan cheese. Remove from heat, leaving covered for a few minutes. Transfer to serving dish, and sprinkle with remaining ¼ cup cheese. Serves 12.

Peppery Grits

A Southern staple goes glamorous, stuffed in red bell peppers.

Vegetables & Side Dishes

4	red bell peppers, uniform in size
	olive oil
4	cups water, lightly salted
1	cup old-fashioned grits
2-4	tablespoons butter
1	medium jalapeño pepper, minced
2	dashes Tabasco
1	cup heavy cream or half-and-half
	salt
	freshly ground black pepper
½	cup dry bread crumbs

Cut bell peppers in half, discarding stems and seeds. Rub the peppers with olive oil. Place them cut side down on lightly greased baking sheet and broil, turning once, until they just begin to char. Set aside. Bring water to a boil in large pot, and slowly stir in grits. Reduce heat, cover, and simmer about 20 minutes, stirring occasionally, until grits are smooth and thick. In a separate pan, sauté jalapeño in melted butter until softened, about 2 minutes. Stir butter, jalapeño, Tabasco, and cream into cooked grits. Season to taste with salt and pepper. Sprinkle half the bread crumbs inside pepper cups. Spoon grits into the cups, mounding them slightly. Sprinkle remaining crumbs on top. Bake about 15 minutes, until hot. Serves 8.

"In these days of calorie counting we don't have grits every day but when there's company or time for a leisurely breakfast and especially when there's grief or trouble in the family, I find myself turning automatically to grits. There's something comforting about grits--hot and creamy and bland, resting beneficently on the tired and troubled stomach.

"A few years ago I embroiled myself in a controversy by referring to grits as 'they.' Readers chose up sides and bombarded me with letters on the subject. When the tumult and the shouting died down and I had sorted over the letters I came to the conclusion that those who saw grits as a singular noun were perhaps more knowledgeable about grammar. But those who regard grits as plural were the true grits fans."

-Celestine Sibley,
A Place Called Sweet Apple

Vegetables & Side Dishes

Macaroni and Cheese Mold

4 cups macaroni, uncooked
¼ cup chopped onion
2 tablespoons butter or margarine
1 cup stuffed green olives, sliced
4 eggs, slightly beaten
1¼ cups light cream
1 tablespoon salt
½ teaspoon black pepper
1 cup Parmesan cheese
1 (12-ounce) package grated cheddar cheese

Prepare macaroni according to package directions; drain and set aside. Sauté onion in butter in large pot; add olives, eggs, cream, salt, and pepper. Combine with macaroni and stir in cheeses. Spray or butter a 12-cup Bundt pan and dust lightly with flour. Fill with macaroni mixture and bake at 350° for 40-45 minutes. Cool 10 minutes. Loosen edges with spatula and invert onto platter. Serves 6-8.

Unfried Fries

A simple, low-fat alternative to the all-American classic

- 4 medium potatoes, with or without skins
- 1 tablespoon olive oil
  sprinkling of salt or Parmesan cheese (optional)

Slice potatoes lengthwise to ¼-inch thickness. Pour olive oil into plastic bag, add potatoes, and shake until coated. Place on broiler pan lined with aluminum foil; broil in oven until crisp. Sprinkle with salt or cheese. Serves 4.

Parmesan Potato Bake

4-6 potatoes
¼ cup flour
¼ cup Parmesan cheese
    salt to taste
    sprinkling of black pepper
⅓ cup butter or margarine
    chopped parsley (optional)

Peel potatoes and cut into quarters or slice ½ inch thick. Combine flour, cheese, salt, and pepper in large zip-top plastic bag. Moisten potatoes with water, add to bag, and shake well to coat. Melt butter in 13x9-inch baking dish. Add potatoes, and bake at 375° for 40-60 minutes, turning once. When brown, garnish with parsley. Serves 6-8.

Mediterranean Potatoes

3 pounds unpeeled baking potatoes, scrubbed
2 tablespoons olive oil
2-3 medium onions, chopped
2 large cloves garlic, minced
2 cups fresh chopped tomatoes or 1 (16-ounce) can of tomatoes, with juice
1 (6-ounce) can tomato paste
⅓ cup chopped parsley
1 bay leaf
1½ teaspoons basil
1 teaspoon oregano
1 teaspoon salt
½ teaspoon thyme
   freshly ground black pepper

Cube potatoes into bite-sized pieces; put in greased 3-quart casserole and set aside. In large skillet heat oil. Sauté onion and garlic until soft. Add tomatoes, tomato paste, and seasonings. Simmer covered for 15 minutes, stirring once or twice. Remove bay leaf. Pour tomato mixture over potatoes, coating well. Cover with lid or foil. Bake 1-1¼ hours until potatoes are soft. Serves 8-10.

Vegetables & Side Dishes

"When we peel the potatoes, scorch the bacon, toss the salad, and in other ways labor frankly and earnestly over the food that cannot fully satisfy, we can make an offering of ourselves and our work. With glad and grateful hearts we return the gift of the Giver of all things; He blesses our offering and makes it holy. Thus in a very real sense, among the pots and pans, the peanut butter and the lobster thermidor, we are indeed laboring for the food which endures to eternal life."

-Ann Jarvis Vest.

Vegetables & Side Dishes

Tip:

Wrap stuffed potatoes in foil and freeze. To serve, thaw and heat at 350° for 30-45 minutes. Garnish with shredded cheese and additional bacon.

Stuffed Baked Potatoes

4	large potatoes
8	slices bacon, chopped
½	cup chopped green onions
3	tablespoons bacon drippings, reserved
4	tablespoons Parmesan cheese
1	cup sour cream
1	teaspoon salt
½	teaspoon black pepper
	sprinkling of paprika

Bake potatoes in 400° oven for 1 hour or more, until softened. In large skillet fry bacon until crisp; drain on paper towels and set aside. Sauté green onions in reserved bacon drippings and remove from heat. Cut shallow, lengthwise slice from each potato. Carefully spoon out inside of potato and add to onions in skillet. Add Parmesan cheese, sour cream, salt, and pepper. Mash and blend thoroughly, then add bacon. Return to low heat until hot. Stuff mixture into potato skins. Sprinkle with paprika. Bake at 350° for 15-20 minutes, until heated through. Serves 4.

Variation:

Top with a mixture of 1 cup brown sugar, ⅓ cup flour, ⅓ cup melted butter, and 1 cup chopped pecans. Bake and serve.

Sweet Potato Supreme

5-6	large sweet potatoes
½	cup sugar
⅓	cup butter or margarine, softened
2	eggs, beaten
½	cup milk or half-and-half
1	teaspoon vanilla
	dash of salt
½	teaspoon nutmeg (optional)

Cook potatoes; peel. Whip with electric mixer until smooth, discarding any stringy portion that clings to the beaters. Add sugar, butter, eggs, milk, vanilla, salt, and nutmeg. Turn into 13x9-inch casserole and bake at 350° for 30 minutes. Serves 10.

Potato Croquettes

4 cups cooked, mashed potatoes
2 eggs, beaten
2-4 tablespoons buttermilk
4 tablespoons chopped fresh chives, divided
1 teaspoon salt
¼ teaspoon white pepper
1½ cups crushed crumbs from round buttery crackers
¼ cup butter or margarine, melted
½ teaspoon paprika

Combine potatoes with eggs, buttermilk, 3 tablespoons chives, salt, and pepper; mix well. Divide mixture into 8 portions, and make 8 round or cylinder-shaped croquettes. Roll in cracker crumbs. Place on lightly greased jelly-roll pan, cover, and refrigerate up to 24 hours. Combine butter and paprika; drizzle over croquettes. Bake at 375° for 20-25 minutes, or until golden. If frozen before baking, allow additional baking time. Garnish with remaining chives. Serves 8.

Yam and Cranberry Bake

This dish adds beautiful color to a holiday dinner.

1 (12-ounce) package whole cranberries
1¼ cups sugar
1 small orange, sliced thinly
½ cup pecan halves
¼ cup orange juice
¾ teaspoon cinnamon
½ teaspoon nutmeg
1 (40-ounce) can yams, drained

Combine cranberries, sugar, orange slices, pecan halves, orange juice, and spices in 2-quart casserole. Bake uncovered at 375° for 30 minutes. Stir yams into cranberry mixture. Bake until hot, about 15 minutes. Serves 10-12.

Vegetables & Side Dishes

Creamy Potato Puff

4 cups hot mashed potatoes
1 (8-ounce) package cream cheese, softened
¼ cup butter, softened
1 egg, beaten
½ cup finely chopped onion
1 teaspoon salt
  dash of white pepper
⅓ cup freshly grated Swiss cheese

Combine potatoes with cream cheese and butter. Blend well with egg, onions, salt, and pepper. Place in buttered 2-quart casserole and top with Swiss cheese. Bake at 350° for 45 minutes. Serves 12.

Caramel Potatoes.

Boil sweet potatoes in salted water. Peel and cut in rather thick slices; dip each slice into melted butter and then roll it in a stiff syrup of melted brown sugar and water and put in the oven to glaze.

Gate City Cook Book

Simply Divine

Vegetables & Side Dishes

Cranberry Apple Crunch

This slightly tart dish may be served warm or cold.

4 cups peeled, chopped cooking apples
2 cups fresh cranberries
1½ teaspoons lemon juice
1 cup sugar
1⅓ cups quick-cooking oatmeal, uncooked
1 cup chopped walnuts
⅓ cup firmly packed light brown sugar
½ cup butter or margarine, melted

Combine apples and cranberries in a lightly greased 13x9-inch rectangular baking dish. Sprinkle with lemon juice and top with sugar. Set aside. Mix oatmeal, walnuts, brown sugar, and margarine until moistened and crumbly. Sprinkle over fruit. Bake uncovered at 325° for 1 hour. Serves 8.

Scalloped Pineapple

Delicious side dish with ham or poultry

¾ cup margarine, softened
1½ cups sugar
3 eggs, slightly beaten
   pinch of salt
1 cup evaporated milk
1 (20-ounce) can crushed pineapple in natural juices, drained well
4 cups fresh white bread cubes, with crust

Cream margarine and sugar. Add eggs and salt, mixing well. Add milk, pineapple, and bread cubes, stirring until combined. Pour into greased 8-inch square baking pan or soufflé dish. Bake at 350° for 50 minutes. Serves 6-8.

Hot Mixed Fruit

1	(17-ounce) can apricot halves
1	(16-ounce) can pear halves
1	(16-ounce) can peach halves
1	(20-ounce) can sliced pineapple
1	(16-ounce) can dark sweet cherries or large pitted, cooked prunes
1	cup juice from fruit, primarily pineapple
¼	cup margarine
½	cup brown sugar
1½	tablespoons cornstarch

Drain fruit, reserving pineapple juice and enough of other juices to make 1 cup. In a saucepan combine the cup of juice with margarine, brown sugar, and cornstarch. Cook, stirring constantly, until thickened. Arrange fruit in a rectangular baking dish with pineapple slices on the bottom, alternating apricots, pears, and peaches with hollow side up, placing cherries or prunes in hollows. Pour juice mixture over fruit and refrigerate overnight. Bake at 350° about 20 minutes, until bubbly. Serves 12.

Vegetables & Side Dishes

Curried Fruit

1	(16-ounce) can peach halves
1	(16-ounce) can pear halves
1	(16-ounce) can apricot halves
3	(8-ounce) cans pineapple chunks
10	maraschino cherries
¼	cup butter, melted
¾	cup light brown sugar
2	teaspoons curry powder

Arrange fruit in a baking dish. Mix butter, brown sugar, and curry. Distribute evenly over fruit. Bake at 325° for 1 hour, basting frequently. Refrigerate overnight and warm to serve at 350° for 30 minutes.

Simply Divine

Vegetables & Side Dishes

"I like my mom's dressing. I like to eat it with turkey. She makes it nice and warm."

Reid Terry, age 9.

Celery Amandine

Celery assumes a starring role

3-4 tablespoons butter
4 cups sliced celery
1 teaspoon salt
1 tablespoon minced chives
1 small onion, minced
4 tablespoons flour
1 cup half-and-half
½ cup chicken broth
1 cup slivered almonds
2 tablespoons pimiento
¼ cup freshly grated Parmesan cheese

Melt butter in skillet; add celery. Cover and cook 15 minutes until tender. Add salt, chives, and onion; stir. Sprinkle with flour; stir in half-and-half and broth; and cook until thick. Add almonds and pimiento. Place in 2-quart baking dish; top with cheese. Bake at 375° for 10 minutes. Serves 8.

Country Chicken Dressing

Ample fare for Sunday night supper, with a salad

6 pieces of chicken breast or 1 whole chicken, reserving broth
3 large squares of cornbread
1 (8-ounce) package herb seasoned stuffing
1 onion, chopped
½ cup chopped celery
1 tablespoon sage
1 teaspoon poultry seasoning
¼ cup oil
2 eggs

Cook chicken until tender, discard skin and bones, and cut into small pieces. In a large bowl crumble cornbread and mix with stuffing, onion, celery, and seasonings. Add enough broth to make a soupy mixture; then add oil, eggs, and cut-up chicken, mixing well. Pour into greased 2-quart baking dish and bake at 450° for 45 minutes, until firm. Serves 10-12.

Simply Divine

Cornbread Dressing Gone Wild

Vegetables & Side Dishes

1	cup wild rice
1½	cups water
½	teaspoon salt
4	green onions, sliced
1	(8-ounce) package fresh mushrooms, sliced
¼	cup plus 2 tablespoons butter or margarine
2	(6-ounce) boxes cornbread stuffing mix with vegetable/seasoning packets
3	cups poultry broth
¾	cup chopped pecans
2	Granny Smith apples, chopped to about ¼-inch cubes

Wash and soak wild rice; cook in salted water until tender and water is absorbed, about 35 minutes. Sauté onions and mushrooms in ¼ cup butter. In a large bowl combine onions and mushrooms, stuffing mix, and contents of seasoning packets. Boil broth and pour over mixture. Add cooked rice, pecans, and apples. Place in 3-quart casserole and dot with 2 tablespoons butter. Bake covered at 350° for total time of 25 minutes, uncovering the last 10 minutes. Serves 12-14.

Tip:

Wild rice, known for its nutty flavor and chewy texture, is not rice at all. It is a long-grain marsh grass and needs to be cleaned before cooking. Place rice in a bowl and fill with cold water. Stir; discard any debris that floats to the surface.

Vegetables & Side Dishes

Turkey Dressing.

Cut the brown crust from slices or pieces of stale bread until you have as much as the inside of a pound loaf, put it in a suitable dish, and pour tepid water (not warm, for that makes it heavy) over it, let stand one minute, as it soaks very quickly. Now take up a handful at a time and squeeze it hard and dry with both hands, placing it as you go along in another dish. This process makes it very light. When all is pressed dry, toss it all up lightly through your fingers. Now add salt and pepper, about a teaspoonful, also a teaspoonful of powdered savory, the same amount of sage, or the green herb minced fine, add a half cup of melted butter and a well-beaten egg, work thoroughly all together and it is ready to stuff the fowl with. It is much improved by adding a pint of oysters without their beards.

Gate City Cook Book

Quick Cornbread Dressing

1	(8½-ounce) box cornbread mix
3	eggs
½	cup milk
1	(10¾-ounce) can cream of chicken soup
3	slices bread, diced
	salt to taste
½	teaspoon coarsely ground black pepper
½	teaspoon sage
1-2	onions, chopped
½	cup celery, chopped
½	cup margarine
6	ounces chicken broth

Bake cornbread mix, using 3 eggs and ½ cup milk. When cool, break into large bowl and add soup, bread, salt, pepper, and sage. Melt margarine and sauté onions and celery; add to mixture. Thin with chicken broth. Pour into greased 13x9-inch baking pan. Bake at 375° until brown, about 30 minutes. Serves 5-6.

Cakes & Cookies

"How sweet are your promises to my taste, sweeter than honey to my mouth!"

Psalm 119:103

Cakes & Cookies

CAKES

Butter Pecan Cheesecake	215
Mama Bootle's Nut Cake	216
Cream Cheese Pound Cake	216
Brownulated Sugar Pound Cake	217
Buttermilk Pound Cake	218
Sour Cream Pound Cake	218
Chocolate Pound Cake	219
Sour Cream Coconut Cake	219
Fresh Apple Cake	220
Pineapple Party Cake	221
Carrot Cake	222
Hummingbird Cake	223
German Chocolate Cake	224
Italian Cream Cake	225
Lemon Berry Cake	226
Holiday Fruitcake	227
Lemonade Cake	227
Chocolate Eclair Cake	228
Cinnamon Swirl Cake	229
Chocolate Gâteau	230
Spice Cake	231
Quick Fudge Cake	231
Soft Gingerbread	232
Macaroon Cupcakes	232
Black Bottom Cupcakes	233

FROSTINGS AND ICINGS

Easy Caramel Frosting	217
Glaze	220
Cream Cheese Frosting	222

BROWNIES AND BARS

Best Brownies in America	234
Glorified Brownies	235
Mocha Brownies	236
Lethal Layered Brownies	237
Gold Rush Bars	237
Congo Bars	238
Lemon Bars	239
Apricot Bars	240
Apple Bars	241
Pound Cake Squares	242
Mocha Crunch	243
South African Crunchies	243

COOKIES

Peach Refrigerator Cookies	241
Sugar Cookies	242
Miss Connie's Oatmeal Cookies	244
Cinnamon Crisps	244
Rita's Famous Oatmeal Cookies	245
Oatmeal Chocolate Chip Cookies	246
Cashew Cookies	247
Christmas Cookies	248
Tea Cakes	249
Mandelbrot	250
Marcine's Meringues	250

HERITAGE RECIPES

Pound Cake	218
Soft Ginger Bread	231
Tea Cakes	249

Butter Pecan Cheesecake

Cakes & Cookies

2	cups shortbread cookies with crunchy pecans
¼	cup margarine, melted
3	(8-ounce) packages cream cheese, softened
1	cup brown sugar
½	cup sugar
3	eggs
2	cups sour cream
1	teaspoon vanilla
1	cup finely chopped pecans, toasted

Crush cookies and combine with melted margarine. Reserve ½ cup and press remainder in bottom of a 9-inch springform pan. Beat cream cheese until light and fluffy and add sugars, mixing well. Add eggs one at a time, mixing well after each addition. Blend in sour cream and vanilla. Stir in pecans. Spoon batter into pan on top of crumb mixture. Bake at 475° for 10 minutes. Reduce temperature to 300° and bake an additional 50 minutes or until top of cheesecake cracks. Cool to room temperature and sprinkle reserved crumb mixture on top of cheesecake. Chill until ready to serve. Serves 10.

Tip:

To toast pecans, spread nuts on a shallow pan and bake at 250° for 12-15 minutes. As soon as nuts begin to color, watch carefully, as they will brown quickly.

Simply Divine

Cakes & Cookies

"Mama always made this cake at Christmas."

-Luther Bootle. Luther is Second-Ponce's Renaissance man: video librarian, artist, bell ringer, sound engineer, historian, photographer, expert at flag protocol, and an accomplished cook.

Mama Bootle's Nut Cake

1	cup butter, softened
2	cups sugar
6	eggs
4	cups flour
1	cup milk
1	teaspoon lemon extract
2	teaspoons vanilla
4	cups chopped pecans

Cream butter and sugar. Add eggs one at a time, beating well after each addition. Add flour and milk alternately, continuing to beat. Add lemon extract, vanilla, and nuts. Beat well. Bake in a greased and floured tube pan or large Bundt pan at 325° for 1½ hours. Cool 15 minutes before removing from pan.

Variation:

Divide batter into two or three small foil pans. The petite pound cakes make great gifts.

Cream Cheese Pound Cake

2	cups butter, softened
1	(8-ounce) package cream cheese, softened
3	cups sugar
6	eggs
3	cups flour
2	teaspoons vanilla
1	teaspoon butter flavoring (optional)

Combine butter and cream cheese. Add sugar and beat until light and fluffy. Add eggs one at a time, beating well after each one. Add 1 cup of flour at a time, beating well after each addition. Mix in vanilla. Pour batter into buttered and floured 10-inch tube pan or 2 small loaf pans. Bake at 325° for 1-1½ hours until cake tests done.

Brownulated Sugar Pound Cake

An old family recipe

1   cup margarine or butter
½   cup shortening
1   box brownulated sugar
5   eggs
1   teaspoon baking powder
1   cup milk
1   teaspoon vanilla
3   cups flour

Frosting
1   box light brown sugar
1   (5-ounce) can evaporated milk
½   cup margarine

Cream margarine, shortening, and sugar. Add eggs, baking powder, milk, vanilla, and flour. Mix thoroughly. Bake in tube pan at 350° for 1½ hours. To make frosting, combine sugar, milk, and margarine. Bring to hard boil. Boil 2 minutes, remove from heat, and beat. Spread on cooled cake.

Cakes & Cookies

Tip:

Brownulated sugar is a granulated brown sugar product that pours and measures easily. It may not be used interchangeably in recipes with regular brown sugar.

Easy Caramel Frosting

5⅓   tablespoons margarine
½   cup dark brown sugar
2   tablespoons milk
⅔   box powdered sugar
1   teaspoon vanilla

Melt margarine and brown sugar in saucepan over medium heat. Simmer 3-4 minutes. Stir in milk. Blend well. Add to powdered sugar and stir until smooth. Add vanilla. If too thick, add more milk. Spread on cooled cake.

Simply Divine

Cakes & Cookies

Buttermilk Pound Cake

1¼ cups shortening
3 cups sugar
7 eggs
3 cups flour
¼ teaspoon baking soda
¼ teaspoon salt
1 cup buttermilk
1 teaspoon vanilla

Cream together shortening and sugar. Add eggs one at a time. Combine flour, soda, and salt. Add flour mixture and buttermilk alternately to batter, beginning and ending with flour. Add vanilla. Bake in greased and floured tube pan at 325° for 1 hour and 20 minutes. Serves 14.

Sour Cream Pound Cake

Pound Cake.

Ten eggs, one pound sugar, one pound CAPITOLA flour, one pound butter, light weight, half cup of water, one light teaspoonful of powder, half teaspoonful of vanilla and one-half of lemon. Bake slowly.

Gate City Cook Book

1 cup butter, softened
3 cups sugar
6 eggs
3 cups flour
½ teaspoon baking soda
1 cup sour cream
2 teaspoons vanilla
1 teaspoon lemon extract

Blend butter and sugar. Add eggs one at a time, beating after each addition. Sift together flour and soda and add sour cream, vanilla, and lemon extract. Stir together. Spoon batter into greased Bundt pan. Bake at 325° for 1 hour and 15 minutes.

Chocolate Pound Cake

Cakes & Cookies

3 cups plain flour, sifted
½ cup cocoa
¼ teaspoon salt
½ teaspoon baking powder
½ cup shortening
1 cup butter
3 cups sugar
5 eggs
1 cup milk
1 teaspoon vanilla

"I like cocolate cake because it is very sweet."
Robbie Watts, age 12.

Sift together flour, cocoa, salt, and baking powder. Set aside. Cream shortening, butter, and sugar together with mixer. Add eggs one at a time to sugar mixture, beating after each addition. Add flour mixture and milk alternately and mix together. Add vanilla. Pour batter into greased and floured tube pan. Bake at 300-325° for 1½ hours. May frost with Fudge Frosting on page 230.

Sour Cream Coconut Cake

Make frosting the day before.

Frosting
2 cups sour cream
2 cups sugar
2 (6-ounce) packages frozen fresh coconut, thawed
½ cup crushed pineapple, drained well
1 box yellow cake mix

Tip:

Use a food processor to grate or chop the meat of fresh coconut. One medium coconut yields 3-4 cups grated coconut and can be frozen for up to 6 months.

In a large glass bowl combine sour cream, sugar, coconut, and pineapple. Mix well. Cover and refrigerate overnight. Prepare yellow cake mix according to package directions and bake in 8-inch round or square cake pans. Cool completely. Slice layers to make four thin layers. Frost layers and keep refrigerated. Serves 10.

Cakes & Cookies

Variation:

For a tropical flavor, increase the oil to 1½ cups, omit all spices except cinnamon, and add 1 (8-ounce) can crushed, undrained pineapple, plus 1 cup coconut.

Glaze

½ cup margarine or butter
1 cup light brown sugar
¼ cup milk
1 teaspoon vanilla

Melt butter in a saucepan. Add sugar, milk, and vanilla, stirring well, until glaze boils 1 minute. Drizzle over cake.

Fresh Apple Cake

Wonderful for breakfast, dessert, or a snack

1 cup vegetable oil
3 eggs
2 cups sugar
1 teaspoon vanilla
3 cups flour
1 teaspoon salt
1 teaspoon baking soda
1 teaspoon ground cinnamon
1 teaspoon ground nutmeg
1 teaspoon ground cloves
3 cups diced apples
1 cup chopped pecans

Mix oil, eggs, sugar, and vanilla. Stir well. Sift together flour, salt, soda, and spices and add to egg mixture to make a thick batter. Fold in apples and nuts. Pour into a greased and floured Bundt pan. Place in cold oven. Bake at 350° for 1 hour 10 minutes. Cool cake slightly before removing from pan. While cake is still warm, add Glaze (see recipe).

Pineapple Party Cake

Refrigerate for easy slicing.

½	cup butter or margarine, softened
1	tablespoon vanilla
1	cup sugar
2	egg yolks
2	teaspoons baking powder
¼	teaspoon salt
2	heaping cups finely crushed graham crackers
1	scant cup milk
½	cup chopped pecans
2	egg whites, beaten stiff

Topping

1	cup sugar
1	(8-ounce) can crushed pineapple

Cream butter, vanilla, and sugar. Add egg yolks. In a separate bowl mix baking powder, salt, and graham crackers. Add to butter mixture alternately with milk. Add nuts and fold in beaten egg whites. Bake in a 9x5-inch loaf pan, lined with wax paper, at 350° for 45 minutes or until cake pulls away from sides of pan. Remove loaf from pan, peeling away wax paper. Boil sugar and pineapple for 10-15 minutes. Pour over hot cake. Refrigerate overnight. Serves 8-10.

Cakes & Cookies

"The most superb cake I have ever eaten in my life was Mother's almond cake... One of the regrets of my life is that I did not procure the recipe while Mother was alive... I cannot understand how I failed to have her write down the recipe for this confection that makes all other cakes seem like sawdust... The cake, as white as a virgin's breast, as tender as a mother's heart, was made in four layers. I can taste it still. I have never, from memory, duplicated it."
-Marjorie Kinnan Rawlings,
Cross Creek Cookery

Cakes & Cookies

Tip:

For the most flavorful carrot cake, use full-grown, not baby carrots. Baby carrots are tender, but because they are immature they lack flavor.

Cream Cheese Frosting

1	(8-ounce) package cream cheese, softened
½	cup butter or margarine, softened
1	box powdered sugar, sifted
1	teaspoon vanilla
½	cup chopped nuts (optional)

Beat cream cheese and butter. Gradually add powdered sugar, beating until light and fluffy. Stir in vanilla. Nuts may be mixed with the frosting or sprinkled on top of the cake.

Carrot Cake

A popular cake in the U.S. since the 1960s

2	cups sifted flour
2	teaspoons baking powder
1½	teaspoons baking soda
1	teaspoon salt
2	teaspoons cinnamon
2	cups sugar
1½	cups vegetable oil
4	eggs
2	cups finely grated carrots
1	(8-ounce) can crushed pineapple, drained
½	cup chopped pecans coated in 1 tablespoon flour
1	(3-ounce) can coconut

Sift together flour, baking powder, soda, salt, and cinnamon. Add sugar, oil, and eggs, mixing thoroughly. Stir in carrots, pineapple, nuts, and coconut. Pour into 3 greased and floured 9-inch round cake pans. Bake at 350° for 35 minutes. Cool 10 minutes in pans. Then, turn layers onto waxed paper. Frost when completely cool with Cream Cheese Frosting (see recipe).

Hummingbird Cake

A moist, luscious cake

3	cups flour
2	cups sugar
1	teaspoon baking soda
½	teaspoon salt
1	teaspoon ground cinnamon
3	eggs, beaten
¾	cup vegetable oil
1½	teaspoons vanilla
1	(8-ounce) can crushed pineapple, undrained
1	cup chopped pecans
1¼	cups mashed bananas

In a large bowl combine flour, sugar, soda, salt, and cinnamon. Add eggs and oil, stirring until dry ingredients are moistened. Do not beat. Stir in vanilla, pineapple, nuts, and bananas. Pour batter into 3 greased and floured 9-inch round cake pans. Bake at 350° for 25-30 minutes or until wooden pick inserted in the center comes out clean. Cool in pans for 10 minutes; remove from pans and cool completely on wire racks. Frost with Cream Cheese Frosting on page 222.

Cakes & Cookies

Variation:

For a change of pace, bake Hummingbird Cake in a loaf pan, Bundt pan, muffin tins, or a sheet cake pan. Adjust baking times accordingly.

"What do you like doing best in the world, Pooh?"

"Well," said Pooh, "what I like best —" and then he had to stop and think. Because although Eating Honey was a very good thing to do, there was a moment just before you began to eat which was better than when you were, but he didn't know what it was called."

-A.A. Milne,
The House at Pooh Corner

Simply Divine

Cakes & Cookies

Tip:

Choose vanilla flavoring carefully. Pure vanilla extract is made from vanilla beans and is dark and intensely aromatic. Imitation vanilla is made from artificial flavorings, most of which are chemically-treated by-products from the paper industry. While imitation vanilla is less expensive, it lacks the quality of pure vanilla extract.

German Chocolate Cake

A *blue-ribbon winner at the South Carolina State Fair*

4	(1-ounce) squares bittersweet chocolate
½	cup boiling water
1	cup butter or margarine, softened
2	cups sugar
4	egg yolks
1	teaspoon vanilla
1	teaspoon salt
1	teaspoon baking soda
2½	cups sifted cake flour
1	cup buttermilk
4	egg whites

Frosting

1	cup evaporated milk
1	cup sugar
3	egg yolks
½	cup margarine
1	teaspoon vanilla
1⅓	cups coconut
1	cup chopped pecans

Melt chocolate in ½ cup boiling water and set aside to cool. Cream butter and sugar until light and fluffy. Add egg yolks and beat well. Add melted chocolate and vanilla. In separate bowl sift together salt, soda, and flour. Add alternately with buttermilk to chocolate mixture. Beat egg whites until stiff and fold into the batter. Line the bottom of three 8-inch or 9-inch cake pans with wax paper and add batter. Bake at 350° for 35 to 45 minutes.

To prepare frosting, combine in a saucepan evaporated milk, sugar, egg yolks, margarine, and vanilla. Cook over medium heat until mixture thickens, stirring constantly, approximately 12 minutes. Add coconut and chopped pecans. Beat until cool and thick. Spread on layers.

Italian Cream Cake

- ½ cup margarine, softened
- ½ cup shortening, softened
- 2 cups sugar
- 1 teaspoon baking soda
- 2 cups flour
- 5 eggs
- 1 cup buttermilk
- 1 teaspoon almond extract
- 1 (3.5-ounce) can coconut
- 1 cup chopped pecans

Frosting
- ¼ cup margarine, softened
- 1 (8-ounce) package cream cheese, softened
- 1 box powdered sugar
- 1 teaspoon almond extract
- ½ cup pecans
- 1 (3.5-ounce) can coconut

Cream together margarine, shortening, and sugar. Add soda and flour. Add eggs, one at a time, beating after each addition. Stir in buttermilk and almond extract. Add coconut and pecans. Pour batter into three 8-inch cake pans. Bake at 350° for approximately 25 minutes. To frost layers, cream together margarine and cream cheese. Add powdered sugar, almond extract, pecans, and coconut and spread on cake. Serves 10.

Cakes & Cookies

"For a century or more, tea, coffee, bananas, pineapples, and coconuts have played a significant role in the culinary history of the South—and virtually all of those foods have come to us from overseas.... I have a 150-year-old Kentucky cookbook with a coconut cake recipe in it. 'Having removed the hull and dark skin from a cocoanut,' the instructions begin, 'weigh a pound of it and grate it fine.' That's still the best way to do it."

—John Egerton,
Side Orders

Cakes & Cookies

Tip:

The cake is finished baking when the top springs back when lightly touched.

Lemon Berry Cake

1 cup flour
1 teaspoon baking powder
3 tablespoons butter
½ cup heavy cream
5 eggs
¾ cup sugar
2 teaspoons grated lemon zest
1 teaspoon lemon extract
1 teaspoon vanilla

Frosting
4 cups strawberries
½ cup sugar, divided
1½ cups heavy cream, whipped

Mix flour and baking powder. Set aside. Melt butter in cream over low heat and set aside. In a large bowl beat eggs and sugar on high speed for 10 minutes. Fold flour mixture into egg mixture. Add cream mixture, zest, lemon extract, and vanilla. Divide batter between 2 well-greased and floured 9-inch cake pans. Bake at 350° for 22 to 25 minutes. Cool in pans for 5 minutes. Remove from pans and cool thoroughly on racks.

For topping, toss strawberries with ¼ cup sugar. Let stand at room temperature until they draw juice. Whip cream with ¼ cup sugar and spread on each layer. Top with strawberries.

Holiday Fruitcake

1 cup flour
16 ounces chopped pecans
1 (8-ounce) package dates, chopped
8 ounces candied cherries
8 ounces candied pineapple
1 cup sugar
4 eggs, separated
2 teaspoons vanilla
2 tablespoons bourbon
1 teaspoon salt
½ teaspoon baking powder

Mix flour with chopped nuts and fruit. Add sugar. In separate bowl beat egg yolks and add vanilla, bourbon, salt, and baking powder. Combine with fruit and nut mixture. Beat egg whites and fold into batter. Bake in lightly greased and floured tube pan at 250° for 2 hours. Serves 20.

Lemonade Cake

1 box yellow cake mix
1 (3.4-ounce) box lemon pudding mix
4 eggs
⅔ cup vegetable oil
1 cup water
juice of ½ lemon or 1 teaspoon lemon extract

Glaze
⅔ (6-ounce) can frozen lemonade concentrate, thawed
1 cup powdered sugar

Mix cake mix and lemon pudding mix. Add eggs, oil, water, and lemon juice. Beat about 2 minutes until smooth. Bake in greased tube pan at 350° for 45 minutes. Cool in pan 10-15 minutes. To glaze cake, mix concentrate with powdered sugar until smooth and pour over cake.

Cakes & Cookies

Tip:

An essential ingredient in many cakes, baking powder is perishable. To test whether the baking powder on your pantry shelf is still active, place 1 teaspoon baking powder in ⅓ cup of hot water. If the liquid bubbles and fizzes, the baking powder is active.

Simply Divine

Cakes & Cookies

"Whenever I made Chocolate Eclair Cake, my family and friends called this sin #11 to infinity."

-Mamie Ruth Bartlett.
Mamie Ruth was a much-loved Sunday School teacher.

Chocolate Eclair Cake

2   (3.4-ounce) packages instant vanilla pudding mix
3½ cups milk
1   teaspoon vanilla
1   (8-ounce) carton whipped topping
1   (16-ounce) box cinnamon graham crackers

Frosting
5   teaspoons butter
1   tablespoon cocoa
1   teaspoon vanilla
1   tablespoon light corn syrup
2   cups powdered sugar
    milk

Mix instant pudding with milk and vanilla. Allow to set; then, stir in whipped topping. In an 11x7-inch container, place a layer of graham crackers. Spread ½ of pudding mixture over crackers. Cover with a layer of crackers. Add rest of pudding and cover with another layer of graham crackers. To frost cake, melt butter and add cocoa, vanilla, syrup, and sugar; add a little milk as needed to make spreadable. Spread over cake and refrigerate.

Cinnamon Swirl Cake

Serve warm with morning coffee.

- ⅔ cup vegetable oil
- ½ cup sugar
- 4 eggs
- 1 cup sour cream
- 1 box yellow cake mix
- 1 cup brown sugar
- 2 teaspoons cinnamon

Glaze
- 2 cups powdered sugar
- 4 tablespoons milk
- 2 teaspoons vanilla

Mix oil, sugar, eggs, and sour cream with cake mix. Pour one half of batter into a greased 13x9-inch baking pan. Mix brown sugar and cinnamon, and spread one half of this mixture on batter. Add remaining batter and spread rest of filling on top of batter. Swirl with knife blade. Bake at 350° for 35 minutes or until done. Cake will fall in middle when removed. To glaze, mix powdered sugar, milk, and vanilla until smooth and pour over warm cake. Serves 12.

Cakes & Cookies

Angie Watterson calls this the "honey bun" cake because serving it to Jim Watterson resulted in their marriage. She served it. He loved it. They started dating and he realized that she wasn't sharing the recipe unless they got married.

Cakes & Cookies

Chocolate Gâteau

A *devilishly dark cake with rich fudge frosting*

1	cup water
1	cup margarine
3	tablespoons cocoa
2	cups sugar
2	cups self-rising flour
½	teaspoon salt
2	eggs
½	cup buttermilk
1	teaspoon baking soda
1	teaspoon vanilla

Fudge Frosting

½	cup margarine
3	tablespoons cocoa
6	tablespoons milk
1	box powdered sugar
½	cup nuts
1	teaspoon vanilla

Boil together water, margarine, and cocoa. Set aside. Mix sugar, flour, and salt. Add hot mixture to dry ingredients. Add eggs. Mix buttermilk with soda and add to batter. Add vanilla and stir until well blended. Bake in a 13x9-inch pan at 350° for 20 minutes. To prepare frosting, melt margarine and add cocoa and milk. Stir in powdered sugar, nuts, and vanilla. Pour icing over hot cake. Serves 20.

Spice Cake

Even better the second or third day

2½ cups flour
2 cups sugar
2 teaspoons baking soda
2 teaspoons cinnamon
1 teaspoon ground cloves
1 teaspoon nutmeg
1 teaspoon salt
2 eggs
1 cup vegetable oil
1 (16-ounce) can applesauce
1 cup chopped pecans or walnuts
1 cup raisins, soaked in rum or fruit juice

Combine flour, sugar, soda, spices, and salt. Add eggs, oil, and applesauce. Beat two minutes. Stir in nuts and drained raisins. Bake in a greased tube pan at 350° for 1 hour. Serves 15.

Quick Fudge Cake

Not for dieters

4 eggs
2 cups sugar
2 heaping tablespoons cocoa
¾ cup margarine
½ cup flour
1 cup chopped pecans
1 teaspoon vanilla
½ teaspoon salt

Beat eggs well, add sugar, and beat again. Dissolve cocoa in melted margarine and add to egg mixture. Add flour, pecans, vanilla, and salt. Pour batter into ungreased 9-inch square cake pan. Place cake pan into larger pan of cold water. Bake at 350° for 45 minutes.

Cakes & Cookies

Soft Ginger Bread.

One-half cup of sugar, one-half cup of butter, one cup of molasses, two and one-half cups of CAPITOLA flour, two teaspoonfuls of soda in one cup of boiling water; add ginger and allspice to taste; add two eggs well-beaten the last thing.

Gate City Cook Book

Cakes & Cookies

"This one hundred-year-old recipe has been handed down for three generations at Second-Ponce. It originated with my mother, Mrs. G. H. (Brownie) Richardson, who gave it to me, and I passed it to my daughters, Sally Angevine and Susan McKessy."
　　　　　-Florence Angevine.

Soft Gingerbread

Some things should never change.

1	cup water
2	teaspoons baking soda
½	cup sugar
1	cup molasses or cane syrup
½	cup butter or margarine
1	teaspoon ginger
1	teaspoon cinnamon
1	teaspoon ground cloves
2⅔	cups flour
2	eggs, well beaten

Boil water and add soda. Set aside. Mix sugar, molasses, butter, spices, flour, eggs, and water with soda. Batter will be very thin. Bake in a greased and floured 13x9-inch pan at 350° for 30 minutes. Cool in pan for 10 minutes. Cut into squares. Serves 20.

Macaroon Cupcakes

T*ip*:

Make superfine sugar by grinding granulated sugar in a food processor until pulverized. Superfine sugar can be substituted for granulated sugar, cup for cup. Because superfine sugar dissolves almost instantly, it is perfect for sweetening cold drinks or whipping up meringues.

4	egg whites
	pinch of salt
¾	cup superfine sugar, divided
1½	cups flaked coconut
½	cup ground blanched almonds
2	tablespoons flour
1	teaspoon grated lemon zest

Beat egg whites with salt until soft peaks form. Slowly add ½ cup sugar, beating until stiff, shiny peaks form. In a separate bowl combine coconut, ¼ cup sugar, almonds, flour, and zest. Mix well. Fold coconut mixture into egg whites. Spoon into paper-lined muffin tins. Bake at 350° for 25 minutes, or until tops are lightly browned. Makes 12.

Black Bottom Cupcakes

Cakes & Cookies

Filling
- 1 (8-ounce) package cream cheese, softened
- 1 egg
- ⅓ cup sugar
- ⅛ teaspoon salt
- 1 cup nuts, chopped or slivered
- 1 (6-ounce) package chocolate chips

Combine cream cheese and egg. Mix in sugar and salt. Fold in nuts and chocolate chips. Set aside.

- 1½ cups flour
- ¼ cup cocoa
- 1 cup water
- 1 teaspoon vinegar
- 1 teaspoon soda
- ⅓ cup oil
- 1 teaspoon vanilla
- 1 cup sugar
- ½ teaspoon salt

Mix ingredients together to make batter. Fill paper-lined muffin tins ⅓ full, add 1 tablespoon topping to each, and add additional batter to fill muffin tins ⅔ full. Bake at 350° for 25 minutes.

Simply Divine

Cakes & Cookies

Tip:

Unsweetened chocolate is also called baking or bitter chocolate.

Best Brownies in America

Brownies are a rich chocolate cake cut into squares. The name first appeared in print in the 1897 Sears, Roebuck Catalog.

1	cup margarine
2	cups sugar
4	eggs
1⅓	cups flour
4	(1-ounce) squares unsweetened baking chocolate, melted
2	teaspoons vanilla
⅔	cup chopped pecans

Buttercream Frosting

1	box powdered sugar
½	cup butter or margarine, softened
1	teaspoon vanilla
3	tablespoons milk
2	(1-ounce) squares unsweetened baking chocolate, melted

For brownies, cream margarine and sugar. Add eggs, beating well after each, then flour, and mix well. Add chocolate, vanilla, and nuts. Stir until mixed. Bake in greased 13x9-inch pan at 325° for 35-40 minutes. Do not overbake. Brownies are better slightly undercooked. Cool. Do not cut until ready to serve, as brownies dry out quickly.

For frosting, beat together sugar, butter, vanilla, and milk until smooth, adding more milk if needed for spreading consistency. Melt chocolate over very low heat or in microwave oven until just melted. Stir into frosting until smooth. Frost brownies. Makes 3 dozen.

Glorified Brownies

1 box milk chocolate chunk brownie mix

Frosting
1   (1-ounce) square unsweetened baking chocolate
½   cup butter
1   box powdered sugar
2-3 tablespoons milk
1   (10½-ounce) package miniature marshmallows
    Pecan halves, optional

Bake brownies as directed on package. Set aside while making frosting. Melt chocolate and butter in microwave oven on low heat. Blend with powdered sugar, and add milk gradually to make a smooth, spreadable frosting. Beat with mixer until well blended.

Spread marshmallows evenly to cover brownies; broil in oven, watching carefully, until melted golden. Remove from oven and swirl frosting into marshmallows. If desired, top with pecan halves. Makes 20 large squares.

Cakes & Cookies

Tip:

As a rule of thumb, if you want brownies that are moist and chewy, use a 13x9-inch pan. If you prefer them cakelike, bake them in a 9x9-inch pan.

Cakes & Cookies

Tip:

Always cool the melted chocolate before adding it to the sugar and eggs. Adding the chocolate while it is hot will make the brownies heavy and dry.

Mocha Brownies

2	(1-ounce) squares unsweetened baking chocolate
⅓	cup butter or margarine
2	eggs
1	cup sugar
1	teaspoon vanilla
¾	cup sifted flour
½	teaspoon baking powder
¼	teaspoon salt
2	tablespoons instant coffee granules
½-¾	cup chopped walnuts

Frosting

1	(1-ounce) square unsweetened baking chocolate
1	tablespoon butter or margarine
1½	tablespoons very hot and strong coffee
1	cup sifted powdered sugar

For brownies, melt chocolate and butter together over very low heat, stirring constantly. Set aside to cool. Beat eggs until light, gradually add sugar, and continue beating until fluffy. Add vanilla. Combine with chocolate mixture, and mix well. Sift together flour, baking powder, salt, and instant coffee. Stir into chocolate mixture and mix well. Fold in nuts. Pour into greased 8-inch square pan, and bake at 350° for 30 minutes, until slight imprint remains when finger touches center top. Cool while making frosting.

For frosting, melt chocolate with butter over hot water or very low heat, stirring constantly. Blend in hot coffee, then powdered sugar as needed to make a smooth frosting that will spread easily on brownies. Frost brownies, cool, and cut into 2" squares. Makes 16.

Lethal Layered Brownies

½ cup butter
1½ cups firmly packed dark brown sugar, divided
1¼ cups flour, divided
1 cup pecans, chopped
2 eggs
1 teaspoon vanilla
¼ teaspoon salt
1 teaspoon baking powder
1 cup chocolate chips

In food processor with metal blade, combine butter with ½ cup of the sugar and 1 cup of the flour, until crumbly. Pat into a buttered 13x9-inch pan. Bake at 375° for 10 minutes. When cooled, spread pecans evenly over crust. Beat eggs with remaining cup of brown sugar until thick; add vanilla. Combine salt and baking powder with remaining ¼ cup flour, and add to egg mixture. Pour over crust. Sprinkle chocolate chips evenly on top. Bake 20 minutes or until center is done. Cool before cutting. Makes about 2 dozen.

Cakes & Cookies

"Too much of a good thing can be wonderful."
-Mae West.

Gold Rush Bars

½ cup butter
1½ cups graham cracker crumbs
1 (14-ounce) can sweetened condensed milk
1 (3½-ounce) can flake coconut
1 (6-ounce) package chocolate chips
1 cup chopped nuts

Melt butter in oven in 13x9-inch pan. Remove from heat and spread crumbs evenly in pan. Spread condensed milk over surface; then coconut, chips, and nuts, distributing evenly. Bake at 325° for 25 minutes. Makes 4 dozen.

"I like chocolate chip cake because my mom Gay makes it. You put 1 layer of Vanilla Cake Mix in bottom of a pan. Put ¾ cup chocolate chips (scattered). Put 1 layer Chocolate Cake Mix. Put ¾ cup chocolate chips (scattered). Put layer of vanilla. It's delicious."
Jenna Campbell, age 11.
"P.S. You better check the recipe with my mom."

Simply Divine

Cakes & Cookies

Congo Bars

These chunky cookies from John Condra, Second-Ponce's Minister of Music, don't miss a beat.

⅔ cup margarine
1 box light brown sugar
3 eggs
2¾ cups sifted flour
2½ teaspoons baking powder
½ teaspoon salt
1 teaspoon vanilla
1 cup chopped pecans
1 (6-ounce) package chocolate or butterscotch chips (they may be mixed)

Melt margarine and stir into brown sugar. When cooled, add eggs one at a time, beating after each. Sift together flour, baking powder, and salt, and add to mixture. Add vanilla, then pecans and chips. Bake in greased 13x9-inch square pan at 350° for 30-35 minutes. Cool before cutting into bars or squares. Makes about 4 dozen.

238 Simply Divine

Lemon Bars

Crust
½ cup butter
½ cup powdered sugar
1 cup flour

Filling
1 cup sugar
2 eggs, beaten
2 tablespoons lemon juice
1 teaspoon lemon zest
3 tablespoons flour
½ teaspoon baking powder
  pinch of salt

To make crust, cream butter and sugar. Add flour, continuing to beat. Spread in ungreased 8-inch square pan. Bake at 350° for 15 minutes.

To make filling, cream sugar and eggs. Add lemon juice, zest, flour, baking powder, and salt. Mix well and spread over baked crust. Bake at 350° for 25 minutes. Cool, then dust with powdered sugar before cutting. Makes 16 bars.

Cakes & Cookies

Tip:

Many pastry cooks prefer using unsalted butter rather than salted because unsalted butter has a shorter shelf life and is a fresher product. Also, because salted butter is dominated by the flavor of salt, it masks the true flavor of the butter. According to the American Dairy Association, one stick of salted butter contains 937 milligrams of sodium, while unsalted butter contains only 16 milligrams of sodium.

Cakes & Cookies

Variation:

Use dried peaches instead of apricots.

Apricot Bars

Crust
1   cup soft butter
2   cups sifted flour
½   cup sugar

Topping
1½ cups dried, chopped apricots
1   cup water
2   eggs, beaten well
2   cups brown sugar
⅔   cup flour
1   teaspoon baking powder
½   teaspoon salt
1   teaspoon vanilla
2   cups chopped pecans or walnuts

Mix crust ingredients until crumbly. Press into 15x10-inch pan which has been buttered generously. Bake at 350° for 20 minutes, until light brown.

For topping, cook apricots in water 10 minutes. Drain, cool, set aside. Mix beaten eggs with brown sugar. Sift together flour, baking powder, and salt. Stir into egg mixture. Blend in vanilla, nuts, and apricots. Spread over crust. Bake at 350° for 30 minutes. Cool completely. Cut into small bars and roll in powdered sugar. Makes 4 dozen.

Peach Refrigerator Cookies

Served at Georgia's Executive Mansion on many state occasions.

"A lovely way to show our wonderful Georgia peaches."
　　　　　　　　　　-Betty Foy Sanders.

¾	cup butter
1½	cups dark brown sugar
1	egg
¼	cup milk
1	cup chopped dried peaches
2½	cups flour
3	teaspoons baking powder
1	teaspoon salt
1	cup chopped nuts

Cream butter, sugar, and egg. Sift dry ingredients; add to butter mixture, alternately with milk. Add nuts and peaches; mix well. Shape into rolls. Wrap and freeze until ready to cook. Slice thin and bake in 400° oven for 12-15 minutes. Yields 5 dozen.

Apple Bars

1	cup margarine
2	cups flour
⅓	cup milk
1	egg, separated
7	cups thinly sliced apples
1	cup sugar
1	teaspoon cinnamon

Tip:

When beating egg whites, use a stainless steel bowl, not glass, porcelain, or plastic.

Cut margarine into flour with pastry blender. Add milk, then egg yolk, and mix well. Divide in half. Roll out one half to cover the bottom of a jelly-roll pan. Mix apples, sugar, and cinnamon. Spread evenly over dough. Roll out the other half to cover the apples. Beat egg white and spread on top. Bake at 300° for 35-40 minutes. While still warm, drizzle with Glaze on page 220 or a buttercream frosting. When cool, cut into bars with a pizza cutter. Makes 3-4 dozen.

Simply Divine

Cakes & Cookies

Pound Cake Squares

1	box pound cake mix
½	cup butter, softened
2	eggs

Topping
1	(8-ounce) package cream cheese
1	box powdered sugar, divided
2	eggs
1	teaspoon vanilla
½	cup chopped pecans

Combine cake mix, butter, and 2 eggs, mixing until blended. Spread in greased 13x9-inch pan.

Blend cream cheese with powdered sugar, reserving ¼ cup of the sugar. Beat in 2 eggs and vanilla. Spread over cake mixture and sprinkle with pecans. Bake at 350° for 45 minutes. While still warm, sift reserved ¼ cup powdered sugar on top. Cool and cut into squares. Makes 2 dozen.

Sugar Cookies

½	cup margarine
1	cup sugar
1	egg
1½	cups flour
1	teaspoon baking powder
¼	teaspoon salt
1	teaspoon vanilla

Cream margarine and sugar. Add egg and beat well. Mix together flour, baking powder, and salt, and add to creamed mixture. Add vanilla. Drop by teaspoonfuls onto lightly greased cookie sheet. Bake at 350° for 12-15 minutes. Do not overbake. Makes 2½ dozen.

Mocha Crunch

Cakes & Cookies

1	cup butter or margarine
2	tablespoons instant coffee granules
½	teaspoon salt
½	teaspoon almond extract
1	teaspoon vanilla
1	cup sugar
2	cups sifted flour
1	(6-ounce) package semisweet chocolate chips
½	cup almonds or pecans, chopped coarsely

Blend butter with coffee, salt, and flavorings. Gradually beat in sugar, then flour. Add chocolate chips. Spread thinly in ungreased 15x10-inch pan. Sprinkle nuts evenly and press into batter with dampened fingers. Bake at 375° for 20-22 minutes. Cut into squares while hot, or cool on rack and break into irregular pieces. Makes 1¼ pounds.

Tip:

If you don't have chocolate chips, substitute coarsely chopped, high-quality chocolate bars.

"How do they taste? They taste like more."

-H.L. Mencken.

South African Crunchies

Karen Toholsky's parents are missionaries in Capetown, South Africa, where these are called biscuits and are commonly served at teatime.

¾	cup butter or margarine, melted
2	tablespoons light corn syrup
1	teaspoon baking soda
1	cup sugar
1	cup flour
2	cups old-fashioned oatmeal
1	cup coconut

To melted butter, add syrup and baking soda, then all other ingredients. Stir well. Spread into 13x9-inch greased pan. Bake at 300° for 20-25 minutes until golden brown. Cool; then cut into bars. Makes 2 dozen.

Simply Divine

Cakes & Cookies

Tip:

Old-fashioned and quick-cooking oats can be used interchangeably in recipes.

Miss Connie's Oatmeal Cookies

Connie Anderson taught many generations of three-year-olds at Second-Ponce how to spell "L-O-V-E LOVE" on the fingers of one hand.

1	cup butter or margarine
1	heaping cup brown sugar
2	cups flour
1	teaspoon baking soda
	pinch of salt
2	tablespoons honey
2	cups quick-cooking oatmeal

Cream butter and sugar well. Add other ingredients and mix thoroughly. Drop from teaspoon onto greased cookie sheet. Pat as thin as possible with a fork, dipping it in water each time. Bake at 350° about 12 minutes until golden brown. Makes 5 dozen.

Cinnamon Crisps

¾	cup butter or margarine
1	cup granulated sugar
1½	teaspoons ground cinnamon
1	egg, separated
1	teaspoon vanilla
½	teaspoon salt
2	cups flour
1	cup finely chopped nuts

Cream butter. Add sugar and cinnamon while continuing to beat. Add egg yolk, then vanilla and salt. Add flour to make a stiff dough. Knead and pat onto a greased 17x11-inch jelly-roll pan. Spread with unbeaten egg white, brushing off excess. Sprinkle nuts over the top, and press into mixture. Bake at 325° for 25 minutes or until golden brown. While still warm, cut into squares, bars, or triangles. Makes 3 dozen.

Rita's Famous Oatmeal Cookies

Cakes & Cookies

"Everyone tries to make them, but they never turn out like mine—beats me!"

-Rita Picklesimer.

Variation:

Omit the raisins, chocolate chips, and 1 teaspoon cinnamon; add candied orange slices, coconut, and pecans.

1	cup vegetable shortening, butter flavored
1	cup firmly packed brown sugar
½	cup sugar
2	eggs
1	teaspoon vanilla
¼	cup molasses
1½	cups flour
1	teaspoon baking soda
2	tablespoons cinnamon
2	tablespoons coriander
1	teaspoon nutmeg
	pinch of ginger
½	teaspoon salt
3	cups old-fashioned oatmeal
1	cup pecans
1	(12-ounce) package chocolate chips
1	(15-ounce) box raisins
6	ounces coconut

Beat shortening and sugars together. Add eggs, vanilla, and molasses. Mix well. In a separate bowl, sift together flour, baking soda, cinnamon, coriander, nutmeg, ginger, and salt. Slowly beat into sugar mixture. Add oatmeal and stir; batter will be very thick. Blend in any optional additions. Drop by rounded tablespoonfuls on greased cookie sheet. Bake at 350° for 8-10 minutes, checking at 8 minutes for a softer cookie. Remove after a minute's delay. Cool on wax paper. Makes 6 dozen.

Cakes & Cookies

T*ip*:

When baking cookies, let the cookie sheet cool completely between batches. Placing the dough on a warm pan causes the cookie to lose its shape.

Oatmeal Chocolate Chip Cookies

1	cup vegetable shortening, butter flavored
¾	cup light brown sugar
¾	cup sugar
2	eggs
1½	cups flour
1	teaspoon salt
1	teaspoon baking soda
1	teaspoon hot water
1	teaspoon vanilla
2	cups quick-cooking oatmeal
1	cup chopped pecans
1	(6-ounce) package chocolate chip mini morsels

Cream shortening and sugars; add eggs and mix well. Sift together flour and salt; add to sugar mixture. Dissolve soda in hot water and add to mixture, followed by vanilla and oatmeal. Stir in pecans and chocolate chips. Drop by teaspoonfuls on ungreased cookie sheet. Bake at 325° for 10-12 minutes. Do not overbake. Makes 4 dozen.

Cashew Cookies

½   cup butter
1   cup brown sugar
1   egg
½   teaspoon vanilla
2   cups sifted flour
¾   teaspoon baking powder
¾   teaspoon baking soda
¼   teaspoon salt
⅓   cup sour cream
1¾ cups salted whole cashew nuts

Icing
½   cup butter
3   tablespoons cream or whole milk
¼   teaspoon vanilla
2   cups powdered sugar

For cookies, cream butter and sugar. Beat in egg and vanilla. Sift together flour, baking powder, baking soda, and salt, and add to mixture. Beat in sour cream. Fold in nuts. Drop by spoonfuls onto ungreased cookie sheet. Bake at 375° for 10 minutes.

For icing, brown butter lightly. Remove from heat and add cream, vanilla, and powdered sugar. Beat until smooth, and ice the cooled cookies. Makes 3½ dozen.

Cakes & Cookies

"At the tip of the tongue, we taste sweet things; bitter things at the back; sour things at the sides; and salty things spread over the surface, but mainly up front. The tongue is like a kingdom divided into principalities according to sensory talent…. Taste buds wear out every week to ten days, and we replace them, although not as frequently over the age of forty-five–our palates really do become jaded as we get older. It takes a more intense taste to produce the same level of sensation, and children have the keenest sense of taste. A baby's mouth has many more taste buds than an adult's, with some even dotting the cheeks. Children adore sweets partly because the tips of their tongues, more sensitive to sugar, haven't yet been blunted by years of gourmandizing or trying to eat hot soup before it cools."

-Diane Ackerman,
A Natural History of the Senses

Simply Divine

Cakes & Cookies

Christmas Cookies

2	cups dates
6	slices candied pineapple
2	cups candied cherries
¾	pound golden seedless raisins
7	cups pecans, chopped
3	cups flour, divided
1	cup butter
1	cup firmly-packed light brown sugar
3	eggs
½	cup milk
1	teaspoon vanilla
1	teaspoon salt
1	teaspoon cinnamon
1	teaspoon baking soda

Chop dates, pineapple, and cherries. Combine with raisins and nuts, and toss with 1 cup of flour to coat. Set aside. Cream butter and sugar, add eggs one at a time, then milk and vanilla, continuing to beat. Sift together the remaining 2 cups flour with salt, cinnamon, and baking soda. Add to batter gradually and beat until creamy. Stir in coated fruit and nuts. Drop by teaspoonfuls or ice tongs onto greased cookie sheet. Bake at 300° for about 15 minutes. Makes approximately 200 cookies.

Tea Cakes

1 cup margarine
¾ cup sugar
1 egg
3 cups self-rising flour
2 teaspoons vanilla

Optional glaze
1 cup powdered sugar
1 tablespoon each of orange and lemon juice
½ teaspoon each of orange and lemon zest
   Nuts or coconut, if desired

Cream margarine and sugar. Add egg, flour, and vanilla. Put dough in refrigerator an hour or more to stiffen it for rolling. Remove enough to make a large ball at a time, keeping the rest chilled. Place a ball on lightly floured wax paper, sift lightly with flour, and cover with wax paper. With rolling pin, flatten to about ¼-inch thickness. Cut in shapes, transferring with spatula to ungreased cookie sheet. Bake at 325° for 10-12 minutes, until just beginning to brown at the edges. Remove before centers are browned.

Since tea cakes are not very sweet, a glaze is a nice addition: Blend sugar with juice and zest until smooth. Nuts or coconut may be sprinkled atop before glaze is firm. Makes 5 dozen.

Cakes & Cookies

"For the Orphan's Home, besides having furnished the ladies' reception and donated two cows, we have tried to give the children some of the simple pleasures of childhood. We have three or four times given them lawn parties and a frolic."
   -Report from the
Young Ladies Society, 1904.

Always popular at "frolics" were crumbly Tea Cakes.

Tea Cakes.

Three eggs, one quart CAPITOLA flour, one-half teaspoon soda, one cup sugar, one-half cup butter, salt to taste, and two tablespoons butter milk. Roll very thin and bake quickly.
   Gate City Cook Book

Simply Divine

Cakes & Cookies

Tip:

Mandelbrot is similar to the Italian treat biscotti. Both are crunchy, twice-baked cookies, best served with a hot drink.

Mandelbrot

A crisp Jewish bread eaten as a cookie

1	cup sugar
4	eggs
1	cup oil
2	cups flour
1	teaspoon baking powder
½	teaspoon salt
1	teaspoon vanilla
1	teaspoon almond extract
1	teaspoon lemon extract (optional)
1	cup chopped pecans or almonds

Beat sugar and eggs well, using electric mixer. Add oil, then flour, baking powder, and salt. Add flavorings as desired, and nuts. Spoon into 3 greased shallow loaf pans or one 13x9-inch pan. Bake at 350° for 20-25 minutes. Slice while in pans, then remove slices, and place flat on large cookie sheet. Bake at 200° for 2 to 3 hours. Makes about 2 dozen.

Marcine's Meringues

Tip:

To whip up a smooth meringue, separate eggs while they are cold, but let whites come to room temperature before beating.

2	egg whites
¾	cup firmly-packed light brown sugar
1	tablespoon vanilla
	pinch of salt
2	cups chopped pecans

Beat egg whites until stiff peaks form. Gradually add sugar, and beat until well blended. Add vanilla and salt. Fold in pecans. Drop by teaspoonfuls onto greased cookie sheet. Bake at 250° for 30-35 minutes. Makes 3-4 dozen.

Pies & Sweet Temptations

"Taste and see that the Lord is good; blessed is the man who takes refuge in him."

Psalm 34:8

Pies & Sweet Temptations

PIES

Garden of Eden Pie	253
Zesty Lemonade Pie	253
Bill's Buttermilk Pie	254
Baked Alaska	254
Chocolate Meringue Pie	255
Coconut Custard Pie	255
South Carolina Pecan Pie	256
Nutty Lemon Pie	256
Most Excellent Pie Crust	256
Strawberry Chiffon Pie	257
Macaroon Pie	258
Cantaloupe Cream Pie	258
Chocolate Silk Pie	259
Peanut Butter Pie	260
Deep-Dish Apple Pie	261
Angel Pecan Pie	262
Low-Fat Coconut Pie	269

COBBLERS

Strawberry Crumble	257
Blueberry Cobbler	260
Very Cherry Crisp	261
Fresh Fruit Cobbler	263

SWEET TEMPTATIONS

Chocolate Sauce	254
Chocolate-Coated Strawberries	257
Raspberry Sauce, Two Variations	259
Nutmeg Cream	261
Cantaloupe Sundaes with Raspberry Sauce	263
Pears Perfectly Poached	263
Lemon Ice Cream	264
Light Lemon Mousse	264
Mango Sorbet	265
Strawberry Pizza	265
Lovejoy Pecan Tassies	266
Fresh Raspberry and Fig Gratin	266
Creamy Cheesecake Bites	267
Heavenly Chocolate Sauce	267
Peach Tapioca	268
Warm Toffee Dip	268
Crème Fraîche, Two Variations	269
Lemon Filling	270
Praline Grahams	271

CANDIES AND SNACKS

Processor Peanut Butter	260
Peanut Brittle	270
Microwave Fudge	271
Candy-Coated Pecans	272
Trash Snacks	272

HERITAGE RECIPES

Chocolate Pie	255
Queen of Trifles	258
Apple Tapioca	268
Chocolate Fudge	271
When and How to Eat	272

Garden of Eden Pie

Pies & Sweet Temptations

5	large tart apples
1	tablespoon lemon juice
¾	cup sugar
⅓	cup flour
1	teaspoon cinnamon
¼	teaspoon nutmeg
¼	cup butter or margarine
½	cup sour cream, room temperature
1	(9-inch) pie crust

Peel and cut apples in thick slices and arrange in overlapping rows in unbaked pie crust. Sprinkle with lemon juice. In separate mixing bowl, mix sugar, flour, and spices. Cut in butter or margarine with fork or pastry blender until crumbly. Spoon over apples. Spread sour cream over top. Bake at 400° for 25 minutes. Reduce temperature to 350° and bake until apples are tender, 20-25 minutes.

Tip:

More than 3,000 varieties of apples are grown at the National Apple Orchard in Geneva, New York. Among the best varieties for cooking are the Cortland, Stayman, Winesap, and Rome Beauty. When baking, avoid McIntosh and Red Delicious apples because these varieties turn mushy when cooked.

Zesty Lemonade Pie

A *refreshing summer dessert*

1	(16-ounce) container whipped topping
1	(6-ounce) can frozen lemonade concentrate
1	(14-ounce) can condensed milk
	grated zest and juice of 1 lemon
1	(8- or 9-inch) graham cracker pie crust

Combine whipped topping, lemonade, milk, zest, and juice. Mix well. Pour into pie crust and chill or freeze.

Variation:

Use filling in tarts and garnish with mint, berries, or a dollop of whipped cream.

Simply Divine 253

Pies & Sweet Temptations

"This was my son Bill's favorite pie. He got the recipe when he was a student at Rabun Gap Nacoochee School."

-Virginia Selph.

Bill's Buttermilk Pie

3 eggs, beaten
1½ cups sugar
1 tablespoon flour
½ cup buttermilk
½ cup margarine, melted
1 (9-inch) deep-dish pie crust

Beat together eggs, sugar, and flour. Add buttermilk and beat. Add margarine and mix. Pour into unbaked pie crust. Place on a cookie sheet and bake at 350° for 1 hour or until golden brown.

Baked Alaska

Some food historians believe that Baked Alaska was created in 1869 to commemorate the purchase of Alaska by the United States.

1 (9-inch) graham cracker pie crust
1½ quarts vanilla or coffee flavored ice cream or frozen yogurt
5 egg whites
10 tablespoons sugar

Fill crust with softened ice cream and freeze overnight. Beat egg whites, gradually adding sugar. Beat until stiff. Spread over ice cream and bake at 475° for 5 minutes or until meringue is golden. Return to freezer for 4-6 hours.

Chocolate Sauce
2 squares unsweetened chocolate
2 tablespoons butter or margarine
1 cup white corn syrup
½ teaspoon vanilla

Melt chocolate in double boiler or microwave. Add butter and corn syrup and cook for approximately 5 minutes over low heat. Stir in vanilla. Drizzle warm sauce over pie slices when ready to serve. Sauce stores well in refrigerator.

"I never think of spectacular desserts without thinking of my mother. She always planned wonderful treats. One of her favorite sayings was: `Tis the dessert that graces the feast; an ill end disparages the rest.'"

-Peggy Lientz.

Chocolate Meringue Pie

1   cup sugar
2   tablespoons cocoa
3   eggs, separated
2   tablespoons cornstarch
4   tablespoons butter, softened
1½ cups milk
1   teaspoon vanilla
1   (9-inch) pie crust, baked
2   tablespoons sugar
½   teaspoon cream of tartar

Mix sugar, cocoa, egg yolks, cornstarch, and butter; gradually stir in milk. Cook mixture in double boiler until thickened. Add vanilla. Cool and pour into pie crust. Beat egg whites until stiff, adding sugar and cream of tartar gradually during beating. Spread over pie filling. Bake at 350° about 10 minutes until golden brown.

Coconut Custard Pie

1   cup sugar
1   tablespoon flour
6   tablespoons margarine, melted
3   eggs, beaten
½   cup buttermilk
1   teaspoon vanilla
1   (6-ounce) package frozen coconut, thawed
1   (9-inch) deep-dish pie crust

Mix all ingredients and pour into unbaked pie crust. Cook at 400° for 10 minutes; then cook at 350° for 25 minutes or until firm and toasty.

Pies & Sweet Temptations

Tip:

To create shiny, smooth meringues, beat superfine or granulated sugar into the egg whites slowly, one tablespoon at a time.

Chocolate Pie.

Grate one-half tea cup of chocolate, put in a sauce pan with one cup hot water, butter the size of an egg, one teaspoonful vanilla, one cup sugar, the beaten yolks of two eggs, and two tablespoonfuls corn starch, dissolved in as much water. Mix well, cook until thick, stirring constantly. Pour into pie shells and let cool. Make a meringue of the whites of two eggs beaten stiff with two tablespoons powdered sugar. Spread on pie and brown slightly.

Gate City Cook Book

Simply Divine

Pies & Sweet Temptations

"I love to eat pecan pie for breakfast with coffee—hmm-m-m."
　　　　　　　　　　-Sue Stumm.

Most Excellent Pie Crust

1	cup shortening or butter
1	cup cake flour
2	cups all-purpose flour
1	teaspoon salt
1	tablespoon sugar
	milk
1	egg, lightly beaten

Cut shortening into dry ingredients until mixture is coarse. Add milk to egg to make ½ cup liquid; blend into dry mixture. Roll out. Makes two 9-inch pie crusts.

Tip:

Substitute 1 cup minus 2 tablespoons sifted all-purpose flour for 1 cup cake flour.

South Carolina Pecan Pie

Make one to eat and one to share

1	cup light brown sugar
1	cup sugar
10	tablespoons plus 2 teaspoons margarine, melted
4	eggs, lightly mixed
1	tablespoon vanilla
1¼	tablespoons vinegar
1	cup chopped pecans
2	(9-inch) pie crusts, lightly browned

Stir all ingredients together well. Divide evenly into pie crusts. Cook at 300° for 10 minutes, then at 325° for 25-30 minutes or until dark golden color. Top may be decorated with pecan halves before cooking. May be served with vanilla ice cream. Makes 2 pies.

Nutty Lemon Pie

3	scant tablespoons margarine, melted
3	eggs
¾	cup chopped nuts
1½	cups sugar
1	teaspoon lemon extract
	grated zest and juice of 1 lemon
1	(9-inch) pie crust

Mix all ingredients together and pour into unbaked pie crust. Bake at 400° for 10 minutes. Reduce heat to 325° and bake for about 40 minutes.

Strawberry Crumble

A *sweet solution for unexpected company*

1   can strawberry or cranberry-cherry pie filling
1   cup self-rising flour
1   cup sugar, or less to taste
½   cup butter

Spread pie filling evenly over bottom of 9-inch pie pan sprayed with nonstick cooking spray. Mix together flour and sugar. Cut in butter with fork or pastry blender until mixture is crumbly. Spread over filling. Bake 20-30 minutes or until top is nicely browned.

Pies & Sweet Temptations

Self-Rising Flour

1   cup all-purpose flour
1¼   teaspoons baking powder
¼   teaspoon salt

Gently mix all ingredients together.

Strawberry Chiffon Pie

½   cup sugar
1   envelope gelatin
½   cup water
1   (10-ounce) package frozen strawberries
    juice of ½ lemon
1   cup heavy cream, whipped
⅛   teaspoon almond extract
1   (9-inch) pie crust, baked

In a saucepan, stir sugar with gelatin. Stir in water and cook over low heat, stirring until just below the boiling point. Remove from heat. Add frozen berries and lemon juice. Stir until thawed and mixture thickens. Fold extract and berry mixture into whipped cream. Pour into pie crust. Refrigerate 30 minutes.

Chocolate-Coated Strawberries

    imported bittersweet chocolate
    fresh whole strawberries

Melt chocolate slowly in top of double boiler over hot, not simmering, water. Using toothpicks, dip each fruit in chocolate, twirling to coat; let excess drip off. Stand toothpicks upright in a piece of Styrofoam covered with foil. Chill to harden.

Simply Divine

Pies & Sweet Temptations

Queen of Trifles.

Take macaroons and lady fingers and spread them with a tart jelly. Put a tablespoonful of port wine on each one, spread in the bottom of a dish and sprinkle with crystallized cherries. Pour over this a boiled custard with almonds, blanched and chipped up, in it. Make as many layers of this as you need, cover with whipped cream, sweetened and made pink with port wine. Fifteen cents worth each of macaroons, lady fingers, almonds and cherries will be sufficient for ten people.

Gate City Cook Book

Macaroon Pie

12	dates, chopped
½	cup nuts, chopped
12	unsalted saltines, rolled very fine
¼	teaspoon baking powder
1	cup sugar
3	egg whites, beaten until stiff
1	teaspoon almond extract
	whipped cream (No substitutions, please)

Mix together dates, nuts, saltines, baking powder, and sugar. Fold in egg whites. Fold in almond extract. Bake in well-greased 9-inch glass pie pan at 350° for 30 minutes. Serve with whipped cream.

Cantaloupe Cream Pie

1	cup sugar
2	tablespoons flour
3	eggs, beaten
1	cup pureed cantaloupe (approximately half of medium-size cantaloupe)
1	teaspoon vanilla
2	tablespoons butter or margarine
1	(8- or 9-inch) graham cracker crust or baked pie crust
1	cup whipped cream or whipped topping

Combine sugar and flour in saucepan. Add eggs. Mix well. Stir in cantaloupe. Cook over medium heat 8-10 minutes, stirring constantly until mixture boils. Remove from heat and add butter and vanilla. Cool. Pour into pie crust. Top with whipped cream.

Chocolate Silk Pie

Smooth, luxurious

Crust
- 2 egg whites
- ½ cup sugar
- ⅛ teaspoon cream of tartar
- ½ cup finely chopped pecans

Beat egg whites until stiff but not dry. Sift sugar with cream of tartar. Add mixture to egg whites slowly, continuing to beat egg whites. Fold in pecans. Line buttered 10-inch pie pan with mixture to form the pie crust. Cook for 1 hour at 275°.

Filling
- ¾ cup semisweet chocolate chips
- 3 tablespoons water
- ½ teaspoon almond extract
- 1 cup whipping cream

Melt chocolate chips with water. Cool until thickened. Add almond extract. Beat whipping cream until stiff. Fold in chocolate mixture. Pour into crust. Refrigerate 2-3 hours before serving.

Pies & Sweet Temptations

Raspberry Sauce, Two Variations

Variation One
- 1 cup fresh raspberries
- ⅓ cup powdered sugar
- 2 teaspoons lemon juice

Puree berries. Add sugar and lemon juice. Strain, discarding seeds. Makes ¾ cup.

Variation Two
- 1 (10-ounce) package frozen raspberries, thawed
- 1½ teaspoons cornstarch
- ½ cup currant jelly

In medium saucepan, combine berries, cornstarch, and jelly. Bring to boil; cook and stir until clear and thick. Strain. Makes 1 cup.

Simply Divine

Pies & Sweet Temptations

Processor Peanut Butter

Fresh roasted flavor, no added sweeteners

1   cup roasted unsalted peanuts
¼-½ teaspoon salt
1-2 tablespoons vegetable oil

Place ingredients in food processor or blender. Process about 3-5 minutes, stopping occasionally to scrape sides of container. Store in refrigerator; stir before serving. Makes ½ cup.

Peanut Butter Pie

1   (8-ounce) package cream cheese, softened (do not substitute with low-fat cream cheese)
¾   cup powdered sugar
2   tablespoons milk
½   cup crunchy peanut butter
1   (8-ounce) container whipped topping
1   (6-ounce) chocolate pie crust
    chocolate shavings or dry roasted peanuts (optional)

Beat together cream cheese and sugar. Stir in milk and peanut butter. Fold in whipped topping. Pour into pie crust. Garnish with optional items or Heavenly Chocolate Sauce on page 267. Makes 1 very rich pie.

Blueberry Cobbler

In colonial New England, this was sometimes called a slump or a grunt.

2   cups blueberries
1½   cups sugar, divided
½   cup butter
¾   cup flour
2   teaspoons baking powder
¼   teaspoon salt
¾   cup milk

Variation:

To add color and flavor, make cobblers using fruits in combinations, such as strawberry-raspberry-blueberry, raspberry-currant, blueberry-peach, or apple-blackberry.

Tip:

Wash all berries just before using. Rinse them gently; never soak them. Soaking turns berries mushy.

Mix blueberries with ¾ cup sugar. Let stand. Melt butter in 8-inch square dish in 325° oven. Combine flour, remaining sugar, baking powder, and salt. Sift into milk and stir gently, just until mixed. Pour over melted butter. Do not stir. Spoon blueberries on top of batter. Do not stir. Bake at 325° for 1 hour. Serves 6-8.

Deep-Dish Apple Pie

Pies & Sweet Temptations

6-8 cups peeled and sliced apples
1½ cups sugar
2 cups water
½ cup margarine, divided
crusts for 2 pies

Melt ¼ cup margarine in bottom of 13x9-inch baking dish. Roll pie crusts into rectangular shapes. Put one crust in dish. Put apples on bottom crust. Heat water, sugar, and remaining ¼ cup margarine in saucepan. Pour over apples. Place second crust on top. Cook at 400° for 40-45 minutes until crust is lightly browned. Serves 10-12.

Very Cherry Crisp

⅓ cup flour
¾ cup old-fashioned oatmeal, uncooked
3 scant tablespoons margarine, softened
⅔ cup sugar, divided
3 tablespoons cornstarch
⅛ teaspoon cinnamon
⅛ teaspoon nutmeg
1 tablespoon lemon juice
2 (16-ounce) cans pitted sour cherries, drained, juice reserved

Combine flour and oatmeal. Cut in margarine until crumbly and add ⅓ cup sugar. Set aside for topping. In a saucepan combine remaining sugar with cornstarch, spices, and lemon juice. Slowly blend in juice from cherries. Cook over low heat, stirring constantly until thick and clear. Remove from heat. Add cherries. Pour into greased 8-inch square pan. Sprinkle with topping. Bake at 375° for 30 minutes. Serve warm with Nutmeg Cream (see recipe). Serves 4.

Nutmeg Cream

1 cup heavy whipping cream
1 teaspoon freshly grated nutmeg
2 tablespoons powdered sugar
½ cup sour cream

Beat whipping cream until soft peaks form; beat in nutmeg and sugar. Fold in sour cream. Chill. Makes 2½ cups.

Pies & Sweet Temptations

Tip:

To test for freshness, place eggs in a pan of cold water. A fresh egg will sink to the bottom; an older egg will float. Because older eggs have a tendency to run during the poaching process, use the freshest eggs available. Reserve older eggs for hard cooking; they are easier to peel than fresh eggs.

Angel Pecan Pie

3	egg whites
1	cup sugar
1	teaspoon baking powder
1	pinch salt
⅛	teaspoon lemon juice
22	round, buttery crackers, coarsely crumbled
1	cup pecans, chopped
1	cup cream, whipped
1	teaspoon vanilla

Beat egg whites until they start to stiffen. Slowly add sugar, baking powder, salt, and lemon juice. Continue beating until stiff but not dry. Carefully fold in cracker crumbs and pecans. Put mixture in greased and lightly floured 9-inch pie pan. Bake for 30 minutes at 350°. Cool and top with slightly sweetened whipped cream flavored with vanilla.

Topping

3	round buttery crackers, crumbled fine
2	tablespoons pecans, chopped
1	tablespoon sugar
½	teaspoon cinnamon

Combine ingredients and sprinkle over whipped cream.

Fresh Fruit Cobbler

Make with your choice of fruit

½ cup butter
6 cups sliced apples or other fruit
1 cup sugar
1 teaspoon cinnamon or to taste
1 tablespoon water
1 cup self-rising flour
1 cup sugar
1 cup buttermilk

Melt butter in a large baking dish. Combine fruit, sugar, cinnamon, and water. Spread over melted butter. Mix flour, sugar, and buttermilk. Spoon over fruit. Bake at 400° for 5 minutes; then bake at 350° for 30 minutes. Serves 10.

Cantaloupe Sundaes with Raspberry Sauce

2 tablespoons cornstarch
2 tablespoons water
1 (10-ounce) package frozen raspberries, thawed but not drained
1 cantaloupe, peeled and cut into 8 wedges
1 quart vanilla ice cream scooped into 8 balls
   fresh raspberries (optional)

Combine cornstarch and water in a saucepan. Stir well. Add thawed raspberries. Cook 1 minute, stirring constantly. Cool. Fill each cantaloupe wedge with a scoop of ice cream. Top with raspberry sauce. Garnish with raspberries if desired. Serves 8.

Pies & Sweet Temptations

Pears Perfectly Poached

Elegant presentation

½ cup sugar
6 cups cranberry-raspberry juice
1 cinnamon stick
6 ripe pears, peeled
   whipped cream or sour cream
   fresh raspberries

In large saucepan, boil sugar and juice briefly, stirring to mix. Add cinnamon stick and pears. Simmer gently, occasionally turning fruit. Cook about 20 minutes until pears are tender. Remove pan from heat and allow to cool, turning pears once or twice. Drain pears and set aside, reserving 3 cups liquid. Boil reserved liquid until reduced to about 1 cup; set aside to cool. To serve, spoon a little syrup onto each plate, top with a pear, and drizzle syrup over fruit, coating each. Garnish with cream and raspberries.

Simply Divine 263

Pies & Sweet Temptations

Tip:

Grate zest first, then squeeze for juice. Freeze any extra zest or juice for another project.

"My favorit food is ice cream because . . . you can put lots of toppings & treats on top."

Blair Gaddis, age 12.

Lemon Ice Cream

4 cups sugar
   juice of 8 lemons
2 tablespoons grated lemon zest
4 pints half-and-half

Stir together sugar, juice, zest, and half-and-half until sugar dissolves. Freeze in an ice cream freezer. Mixture will not freeze solid. Pour into separate container and freeze overnight in freezer. Remove from freezer 18 minutes before serving. Serves 10.

Light Lemon Mousse

A *light refreshing dessert*

1   (12-ounce) can evaporated milk, thoroughly chilled
1   (3-ounce) package lemon jello
¾   cup sugar
¾   cup hot water
    grated zest and juice of 3 lemons
⅛   teaspoon salt
    lemon twists

Place can of evaporated milk in freezer two hours prior to making dessert or put in refrigerator overnight. Dissolve jello and sugar in hot water and cool. Add lemon juice (six tablespoons), zest, and salt to mixture. Whip the cold milk in a large mixing bowl until stiff and slowly fold into jello mixture. Pour into a 3-quart soufflé dish or serving bowl and refrigerate. Before it congeals fully, fold again to reincorporate any lemon mixture that may have settled. Return to refrigerator to congeal. Garnish with lemon twists. Serves 8.

Mango Sorbet

A *dessert with a gorgeous color*

2	cups peeled and diced mangoes
8	ounces nonfat vanilla yogurt
¼-½	teaspoon fresh lime juice
	pinch sugar
	fresh mint

Freeze mango for about 3 hours. Place mango, yogurt, lime juice, and sugar in food processor. Pulse using on-off technique until coarsely pureed (30-50 seconds). Spoon into 4 stemmed glasses and garnish with fresh mint. Serves 4.

Strawberry Pizza

1	cup self-rising flour
¼	cup powdered sugar
½	cup margarine, melted
1	(8-ounce) package cream cheese, softened
1	(14-ounce) can sweetened condensed milk
⅓	cup lemon juice
1	teaspoon vanilla
½	cup sugar
2	tablespoons cornstarch
½	cup water
2	pints strawberries, cut in half

Combine flour and powdered sugar. Add margarine. Mix well. Spread dough on a 14-inch pizza pan. Bake at 350° for 10 minutes. Combine cream cheese, milk, lemon juice, and vanilla. Spread on cooled crust. Chill thoroughly. Combine sugar and cornstarch in a large saucepan. Add water and mix until smooth. Cook over medium heat about 5 minutes, stirring until thickened. Add strawberries. Cool completely. Spread strawberry glaze over cream cheese layer. Refrigerate for several hours before serving. Makes 8 slices.

Pies & Sweet Temptations

Variation:

Substitute a combination of bananas and strawberries for the mangoes.

Variation:

Use peaches and almond flavoring in place of strawberries and vanilla.

Pies & Sweet Temptations

"This is one of my very favorite recipes. I am honored to share it with you."

-Betty Talmadge.
Betty, a gracious lady who has exercised at Second-Ponce's Family Life Center, was the wife of former Georgia governor, Herman Talmadge. She is a gourmet cook and the author of two cookbooks.

Lovejoy Pecan Tassies

Crust
1   (3-ounce) package cream cheese, softened
½   cup butter, softened
1   cup flour, sifted

Mix crust ingredients. Chill at least 2 hours. Pinch off dough, shaping into 2 dozen 1-inch balls. Press each ball into bottom and side of 1¾-inch muffin pans. Set aside.

Filling
1   egg, slightly beaten
¾   cup brown sugar
1   tablespoon butter, softened
1   teaspoon vanilla
⅔   cup pecan pieces

Combine all ingredients. Fill each crust ¾ full. Bake at 325° for 25 minutes. Cool and remove from pan. Makes 2 dozen.

Fresh Raspberry and Fig Gratin

A blending of delicate flavors

"He that is of a merry heart hath a continual feast."

-Proverbs 15:15.

1   pint fresh raspberries
6   fresh figs, quartered
8   ounces sour cream
¼   teaspoon grated orange zest
½   cup firmly packed dark brown sugar
     mint sprigs

Arrange raspberries and figs in 10-inch broiler-proof baking dish. Stir sour cream with zest until smooth. Spoon evenly over fruit. Sprinkle with brown sugar. Broil close to heat until brown, about 4 minutes. Garnish with mint. Serves 4.

Creamy Cheesecake Bites

Pies & Sweet Temptations

1	(8-ounce) package cream cheese, softened
¾	cup sugar
3	eggs, separated
	graham cracker crumbs

Beat together cream cheese and sugar. Add egg yolks one at a time, beating well. In a separate bowl beat egg whites until very stiff. Fold into cream cheese mixture. Butter miniature muffin tins and lightly coat with crumbs. Fill almost to top with mixture. Bake in upper third of oven at 350° for 15 minutes. Cool. Cakes will sink in middle.

Topping
2	cups sour cream
2½	tablespoons sugar
1	teaspoon vanilla
	small strawberries, sliced

Mix sour cream, sugar, and vanilla. Drop 1 teaspoon of mixture on top of each cake. Bake 5 minutes at 400°. Cool. Top each with a strawberry. Makes 48.

Tip:

To do ahead, bake cheesecake in miniature muffin tins and freeze. Before serving, thaw, add topping, and garnish.

Heavenly Chocolate Sauce

A chocolate lover will pour this on anything!

½	cup butter
4	(1-ounce) squares unsweetened chocolate
3	cups sugar
½	teaspoon salt
1	(13-ounce) can evaporated milk

Melt butter and chocolate in double boiler. Stir in sugar, salt, and milk. Cook over medium heat, stirring constantly until sugar is dissolved and sauce is smooth, about 20 minutes. Serve warm or cold. Keeps well in refrigerator. Makes 4 cups.

"The nutritionists are ruining our food!"
                                    -Julia Child.

Simply Divine

Pies & Sweet Temptations

Apple Tapioca.

To one cup of granulated tapioca add two cups of cold water; soak one hour. Put into a porcelain kettle and add two cups of water. Let cook till clear as jelly. Add one heaping cup sugar, boil a few minutes then take from stove. Add six large, mellow apples cut up fine, pour in pan and bake until apples are tender. Serve with cream, either whipped or plain, as preferred. Very superior.

Gate City Cook Book

Peach Tapioca

Zero fat, zero cholesterol, and only 80 calories per serving

⅓	cup sugar
3	tablespoons quick-cooking tapioca
1¾	cups water
4	large peaches (about 1½ pounds), divided
½	teaspoon almond extract

In a saucepan combine sugar, tapioca, and water. Set aside. Peel 3 peaches and mash with a fork. Add peaches and their juice to sugar mixture and cook to boiling point. Remove from heat. Peel and dice the fourth peach. Add diced peach and almond extract to cooked mixture. Stir gently to combine. Spoon into custard cups. Cover and chill. Serves 6.

Warm Toffee Dip

A winter treat for church gatherings

1	cup butter
2	cups dark brown sugar
1	cup white corn syrup
2	tablespoons water
1	(14-ounce) can sweetened condensed milk
1	teaspoon vanilla
	apple and/or pear slices
	pineapple juice or grapefruit juice

Melt butter in heavy pan. Add sugar, syrup, water, and milk. Cook over moderate heat, stirring until thick. Add vanilla. Pour into dish that will keep the mixture warm. Serve hot with fruit slices that have been dipped in juice to prevent browning.

Crème Fraîche, Two Variations

A thickened cream with a tangy, nutty flavor

Variation One
- 1 cup heavy whipping cream
- 2 tablespoons buttermilk

In a glass container, combine cream and buttermilk. Cover and let stand at room temperature until thick, about 12-36 hours. Stir, cover, and refrigerate 24 hours before using. Keeps up to 10 days.

Variation Two
- ½ cup heavy whipping cream
- ½ cup sour cream

In a glass container, gently blend creams together. Then follow directions for Variation One.

Low-Fat Coconut Pie

- ½ cup reduced-fat biscuit baking mix
- ½ cup sugar
- liquid egg substitute equivalent to four eggs
- 2 cups skim milk
- 3 ounces frozen coconut
- 1 teaspoon vanilla
- 2 tablespoons reduced-calorie margarine

Combine all ingredients in blender. Mix well. Pour batter into deep-dish pie pan or quiche dish. Place on lowest rack in oven and bake at 400° for 30 minutes or until custard sets. Serves 8-10.

Pies & Sweet Temptations

Tip:

Spoon this versatile cream over fresh fruit, pudding, warm cobbler, or chocolate desserts. Because crème fraîche does not curdle when boiled, it is a good substitute for sour cream in sauces and soups.

"'How long does getting thin take?' asked Pooh anxiously."

—A.A. Milne,
Winnie-the-Pooh

Pies & Sweet Temptations

Tip:

Zest is the "skin," the peel, or outermost layer of the lemon. To remove the zest, use a paring knife, citrus zester, or vegetable peeler, or lightly rub the fruit over a grater. Whichever method you use, be sure to avoid the pith, the bitter white layer just below the skin.

Variation:

In place of lemons try oranges or limes. Use 9 tablespoons of juice and 6-9 teaspoons of zest.

Lemon Filling

Also called lemon curd

    grated zest and juice of 3 lemons
4   eggs
1½ cups sugar
½   cup margarine

Process zest and juice in food processor. Combine liquid with eggs, sugar, and margarine. Cook in double boiler until thick, stirring constantly. Serve over cake or in small pastry shells.

Peanut Brittle

The national craze for peanuts started during the Civil War when Union soldiers fighting in the South were first introduced to them.

2   cups shelled raw peanuts
     (small red Spanish peanuts preferred)
2   cups sugar
1   cup light corn syrup
1   cup cold water
½   teaspoon baking soda
½   teaspoon salt

Cook peanuts, sugar, syrup, and water over medium heat in heavy saucepan until amber colored, about 30 minutes, being careful not to burn. If a candy thermometer is used, it should reach 300°, hard-crack stage. Remove from heat and add baking soda and salt. Pour onto greased platter or marble slab, working quickly. Pull around edges until thin and brittle. Makes 2½ pounds of broken pieces.

Microwave Fudge

Easy and delicious!

1	box powdered sugar
½	cup margarine
⅓	cup cocoa
¼	cup milk
1	teaspoon vanilla
½	cup crunchy peanut butter (optional)
1	cup chopped nuts (optional)

Place sugar, margarine, cocoa, and milk in a mixing bowl in microwave oven for approximately 5 minutes. Remove and beat well to blend. Add vanilla, peanut butter, and/or nuts. Pour into greased 8-inch square pan, or use a larger pan for thinner pieces. Cool before cutting into squares.

Praline Grahams

1	package (⅓ of 16-ounce box) graham crackers
½	cup butter
½	cup margarine
½	cup sugar
1	cup chopped pecans

Break each graham cracker along scoring into 4 rectangular sections. In a greased jelly-roll pan, 15x11-inch or larger, arrange rectangles with sides touching, using more crackers if needed to cover the entire pan surface. Melt butter and margarine, stirring in sugar and pecans. Bring to a boil and cook 3 minutes, stirring or whisking constantly. Spread evenly over graham crackers. Bake at 300° for 12-15 minutes. Remove separated crackers to wax paper for cooling. Makes 40-50.

Pies & Sweet Temptations

Chocolate Fudge.

Three cups of sugar, one and one-half cups of rich sweet milk, one tablespoonful of butter, cook this mixture slowly until it begins to boil, then put into it nearly a half of a cake of Walter Baker's chocolate, grated, cook, constantly trying a little of it in a cup of cold water. It is done when the candy forms a little soft ball in the bottom of the cup. When taken from the fire it must be beaten until perfectly creamed and begins to be heavy, then pour in a buttered plate and when cool cut in little blocks.
   Gate City Cook Book

Simply Divine   271

Pies & Sweet Temptations

Candy-Coated Pecans

1   cup brown sugar
½   cup sugar
½   cup sour cream
1   teaspoon vanilla
2½ cups pecan halves

Butter sides of a heavy saucepan. In it mix sugars and sour cream. Stir until sugar melts. Cook to soft-ball stage, 236° on a candy thermometer. Remove from heat and add vanilla. Beat until mixture begins to thicken. Add nuts and stir until well coated, working quickly. Turn out on a greased platter or cookie sheet, separating into individual pieces. Makes 1 pound.

In addition to recipes, vintage cookbooks often included advice on healthful living. Here is a final entry from the Gate City Cook Book.

When and How to Eat

One should not eat when tired, angry, or laboring under a mental strain, nor should the mind be preoccupied with business or other cares. There would be fewer dyspeptics if every one could have absolute rest thirty minutes before, and one hour after each meal. One should think of how he shall enjoy a meal before eating [it], how he is enjoying it while eating, and how he did enjoy it when he is through.

                    Gate City Cook Book

Trash Snacks

1   (14-ounce) box graham cereal squares
1   (16-ounce) box raisins
8   ounces chopped dates
4-5 cups mixed nuts
1   (12-ounce) bag semisweet chocolate chips
½   cup butter or margarine, melted
14   ounces peanut butter
½   teaspoon salt
2   teaspoons almond extract
1   box powdered sugar

Pour cereal squares, raisins, dates, nuts, and chocolate chips into a large plastic bag. Mix butter, peanut butter, salt, and almond extract. Pour over dry ingredients in the plastic bag. Close bag and push back and forth to coat mixture. Open bag and pour in unsifted sugar, then shake repeatedly until everything is coated white. Store in airtight container. Do not freeze or refrigerate.

Simply Divine

Index

A

Almond Tea 30
ALMONDS
    Celery Amandine 210
    Chicken Almond Salad 94
    Frozen Queen Anne Salad 102
    Mandarin Green Salad with Slivered Almonds 88
    Sugared Almonds 97
Angel Pecan Pie 262
Anointed Quail 136
APPETIZERS (See also Spreads and Dips)
    Artichoke Quiche Squares 14
    Bacon-Wrapped Scallops 13
    Bruschetta for Two 86
    Cream Cheese Pastry 13
    Ham Rolls 17
    Honey-Mustard Chicken 14
    Hot Bacon Roll-Ups 15
    Hot Salami 16
    Marinated Broccoli and Cauliflower 24
    Mexican Pinwheels 26
    Old-Fashioned Cheese Straws 26
    Open-Faced Veggie Squares 25
    Petite Quiche Lorraines 13
    Stuffed New Potatoes 25
    Zucchini Triangles 15
APPLES
    Apple Ambrosia 102
    Apple Bars 241
    Apple Bran Muffins 50
    Apple Chicken Curry 160
    Apple Chutney 135
    Apple Salad with Honey Lime Dressing 106
    Apple-Glazed Brisket 118
    Chicken Breasts Stuffed with Apples and Gouda ... 148
    Cornbread Dressing Gone Wild 211
    Cranberry Apple Crunch 208
    Deep-Dish Apple Pie 261
    Fresh Apple Cake 220
    Fresh Fruit Cobbler 263
    Fruit Salad 106
    Garden of Eden Pie 253
APRICOTS
    Apricot Bars 240

    Apricot Butter 35
    Apricot Freeze 100
    Curried Fruit 209
    Fruit Bread 35
    Hot Mixed Fruit 209
    Morning Glory Muffins 51
ARTICHOKES
    Artichoke Quiche Squares 14
    Artichoke Rice Salad 94
    Hickory Smoked Chicken and
        Artichoke Pasta 154
    Spinach with Artichokes 189
ASPARAGUS
    Asparagus As Is 182
    Asparagus Stir-Fry 183
    Awesome Asparagus Casserole 182
    Saucy Chicken and Asparagus 158
    Tangy Congealed Asparagus 92
Aunt Ruth's Cheese Biscuits 38

B

Baby Greens with Feta and Sugared Walnuts 83
Bacon-Wrapped Scallops 13
Baked Alaska 254
Baked Blintz 54
Baked Vegetable Quartet 181
Baked Venison Loaves 135
Balsamic Vinaigrette 84
BANANAS
    Banana Bread 35
    Banana Nut Bread 36
    Hummingbird Cake 223
    Patio Punch 27
Baptized Quail 137
Barbecued Ribs 125
Barbecued Shrimp 174
Barley Soup 64
Basic Broccoli 184
Basic Refrigerator Rolls 41
Basque Bean Cassoulet 69
BEANS
    Basque Bean Cassoulet 69
    Chunky Chicken Chili 70
    Cincinnati 5-Way Chili 71

Simply Divine   273

Index

Garbanzo Bean Salad with Balsamic Vinegar 100
Hot and Spicy Bean Dip 17
Jim Denison's Mexican Stew 77
Mexican Black Beans on Rice 197
New Orleans Red Beans and Rice 196
Nine Bean Soup 65
Nine Bean Soup Mix 65
Piquant Green Beans 186
Polish Potato Soup 67
Pseudo-Southern Green Beans 186
Seven Layer Taco Dip 16
Southwest Crab Cakes 171
Three Bean Chili 72

BEEF
Apple-Glazed Brisket 118
Beef Tenderloin in a Blanket of Herbs 110
Braised Beef à la Hendrix 120
Brunswick Stew 75
Cheesy Pizza Loaf 128
Cincinnati 5-Way Chili 71
Fabulous Fajitas 116
Family Stroganoff 119
Fiesta Cornbread 127
Granny's Pot Roast 114
Grilled Flank Steak 120
Homemade Spaghetti Sauce 129
Jim Denison's Mexican Stew 77
Kebabs 124
Not a Traditional Meat Loaf 126
Old Joe's "Lundun Broyll" Pot Roast 113
Rib Roast and Yorkshire Pudding 109
Rotini and Beef Bake 128
Spaghetti Pie 131
Steak and Mushroom Soup 62
Stuffed Eggplant 134
Stuffed Shells Florentine 130
Super Supper Nachos 126
Swedish Meat Balls and Gravy 132
Sweet and Sour Beef 117
Vegetable Beef Soup 63

Berry Vinegar 85
Best Brownies in America 234

BEVERAGES
Almond Tea 30
Cranberry Percolator Punch 30
Cranberry Tea 31
German Coffee 31
Hot Cider 32
Mint Water 28

Miss Rubye's Summer Punch 27
Mocha Mix 32
Mocha Punch 28
Patio Punch 27
Peach Punch 29
SPdL Mint Tea 28
Strawberry Punch 29

Bill's Buttermilk Pie 254
Bistro Oakleaf Salad 82
Black Bottom Cupcakes 233
Black-Eyed Pea Relish 138
Blackened Tuna 169
Blue Chip White Salsa 18
Blueberry Cobbler 260
Boursin 20
Braised Beef à la Hendrix 120
Braised Chicken with Mushrooms 157
Braised Pork with Spiced Cranberries 112

BREADS *(See also Muffins)*
Aunt Ruth's Cheese Biscuits 38
Banana Bread 35
Banana Nut Bread 36
Basic Refrigerator Rolls 41
Broccoli Cornbread 41
Butter-Me-Nots 53
Cheese Buttermilk Biscuits 39
Country Spoon Bread 40
Dill Bread 44
Dinner Rolls 42
Easy Cheese Bread 38
Fruit Bread 35
Grandma Stone's Company Cornbread 40
Mrs. Charles' Scones 39
No Need to Knead Wheat Bread 45
Poppy Seed Bread 37
Pumpkin Bread 37
Sally Lunn 43
Seven-Grain Bread 46
Zucchini Bread 36

BROCCOLI
Basic Broccoli 184
Broccoli Bake 185
Broccoli Cauliflower Salad 91
Broccoli Coleslaw 89
Broccoli Cornbread 41
Cheesy Broccoli and Rice 184
Easy Broccoli Soufflé 185
Marinated Broccoli and Cauliflower 24
Marinated Broccoli with Crumbled Feta 90

274 *Simply Divine*

Index

Broiled Lamb Chops 114
BROWNIES AND BARS
    Apple Bars 241
    Apricot Bars 240
    Best Brownies in America 234
    Congo Bars 238
    Glorified Brownies 235
    Gold Rush Bars 237
    Lemon Bars 239
    Lethal Layered Brownies 237
    Mocha Brownies 236
    Mocha Crunch 243
    South African Crunchies 243
Brownulated Sugar Pound Cake 217
BRUNCH
    Baked Blintz 54
    Crab Quiche 56
    Granola 49
    Ham Hash 58
    Mexican Breakfast Bake 55
    Peggy Durrett's Charleston Cheese Grits 55
    Poached to Perfection 58
    Saturday Morning Omelet 57
    Sausage Egg Strata 54
    Tomato Gravy and Grits 56
    Ungspankaka 58
Brunswick Stew 75
Bruschetta for Two 86
Buffet Chicken Breasts 149
Butter Pecan Cheesecake 215
Butter-Me-Nots 53
Buttermilk Pound Cake 218

C

Caesar Salad with Blue Cheese Dressing 85
CAKES
    Black Bottom Cupcakes 233
    Brownulated Sugar Pound Cake 217
    Butter Pecan Cheesecake 215
    Buttermilk Pound Cake 218
    Carrot Cake 222
    Chocolate Eclair Cake 228
    Chocolate Gâteau 230
    Chocolate Pound Cake 219
    Cinnamon Swirl Cake 229
    Cream Cheese Pound Cake 216
    Fresh Apple Cake 220
    German Chocolate Cake 224

    Holiday Fruitcake 227
    Hummingbird Cake 223
    Ida's Oatmeal Coffee Cake 47
    Italian Cream Cake 225
    Lemon Berry Cake 226
    Lemonade Cake 227
    Macaroon Cupcakes 232
    Mama Bootle's Nut Cake 216
    Pineapple Party Cake 221
    Quick Fudge Cake 231
    Soft Gingerbread 232
    Sour Cream Coconut Cake 219
    Sour Cream Coffee Cake 48
    Sour Cream Pound Cake 218
    Spice Cake 231
    Texas Coffee Cake 49
Candy-Coated Pecans 272
Cantaloupe Cream Pie 258
Cantaloupe Sundaes with Raspberry Sauce 263
Caramelized Pecans 87
CARROTS
    Carrot Cake 222
    Fresh Carrot Puree 187
    Marinated Carrots 91
Cashew Cookies 247
CASSEROLES
    Awesome Asparagus Casserole 182
    Baked Vegetable Quartet 181
    Broccoli Bake 185
    Cauliflower à la Polonaise 188
    Cauliflower Bake 187
    Celery Amandine 210
    Cheesy Broccoli and Rice 184
    Chicken Salad Gratinée 164
    Chicken with Wild Rice 161
    Confetti Rice 201
    Cornbread Dressing Gone Wild 211
    Country Chicken Dressing 210
    Cranberry Apple Crunch 208
    Creamed Spinach au Gratin 190
    Creamy Potato Puff 207
    Microwaved Spaghetti Squash 192
    Posh Squash 191
    Quick Cornbread Dressing 212
    Rotini and Beef Bake 128
    Scalloped Pineapple 208
    Shellfish with Wild Rice 176
    Spaghetti Pie 131
    Spinach with Artichokes 189

Index

Squash Deluxe 191
Sweet Potato Supreme 206
Vegetarian Medley 181
Yam and Cranberry Bake 207
Catfish Crisp 168
CAULIFLOWER
Broccoli Cauliflower Salad 91
Cauliflower à la Polonaise 188
Cauliflower Bake 187
Marinated Broccoli and Cauliflower 24
Caviar Mousse 23
Celery Amandine 210
CHEESE
Artichoke Quiche Squares 14
Aunt Ruth's Cheese Biscuits 38
Cheese Buttermilk Biscuits 39
Cheese Grits 173
Cheese Soup 66
Cheesy Broccoli and Rice 184
Cheesy Pizza Loaf 128
Chèvre Persillade 20
Chicken Enchiladas 162
Crab Quiche 56
Curried Cheese Log 22
Easy Cheese Bread 38
Homemade Pimiento Cheese 22
Liptauer Cheese Spread 21
Macaroni and Cheese Mold 204
Mexican Breakfast Bake 55
Old-Fashioned Cheese Straws 26
Peggy Durrett's Charleston Cheese Grits 55
Saturday Morning Omelet 57
Sausage Egg Strata 54
Stuffed Shells Florentine 130
Super Supper Nachos 126
Vidalia Onion Spread 16
White Cheddar Raspberry Ring 24
Cherry Coke Salad 104
CHICKEN (See also Poultry)
Apple Chicken Curry 160
Braised Chicken with Mushrooms 157
Brunswick Stew 75
Buffet Chicken Breasts 149
Chicken Almond Salad 94
Chicken Breasts Stuffed with Apples and Gouda 148
Chicken Bundles 152
Chicken Cheese Quartet 151
Chicken Dijon 146
Chicken Enchiladas 162
Chicken Italiano 150
Chicken Olé 156
Chicken Pasta Salad 92
Chicken Pie in Puff Pastry 155
Chicken Salad Gratinée 164
Chicken with Figs 159
Chicken with Wild Rice 161
Chinese Chicken Salad 97
Chunky Chicken Chili 70
Cornish Hens with Seasoned Stuffing 163
Country Chicken Dressing 210
Creole Pasta 153
Crockpot Brunswick Stew 76
Hickory Smoked Chicken and Artichoke Pasta 154
Honey-Mustard Chicken 14
Lean and Spicy Chicken 146
No-Fat Fried Chicken 145
Nutty Coconut Chicken Salad 96
Oriental Sesame Chicken 99
Pineapple Chicken Salad with Ginger Dressing 95
Roasted Sticky Chicken 145
Rock of Ages Pot Pie 156
Royal Chicken with Chilies 147
Saucy Chicken and Asparagus 158
CHILI
Chunky Chicken Chili 70
Cincinnati 5-Way Chili 71
Three Bean Chili 72
CHOCOLATE
Baked Alaska 254
Best Brownies in America 234
Black Bottom Cupcakes 233
Chocolate Eclair Cake 228
Chocolate Gâteau 230
Chocolate Meringue Pie 255
Chocolate Pound Cake 219
Chocolate Sauce 254
Chocolate Silk Pie 259
Chocolate-Coated Strawberries 257
Congo Bars 238
Fudge Frosting 230
German Chocolate Cake 224
Glorified Brownies 235
Gold Rush Bars 237
Heavenly Chocolate Sauce 267
Lethal Layered Brownies 237
Microwave Fudge 271

276   **Simply Divine**

Index

Mocha Brownies 236
Mocha Crunch 243
Mocha Mix 32
Mocha Punch 28
Oatmeal Chocolate Chip Cookies 246
Quick Fudge Cake 231
Christmas Cookies 248
Chunky Chicken Chili 70
Chunky Tomato Sauce 198
Cincinnati 5-Way Chili 71
Cinnamon Crisps 244
Cinnamon Swirl Cake 229
Citrus Marinade 142
Claire's Crudités 179
Classic Caesar Salad 84
Classic Pesto Primavera 200
COCONUT
Coconut Custard Pie 255
Italian Cream Cake 225
Low-Fat Coconut Pie 269
Macaroon Cupcakes 232
Nutty Coconut Chicken Salad 96
Sour Cream Coconut Cake 219
South African Crunchies 243
Coleslaw 89
Confetti Rice 201
Congealed Citrus Buttermilk Salad 105
Congealed Grapefruit Wedges 101
Congo Bars 238
COOKIES
Cashew Cookies 247
Christmas Cookies 248
Cinnamon Crisps 244
Mandelbrot 250
Marcine's Meringues 250
Miss Connie's Oatmeal Cookies 244
Mocha Crunch 243
Oatmeal Chocolate Chip Cookies 246
Peach Refrigerator Cookies 241
Rita's Famous Oatmeal Cookies 245
Tea Cakes 249
Corn Chowder 65
Corn Pudding 188
CORNBREAD
Broccoli Cornbread 41
Corn Muffins 42
Cornbread Dressing Gone Wild 211
Cornbread Salad 97
Country Spoon Bread 40

Grandma Stone's Company Cornbread 40
Cornish Hens with Seasoned Stuffing 163
Country Chicken Dressing 210
Country Spoon Bread 40
CRAB
Crab Quiche 56
Florida Paella 175
Seafood Gumbo 74
Shellfish with Wild Rice 176
Southwest Crab Cakes 171
Tomato Aspic with Crabmeat Salad 93
CRANBERRIES
Braised Pork with Spiced Cranberries 112
Cranberry Apple Crunch 208
Cranberry Company Mold 105
Cranberry Percolator Punch 30
Cranberry Tea 31
Creamy Cranberry Salad 103
Yam and Cranberry Bake 207
Crawfish Fettuccine 170
Crawford Farms Quail with Black-Eyed Pea Relish 138
Cream Cheese Frosting 222
Cream Cheese Pastry 13
Cream Cheese Pound Cake 216
Creamed Spinach au Gratin 190
Creamy Cheesecake Bites 267
Creamy Citrus Dressing 101
Creamy Cranberry Salad 103
Creamy Potato Puff 207
Crème Fraîche, Two Variations 269
Creole Pasta 153
Crockpot Brunswick Stew 76
Curried Cheese Log 22
Curried Fruit 209

D

Deep-Dish Apple Pie 261
DESSERT SAUCES
Chocolate Sauce 254
Crème Fraîche, Two Variations 269
Heavenly Chocolate Sauce 267
Lemon Filling 270
Nutmeg Cream 261
Raspberry Sauce, Two Variations 259
Warm Toffee Dip 268
DESSERTS (See also Brownies and Bars, Cakes, Cookies, and Pies)
Blueberry Cobbler 260

Simply Divine 277

Index

Cantaloupe Sundaes with Raspberry Sauce 263
Chocolate-Coated Strawberries 257
Creamy Cheesecake Bites 267
Fresh Fruit Cobbler 263
Fresh Raspberry and Fig Gratin 266
Lemon Ice Cream 264
Light Lemon Mousse 264
Lovejoy Pecan Tassies 266
Mango Sorbet 265
Microwave Fudge 271
Peach Tapioca 268
Peanut Brittle 270
Pears Perfectly Poached 263
Praline Grahams 271
Strawberry Pizza 265
Trash Snacks 272
Very Cherry Crisp 261
Dill Bread 44
Dilly of a Dip 19
Dinner Rolls 42

E

Easy Broccoli Soufflé 185
Easy Caramel Frosting 217
Easy Cheese Bread 38
Egg Wash 39
EGGS
Artichoke Quiche Squares 14
Cauliflower à la Polonaise 188
Country Spoon Bread 40
Crab Quiche 56
Easy Broccoli Soufflé 185
Mexican Breakfast Bake 55
Petite Quiche Lorraines 13
Poached to Perfection 58
Saturday Morning Omelet 57
Sausage Egg Strata 54
Ungspankaka 58
Zucchini Triangles 15

F

Fabulous Fajitas 116
Family Stroganoff 119
Fiesta Cornbread 127
FIGS
Chicken with Figs 159
Fig Muffins 50

Fresh Raspberry and Fig Gratin 266
Pork Roast with Figs and Veggies 110
FISH
Blackened Tuna 169
Catfish Crisp 168
Caviar Mousse 23
Nut-Crusted White Fish 167
Orange Roughy with Star Fruit Salsa 165
Poached Salmon Steaks with Cucumber
   Dill Sauce 166
Seafood Chowder 73
Smoked Salmon Party Spread 21
Florida Paella 175
Foiled Turkey Breast 164
Franconia Potatoes 109
Fresh Apple Cake 220
Fresh Carrot Puree 187
Fresh Fruit Cobbler 263
Fresh Raspberry and Fig Gratin 266
Fresh Tomatoes with Garlic and Mint 87
Fried Green Tomatoes 195
FROSTINGS AND ICINGS
Cream Cheese Frosting 222
Easy Caramel Frosting 217
Fudge Frosting 230
Glaze 220
Frozen Fruit Cups 101
Frozen Queen Anne Salad 102
FRUIT *(See also Desserts and Pies)*
Apple Ambrosia 102
Apple Salad with Honey Lime Dressing 106
Apricot Freeze 100
Cherry Coke Salad 104
Congealed Citrus Buttermilk Salad 105
Congealed Grapefruit Wedges 101
Cranberry Apple Crunch 208
Cranberry Company Mold 105
Creamy Cranberry Salad 103
Curried Fruit 209
Frozen Fruit Cups 101
Frozen Queen Anne Salad 102
Fruit and Vegetable Medley 181
Fruit Bread 35
Fruit Salad 106
Hot Mixed Fruit 209
Pickled Peach Congealed Salad 104
Quick Cranberry Salad 105
Scalloped Pineapple 208

278   **Simply** Divine

Index

Star Fruit Salsa 165
Strawberry Salad in a Pretzel Crust 103
Fudge Frosting 230

G

GAME
Anointed Quail 136
Baked Venison Loaves 135
Baptized Quail 137
Crawford Farms Quail with Black-Eyed
   Pea Relish 138
Hunter's Stew 77
Pheasant in Seasoned Sauce 137
Roast Venison 136
Garbanzo Bean Salad with Balsamic Vinegar 100
Garden of Eden Pie 253
Garlic Croutons 82
Georgia Barbecue Sauce 142
German Chocolate Cake 224
German Coffee 31
Gingersnap Gravy 136
Glaze 220
Glorified Brownies 235
Gold Rush Bars 237
Grandma Stone's Company Cornbread 40
Granny's Pot Roast 114
Granola 49
Grilled Flank Steak 120

GRITS
Cheese Grits 173
Peggy Durrett's Charleston Cheese Grits 55
Peppery Grits 203
Shrimp with Grits 173
Tomato Gravy with Grits 56

H

HAM
Ham Hash 58
Ham Loaves with Mustard Glaze 121
Ham Rolls 17
New Orleans Red Beans and Rice 196
Heavenly Chocolate Sauce 267
Herb Tomato Broth 63
Herbal Vinegar 84

HERITAGE RECIPES
Apple Tapioca 268
Baked Beans 197

Baked Tomatoes 194
Beaten Biscuit 38
Beef Hash (Very Fine) 133
Boiled Shad with White Sauce 166
Broiled Finnon Haddie 56
Canapé de Sardines 21
Caramel Potatoes 207
Caviar 23
Cheese and Peanut Butter Sandwiches 22
Cheese Fondue, or English Monkey 57
Cheese Straws 26
Chicken Croquettes 151
Chicken Salad 94
Chocolate Fudge 271
Chocolate Pie 255
Cold Slaw 89
Crumpets 43
Fruit Punch 27
"Love in Disguise" 123
Maraschino Cherry Salad 88
Mint Sauce 111
Oysters in Ramekins 170
Peach Pickles 135
Pilau 75
Potato Salad 95
Pound Cake 218
Queen of Trifles 258
Sauce for Barbecue 142
Scalloped Onions 189
Shrimp Pie 176
Soft Ginger Bread 231
Tartare Sauce 168
Tea Cakes 249
Terrapin Soup 61
To Boil a Ham 122
Turkey Dressing 212
Veal or Poultry Stuffing 115
Virginia Corn Bread 40
When and How to Eat 272
Hickory Smoked Chicken and Artichoke Pasta 154
Holiday Fruitcake 227
Homemade Pimiento Cheese 22
Homemade Spaghetti Sauce 129
Honey-Mustard Chicken 14
Honey-Mustard Salad Dressing 85
Horseradish Sauce 134
Hot and Spicy Bean Dip 17
Hot and Vinegar-y Barbecue and Basting Sauces 140

Index

Hot Bacon Roll-Ups 15
Hot Cider 32
Hot Mixed Fruit 209
Hot Salami 16
Hummingbird Cake 223
Hunter's Stew 77

I

Ida's Oatmeal Coffee Cake 47
Italian Cream Cake 225
Italian Pinwheel Loaf 133

J

Jim Denison's Mexican Stew 77
Jim McCranie's Barbecue Sauce 125

K

Kebabs 124

L

LAMB
    Broiled Lamb Chops 114
    Rack of Lamb with Pan Sauce 111
Lean and Spicy Chicken 146
Lemon Bars 239
Lemon Berry Cake 226
Lemon Dressing 81
Lemon Filling 270
Lemon Ice Cream 264
Lemonade Cake 227
Lethal Layered Brownies 237
Light Lemon Mousse 264
Liptauer Cheese Spread 21
Lovejoy Pecan Tassies 266
Low-Fat Coconut Pie 269
"Lundun Broyll" Marinade 113

M

Macaroni and Cheese Mold 204
Macaroon Cupcakes 232
Macaroon Pie 258
Mama Bootle's Nut Cake 216
Mandarin Green Salad with Slivered Almonds 88
Mandelbrot 250
Mango Sorbet 265

Marcine's Meringues 250
Marinade 124
Marinated Broccoli and Cauliflower 24
Marinated Broccoli with Crumbled Feta 90
Marinated Carrots 91
Mediterranean Potatoes 205
Mexican Black Beans on Rice 197
Mexican Breakfast Bake 55
Mexican Pinwheels 26
Mexican Salsa 18
Microwave Fudge 271
Microwaved Spaghetti Squash 192
Mint Water 28
Miss Connie's Oatmeal Cookies 244
Miss Rubye's Summer Punch 27
Mixed Greens with Roquefort and Dried Fruit Terrine . 81
Mocha Brownies 236
Mocha Crunch 243
Mocha Mix 32
Mocha Punch 28
Morning Glory Muffins 51
Most Excellent Pie Crust 256
Mrs. Charles' Scones 39
MUFFINS
    Apple Bran Muffins 50
    Corn Muffins 42
    Fig Muffins 50
    Morning Glory Muffins 51
    Oat and Wheat Bran Muffins 52
    Petite Mayonnaise Muffins 44
    Winter Squash Muffins 53
MUSHROOMS
    Barley Soup 64
    Braised Chicken with Mushrooms 157
    Mushroom and Parsley Salad 88
    Mushroom-Stuffed Tomatoes 194
    Shellfish with Wild Rice 176
    Shrimp with Grits 173
    Steak and Mushroom Soup 62

N

New Orleans Red Beans and Rice 196
New Potato Salad 95
New South Tomato Ketchup 141
Nine Bean Soup 65
Nine Bean Soup Mix 65
No Need to Knead Wheat Bread 45
No-Fat Fried Chicken 145

Index

Not a Traditional Meat Loaf 126
Nut-Crusted White Fish 167
Nutmeg Cream 261
Nutty Coconut Chicken Salad 96
Nutty Lemon Pie 256

O

Oat and Wheat Bran Muffins 52
Oatmeal Chocolate Chip Cookies 246
Old Joe's "Lundun Broyll" Pot Roast 113
Old-Fashioned Cheese Straws 26
Open-Faced Veggie Squares 25
Orange Roughy with Star Fruit Salsa 165
Orange Spread 50
Oriental Sesame Chicken 99
Oriental Shrimp Soup 61
Oven-Roasted Vegetables 180
Oyster Stew 78

P

Parmesan Potato Bake 204
PASTA
    Chicken Pasta Salad 92
    Cincinnati 5-Way Chili 71
    Classic Pesto Primavera 200
    Crawfish Fettuccine 170
    Creole Pasta 153
    Family Stroganoff 119
    Hickory Smoked Chicken and Artichoke Pasta 154
    Macaroni and Cheese Mold 204
    Rotini and Beef Bake 128
    Shrimp and Linguine 169
    Shrimp Jubilee 171
    Sofia's Sauce for Pasta or Potatoes 199
    Stuffed Shells Florentine 130
    Vegetarian Pasta with Chunky Tomato Sauce 198
    Vermicelli Crowned with Veal Parmigiana 123
Patio Punch 27
PEACHES
    Curried Fruit 209
    Hot Mixed Fruit 209
    Peach Punch 29
    Peach Refrigerator Cookies 241
    Peach Tapioca 268
    Pickled Peach Congealed Salad 104
Peanut Brittle 270
Peanut Butter Pie 260

Pears Perfectly Poached 263
PECANS
    Angel Pecan Pie 262
    Butter Pecan Cheesecake 215
    Candy-Coated Pecans 272
    Caramelized Pecans 87
    Lovejoy Pecan Tassies 266
    Mama Bootle's Nut Cake 216
    Nutty Coconut Chicken Salad 96
    Praline Grahams 271
    South Carolina Pecan Pie 256
Peggy Durrett's Charleston Cheese Grits 55
Peppery Grits 203
Pesto Dip 19
Petite Mayonnaise Muffins 44
Petite Quiche Lorraines 13
Pheasant in Seasoned Sauce 137
Pickled Peach Congealed Salad 104
PIES
    Angel Pecan Pie 262
    Baked Alaska 254
    Bill's Buttermilk Pie 254
    Cantaloupe Cream Pie 258
    Chocolate Meringue Pie 255
    Chocolate Silk Pie 259
    Chocolate-Coated Strawberries 257
    Coconut Custard Pie 255
    Deep-Dish Apple Pie 261
    Garden of Eden Pie 253
    Low-Fat Coconut Pie 269
    Macaroon Pie 258
    Most Excellent Pie Crust 256
    Nutty Lemon Pie 256
    Peanut Butter Pie 260
    Self-Rising Flour 257
    South Carolina Pecan Pie 256
    Strawberry Chiffon Pie 257
    Strawberry Crumble 257
    Zesty Lemonade Pie 253
PINEAPPLE
    Congealed Citrus Buttermilk Salad 105
    Curried Fruit 209
    Frozen Fruit Cups 101
    Frozen Queen Anne Salad 102
    Hot Mixed Fruit 209
    Hummingbird Cake 223
    Patio Punch 27
    Pineapple Chicken Salad with Ginger Dressing 95

Simply Divine

Index

Pineapple Party Cake 221
Scalloped Pineapple 208
Piquant Green Beans 186
Poached Salmon Steaks with Cucumber Dill Sauce 166
Poached to Perfection 58
Polish Potato Soup 67
Poppy Seed Bread 37
PORK (See also Ham and Sausage)
Barbecued Ribs 125
Basque Bean Cassoulet 69
Braised Pork with Spiced Cranberries 112
Brunswick Stew 75
Ham Loaves with Mustard Glaze 121
Hot Bacon Roll-Ups 15
Hot Salami 16
Italian Pinwheel Loaf 133
Pork Chops with Seasoned Rice 122
Pork Loin with Garlic and Onion 112
Pork Roast with Figs and Veggies 110
Savory Grilled Pork Chops 124
Posh Squash 191
POTATOES
Basic Refrigerator Rolls 41
Corn Chowder 65
Creamy Potato Puff 207
Franconia Potatoes 109
Mediterranean Potatoes 205
New Potato Salad 95
Parmesan Potato Bake 204
Polish Potato Soup 67
Potato Croquettes 207
Potato Salad with Horseradish Dressing 96
Sofia's Sauce for Pasta or Potatoes 199
Stuffed Baked Potatoes 206
Stuffed New Potatoes 25
Unfried Fries 204
POULTRY (See also Chicken)
Anointed Quail 136
Baptized Quail 137
Cornish Hens with Seasoned Stuffing 163
Crawford Farms Quail with Black-Eyed
   Pea Relish 138
Foiled Turkey Breast 164
Pheasant in Seasoned Sauce 137
Praline Grahams 271
Processor Peanut Butter 260
Pseudo-Southern Green Beans 186
Pumpkin Bread 37
Pumpkin Soup 68

Q

Quick Cornbread Dressing 212
Quick Cranberry Salad 105
Quick Fudge Cake 231

R

Rack of Lamb with Pan Sauce 111
RASPBERRIES
Cantaloupe Sundaes with Raspberry Sauce 263
Fresh Raspberry and Fig Gratin 266
Raspberry Sauce, Two Variations 259
Raspberry Vinaigrette 106
Red Raisin Sauce 163
RELISHES
Apple Chutney 135
Black-Eyed Pea Relish 138
Sassy Sauerkraut 139
Star Fruit Salsa 165
Rib Roast and Yorkshire Pudding 109
RICE
Artichoke Rice Salad 94
Cheesy Broccoli and Rice 184
Chicken Olé 156
Chicken with Wild Rice 161
Confetti Rice 201
Cornbread Dressing Gone Wild 211
Florida Paella 175
Mexican Black Beans on Rice 197
New Orleans Red Beans and Rice 196
Pork Chops with Seasoned Rice 122
Risotto aux Légumes 202
Shellfish with Wild Rice 176
Weezie's Rice Salad with Shrimp 98
Wild Rice Soup 61
Rita's Famous Oatmeal Cookies 245
Roast Venison 136
Roasted Sticky Chicken 145
Rock of Ages Pot Pie 156
Rotini and Beef Bake 128
Royal Chicken with Chilies 147

S

SALAD DRESSINGS
Balsamic Vinaigrette 84
Berry Vinegar 85
Creamy Citrus Dressing 101

282 *Simply Divine*

Index

Garlic Croutons 82
Herbal Vinegar 84
Honey-Mustard Salad Dressing 85
Lemon Dressing 81
Raspberry Vinaigrette 106
SALADS
   Apple Ambrosia 102
   Apple Salad with Honey Lime Dressing 106
   Apricot Freeze 100
   Artichoke Rice Salad 94
   Baby Greens with Feta and Sugared Walnuts 83
   Bistro Oakleaf Salad 82
   Broccoli Cauliflower Salad 91
   Broccoli Coleslaw 89
   Caesar Salad with Blue Cheese Dressing 85
   Cherry Coke Salad 104
   Chicken Almond Salad 94
   Chicken Pasta Salad 92
   Chinese Chicken Salad 97
   Classic Caesar Salad 84
   Coleslaw 89
   Congealed Citrus Buttermilk Salad 105
   Congealed Grapefruit Wedges 101
   Cornbread Salad 97
   Cranberry Company Mold 105
   Creamy Cranberry Salad 103
   Fresh Tomatoes with Garlic and Mint 87
   Frozen Fruit Cups 101
   Frozen Queen Anne Salad 102
   Fruit Salad 106
   Garbanzo Bean Salad with Balsamic Vinegar 100
   Mandarin Green Salad with Slivered Almonds 88
   Marinated Broccoli with Crumbled Feta 90
   Marinated Carrots 91
   Mixed Greens with Roquefort and Dried
      Fruit Terrine 81
   Mushroom and Parsley Salad 88
   New Potato Salad 95
   Nutty Coconut Chicken Salad 96
   Oriental Sesame Chicken 99
   Pickled Peach Congealed Salad 104
   Pineapple Chicken Salad with Ginger Dressing 95
   Potato Salad with Horseradish Dressing 96
   Quick Cranberry Salad 105
   Spinach Salad 86
   Strawberry Salad in a Pretzel Crust 103
   Strawberry Spinach Salad with Poppy
      Seed Dressing 87

   Summer Tomatoes 86
   Tangy Congealed Asparagus 92
   Tomato Aspic with Crabmeat Salad 93
   Weezie's Rice Salad with Shrimp 98
Sally Lunn 43
Sassy Sauerkraut 139
Saturday Morning Omelet 57
SAUCES AND MARINADES (See also Dessert Sauces)
   Chunky Tomato Sauce 198
   Citrus Marinade 142
   Georgia Barbecue Sauce 142
   Gingersnap Gravy 136
   Homemade Spaghetti Sauce 129
   Horseradish Sauce 134
   Hot and Vinegar-y Barbecue and Basting Sauces .. 140
   Jim McCranie's Barbecue Sauce 125
   "Lundun Broyll" Marinade 113
   Marinade 124
   New South Tomato Ketchup 141
   Red Raisin Sauce 163
   Sofia's Sauce for Pasta or Potatoes 199
   Spicy Cajun Seasoning 169
   Steak Marinade 62
Saucy Chicken and Asparagus 158
SAUSAGE
   Basque Bean Cassoulet 69
   Hunter's Stew 77
   New Orleans Red Beans and Rice 196
   Sausage Egg Strata 54
Savory Grilled Pork Chops 124
Scalloped Pineapple 208
SEAFOOD (See also Crab, Fish, and Shrimp)
   Bacon-Wrapped Scallops 13
   Crawfish Fettuccine 170
   Oyster Stew 78
   Seafood Chowder 73
   Seafood Gumbo 74
   Shellfish with Wild Rice 176
Seagoing Shrimp 173
Self-Rising Flour 257
Seven Layer Taco Dip 16
Seven-Grain Bread 46
Shellfish with Wild Rice 176
SHRIMP
   Barbecued Shrimp 174
   Florida Paella 175
   Oriental Shrimp Soup 61
   Seafood Chowder 73

Simply Divine

Index

Seafood Gumbo 74
Seagoing Shrimp 173
Shellfish with Wild Rice 176
Shrimp and Linguine 169
Shrimp Creole 172
Shrimp Jubilee 171
Shrimp with Grits 173
Smoked Salmon Party Spread 21
Sofia's Sauce for Pasta or Potatoes 199
Soft Gingerbread 232
SOUPS AND STEWS
    Barley Soup 64
    Basque Bean Cassoulet 69
    Brunswick Stew 75
    Cheese Soup 66
    Corn Chowder 65
    Crockpot Brunswick Stew 76
    Herb Tomato Broth 63
    Hunter's Stew 77
    Jim Denison's Mexican Stew 77
    Nine Bean Soup 65
    Nine Bean Soup Mix 65
    Oriental Shrimp Soup 61
    Oyster Stew 78
    Polish Potato Soup 67
    Pumpkin Soup 68
    Seafood Chowder 73
    Seafood Gumbo 74
    Steak and Mushroom Soup 62
    Vegetable Beef Soup 63
    Vichyssoise 63
    Wild Rice Soup 61
Sour Cream Coconut Cake 219
Sour Cream Coffee Cake 48
Sour Cream Pound Cake 218
South African Crunchies 243
South Carolina Pecan Pie 256
Southwest Crab Cakes 171
Spaghetti Pie 131
SPdL Mint Tea 28
Spice Cake 231
Spicy Cajun Seasoning 169
SPINACH
    Chicken Cheese Quartet 151
    Creamed Spinach au Gratin 190
    Spinach Salad 86
    Spinach with Artichokes 189
    Steamed Balsamic Spinach 191

Strawberry Spinach Salad with Poppy
    Seed Dressing 87
Stuffed Shells Florentine 130
SPREADS AND DIPS
    Apricot Butter 35
    Blue Chip White Salsa 18
    Boursin 20
    Caviar Mousse 23
    Chèvre Persillade 20
    Curried Cheese Log 22
    Dilly of a Dip 19
    Homemade Pimiento Cheese 22
    Hot and Spicy Bean Dip 17
    Liptauer Cheese Spread 21
    Mexican Salsa 18
    Orange Spread 50
    Pesto Dip 19
    Processor Peanut Butter 260
    Seven Layer Taco Dip 16
    Smoked Salmon Party Spread 21
    Sun-Dried Tomato Log 23
    Vidalia Onion Spread 16
    White Cheddar Raspberry Ring 24
SQUASH (See also Zucchini)
    Baked Vegetable Quartet 181
    Microwaved Spaghetti Squash 192
    Posh Squash 191
    Squash Deluxe 191
    Warmly Dressed Winter Squash 193
    Winter Squash Muffins 53
Star Fruit Salsa 165
Steak and Mushroom Soup 62
Steak Marinade 62
STRAWBERRIES
    Chocolate-Coated Strawberries 257
    Fruit Salad 106
    Lemon Berry Cake 226
    Star Fruit Salsa 165
    Strawberry Chiffon Pie 257
    Strawberry Crumble 257
    Strawberry Pizza 265
    Strawberry Punch 29
    Strawberry Salad in a Pretzel Crust 103
    Strawberry Spinach Salad with Poppy
        Seed Dressing 87
Stuffed Baked Potatoes 206
Stuffed Breast of Veal 115
Stuffed Eggplant 134

Index

Stuffed New Potatoes 25
Stuffed Shells Florentine 130
Stuffed Zucchini 193
Sugared Almonds 97
Summer Tomatoes 86
Sun-Dried Tomato Log 23
Super Supper Nachos 126
Swedish Meat Balls and Gravy 132
Sweet and Sour Beef 117
Sweet Potato Supreme 206

T

Tangy Congealed Asparagus 92
Tea Cakes 249
Texas Coffee Cake 49
Three Bean Chili 72
TOMATOES
    Fresh Tomatoes with Garlic and Mint 87
    Fried Green Tomatoes 195
    Homemade Spaghetti Sauce 129
    Mexican Salsa 18
    Mushroom-Stuffed Tomatoes 194
    New South Tomato Ketchup 141
    Summer Tomatoes 86
    Sun-Dried Tomato Log 23
    Tomato Aspic with Crabmeat Salad 93
    Tomato Gravy and Grits 56
    Tomato Pie 195
    Vegetarian Pasta with Chunky Tomato Sauce 198
Trash Snacks 272

U

Unfried Fries 204
Ungspankaka 58

V

VEAL
    Stuffed Breast of Veal 115
    Vermicelli Crowned with Veal Parmigiana 123
VEGETABLES *(See also individual vegetable listings)*
    Baked Vegetable Quartet 181
    Celery Amandine 210
    Claire's Crudités 179
    Corn Chowder 65
    Corn Pudding 188
    Fresh Carrot Puree 187
    Fruit and Vegetable Medley 181
    Oven-Roasted Vegetables 180
    Pumpkin Soup 68
    Stuffed Eggplant 134
    Sweet Potato Supreme 206
    Vegetable Beef Soup 63
    Vegetarian Medley 181
    Vegetarian Pasta with Chunky Tomato Sauce 198
    Vidalia Pie 189
    Yam and Cranberry Bake 207
Very Cherry Crisp 261
Vichyssoise 63
Vidalia Onion Spread 16
Vidalia Pie 189

W

Warm Toffee Dip 268
Warmly Dressed Winter Squash 193
Weezie's Rice Salad with Shrimp 98
White Cheddar Raspberry Ring 24
Wild Rice Soup 61
Winter Squash Muffins 53

Y

Yam and Cranberry Bake 207
Yorkshire Pudding 109

Z

Zesty Lemonade Pie 253
ZUCCHINI
    Baked Vegetable Quartet 181
    Stuffed Zucchini 193
    Zucchini Bread 36
    Zucchini Triangles 15

Simply Divine

Second-Ponce de Leon Baptist Church
2715 Peachtree Rd. N.E.
Atlanta, GA 30305-2907
404-266-8111

Please send me _____ copies of **Simply Divine**   @ $17.95 each _____

Postage and handling   @ $3.50 each _____

Georgia residents add 7% for sales tax.   @ $1.26 each _____

Total _____

Name _____

Address _____

City _____ State _____ Zip _____

Payable in U.S. funds.
Make checks payable to **Simply Divine**.

Simply Divine

Second-Ponce de Leon Baptist Church
2715 Peachtree Rd. N.E.
Atlanta, GA 30305-2907
404-266-8111

Please send me _____ copies of **Simply Divine**   @ $17.95 each _____

Postage and handling   @ $3.50 each _____

Georgia residents add 7% for sales tax.   @ $1.26 each _____

Total _____

Name _____

Address _____

City _____ State _____ Zip _____

Payable in U.S. funds.
Make checks payable to **Simply Divine**.